William James
and Phenomenology: a Study of
"The Principles of
Psychology"

AMS PRESS
NEW YORK

Bruce Wilshire

William James and Phenomenology: a Study of "The Principles of Psychology"

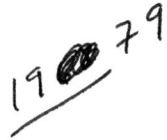

Indiana University Press *Bloomington, London*

Library of Congress Cataloging in Publication Data

Wilshire, Bruce W.
　William James and phenomenology.

　Reprint of the 1968 ed. published by Indiana
University Press, Bloomington.
　Bibliography: p.
　Includes index.
　1. James, William, 1842-1910. The principles
of psychology.　2. Phenomenological psychology.
I. Title.
[BF121.J3W5　1979]　　150'.19'2　　76-6601
ISBN 0-404-15226-0

BF
121
.J3
W5
1979

Copyright © 1968 by Indiana University Press

Reprinted by arrangement with
Indiana University Press

First AMS edition published in 1979.

Reprinted from the edition of 1968, Indiana University Press. [Trim size and text area of the original have been slightly altered in this edition. Original trim size: 15.5 x 23.5 cm; text area: 11 x 18.7 cm.]

MANUFACTURED
IN THE UNITED STATES OF AMERICA

FOR D.W.W.

*Zwei Seelen wohnen, ach! in meiner Brust,
Die eine will sich von der andern trennen.*
FAUST

CONTENTS

Foreword by William Barrett, ix

INTRODUCTION, 3
Why a phenomenological psychology?

ONE, 10
James's dualistic program
for a natural scientific psychology and its failure

TWO, 20
The puzzling opening of "The Principles of Psychology"

THREE, 30
Initial difficulties of psychophysical dualism:
inadequacy of causal theory
for the specification of mental states

FOUR, 68
Further difficulties of dualism: the stream of thought

FIVE, 119
The phenomenological breakthrough in James's psychology:
psychology as field and horizon as well as stream

SIX, 124
James's conception of the self: phenomenology in embryo

SEVEN, 150
Phenomenology: intentionality and worldliness of thought

EIGHT, 217
Conclusion: toward philosophy of mind
and reconciliation of natural science and phenomenology

Bibliography 226, *Notes* 231, *Index* 249

FOREWORD

The figure of William James is slowly gaining a higher and more secure place in the philosophic pantheon. Gone indeed are the days of popular fame, when—in the fresh heyday of pragmatism—he was virtually barnstorming the country as a lecturer and moving students and audiences with his vigorous and infectious personal presence. But the new fame that emerges is of a more significant kind: we are becoming more and more aware of the power of his thought and the depth of his insight on philosophic matters that still concern us.

For survival in philosophy, as in other areas of culture, what counts in the end is a certain quality of vitality. In James's case it would be a mistake to think of this vitality solely in terms of certain endearing, but also relatively superficial, qualities of his writing: the vigorous and almost colloquial prose, his democratic eloquence, the ability to move us by making philosophy sound like one human being talking to another. What we have in mind, rather, is a *vitality of thought:* an energy of mind that can cut through the periphery to the center of its subject, and—holding that center fast

—still keep in its grasp the manifold aspects of that same subject that prevent any false simplification. And of this kind of philosophic vitality James had an abundance.

Thus a rereading of his *Principles of Psychology* is a rather surprising experience—particularly for a reader who has been attentive to the "crisis in fundamentals" that presently besets contemporary psychologists. James's grasp of his subject is astonishing. Not only had he read all the relevant extant literature, but he was also able, while keeping all details in mind, to cut through always to the central issues. More striking still are the candor and energy of mind capable of carrying these issues forward, even to the point of leading us to an impasse. The terms in which James sought to set up a science of psychology may sometimes seem old-fashioned, but the problems he brings us to are those that still face us today in the philosophy of mind. Indeed, a good claim could be made that the *Principles*, though it professes to be a treatise strictly within the then new discipline of psychology, is really the philosophically richest of James's works. One of the virtues of Dr. Wilshire's book—and not an inconsiderable one either—is that, while interesting and significant in itself, it leads us to a rereading of the *Principles*.

What Dr. Wilshire has done is to trace one strand of thought through the complex texture of the *Principles*. This strand of thought, moreover, is one that leads James into puzzlement and mystery—in short, a dead end. So stated, the theme of this book might seem to consign it to that mounting body of specialist literature that is presently accumulating around James. However, the exact opposite is the case. Here, in fact, is an intellectually exciting work, a kind of intellectual detective story, with very broad philosophic implications. There is something of high drama in watching a great philosopher struggle with the octopus-like tentacles of a problem that at first he wishes to avoid raising, because psychology as a self-contained discipline need not ask about its philosophic assumptions; but then that he cannot avoid, as his treatise goes on, until the suppressed problem threatens to destroy his whole initial structure. The single strand of thought, moreover, that Dr. Wilshire has chosen to trace is one that leads us into some of the central concerns of present-day phenomenology in its attempts to establish a more adequate grounding for the various sciences of man. As for the dead end, that should not bother us at all. The thinking of the great philosophers always leads us to some such "dead-end." What matters is the light shed on the way, and whether that light does not open up new paths for fresh thinking (which, of course, will end in its own dead end). Only the second-rate philosophers present us with the image of self-satisfied men who claim to have "solved" completely their particular problems.

As witness to the fact that James's problems still persist, we cite these remarks of Wittgenstein, expressed with his usual aphoristic brilliance:

> The confusion and barrenness of psychology is not to be explained by calling it a "young science"; its state is not comparable with that of physics, for instance, in its beginnings . . . For in psychology there are experimental methods and *conceptual confusion.*
>
> The existence of experimental methods makes us think we have the means of solving the problems which trouble us; though problem and method pass each other by.

More than sixty years lie between these observations of Wittgenstein's and James's *Principles.* James addresses himself to a different historical situation—one in which he and others were struggling eagerly and *optimistically* toward establishing psychology as a laboratory science with its own sophisticated experimental techniques. Yet a careful reading of James—which sometimes means a reading between the lines—would seem to lead us to the same *pessimistic* conclusions as Wittgenstein's. Or, to put the matter the other way around, in those intervening sixty years psychology has developed its own quite intricate experimental techniques, but now it is just the existence of those techniques that lead Wittgenstein to conclude that psychology cannot advance until it deals with those questions that James originally raised in its very beginnings.

My hope for this book is that not only will it help in the present general effort toward a reunderstanding and reassessment of James but that it will also lead to some fresh thinking on the obstacles that currently block the development of the human sciences.

William Barrett

New York University

William James
and Phenomenology: a Study of
"The Principles of
Psychology"

INTRODUCTION

Why a phenomenological psychology?

The central thesis of phenomenology is that the world is comprehensible only in terms of its modes of appearance to mind, and that mind cannot be conceived independently of the world which appears to it. Hence, despite Edmund Husserl's aversion to the word metaphysics, the phenomenological thesis generates implications concerning the structure of reality, and must be considered an outgrowth in the broadest sense of Kant's new metaphysics of experience. It is not that the world exists only in the mind, but that the world can be specified only in terms of what it appears to be to mind. Hence, as well, the phenomenological thesis generates a philosophy of mind: the relationship of mind to world is necessary and internal. Truths about the relationship are necessary and nonempirical and the discipline which discovers them is a nonempirical one. Mind cannot be conceived independently of the world which appears to it. Any phenomenological psychology derives from this fundamental philosophical background.

Probably more has been written about William James than about any other American philosopher. Thus it is startling that his pioneering work in phenomenology and his influence on Husserl went without proper notice for seventy years and has only just recently gained recognition.[1] Husserl's own acknowledgment of James's influence is particularly revealing. He read the bulk of *The Principles of Psychology* in the 1890's and wrote, in 1900, that James's psychology had helped him find his way out of psychologism.[2] This confining view held that since thought is a psychical activity, thought's object or what thought is about must be subject to psychological laws. Because all subject-matter areas are composed of objects-thought-about, psychologism held that psychology is the ultimate discipline.

No better initial stroke to sketch James's phenomenological psychology can be imagined than this admission by Husserl that James helped him overcome psychologism. The central thesis of a phenomenological psychology is that mind and thoughts cannot be conceived independently of the world which appears to mind, and that this phenomenal world can be conceived only through a philosophical investigation of the world's own structures (in Husserl's parlance, essences) as revealed to mind. For example, material objects and formal objects like numbers fall into different regional ontologies; if thought's objects are numbers, say, then at some point in the elucidation of the *thought* a mathematician will have to be called in, not just a psychologist. Although the object belongs to thought and thought is psychical, still the object of thought cannot be given an elucidation that is exclusively psychological. Hence psychology is derivative, not ultimate.

To be sure, modes of being are linked with modes of being presented to mind, but this linkage is not an external, contingent, or causal relationship (not merely factual), hence it cannot be the subject matter of any particular empirical science, e.g., psychology. The linkage is internal—exclusively conceptual. Truths about it are necessary in virtue of their very meaning, and it is apprehended by what Husserl calls a transcendental investigation.

Immanuel Kant first introduced the phrase transcendental exposition, by which he meant the demonstration of the necessary truth of conceptions or principles of judgment through the demonstration that other necessary truths, already in hand, are impossible without the presupposition of the conceptions or principles of judgment in question.[3] What we begin with is actual; therefore that which makes it possible must be the case. The idea was adopted by Husserl and modified in line with his belief that essences (what some might call concepts) and connections of essences comprising necessary truths are *intuited* or seen in some sense. Kant had limited intuition to sensations. By pure phenomenology Husserl means transcendental phenomenology: an exposition of what must be the case in the way of essence if that which is actual in the way of phenomena is to be shown to be possible or intelligible. Husserl's goal is the intuition of necessary truths which lie at the foundation of knowledge. For example, we intuit this: that it is possible for a solid to present itself as a solid in the most fleeting of glimpses only because it is part of the essence of solid (of what we mean by "solid") that it be presented perspectively and incompletely to any given glance. Presuppositions of this sort, says Husserl, are grasped only in a transcendental or reversed method of investigation which goes against the natural empirical grain of the mind.

Indeed, the purpose of Husserl's famous "bracket" is to force investigations into the transcendental channel: to constrain us to give up the question, So we know this fact; now what other facts can we go on to know? and to ask instead, So we know what we take to be this fact; now how is this taking or intending—this *meaning*—possible? The procedure is comparable to Oxford philosophers' throwing language "out of gear." Their purpose in mentioning terms instead of using them and in working on concepts instead of with them is to grasp something about uses and concepts not graspable otherwise—their inherent structures—which includes necessary connections between them.

Now I think that William James's *Principles of Psychology* is one of the best justifications for phenomenological psychology, and I think that Husserl's interest in the book is completely understandable. But it is a strange and often inconsistent work, all fourteen hundred pages of it. It justifies phenomenological psychology as much negatively as it does positively: both the pitfalls of departing from a phenomenological approach and the advantages of hewing to it are exhibited. James's program for the book calls for an autonomous, natural scientific psychology, replete with external, causal, and contingent relationships, and it acknowledges no special difficulty in describing and specifying mind or mental states. But as James progresses it gradually becomes clear that he cannot even begin to talk meaningfully about mental states unless he talks about them in conjunction with the world which appears to them; it becomes clear that he is caught in the phenomenological assumption concerning the mind-world relationship: that it is internal and noncontingent. It is thus absurd for him to talk of brain states causing mental states, as his program demands, before he knows what mental states are. We learn as much from the reversal of his program as we do from his phenomenological insights which occasion the reversal.

But this is not to minimize the fact that there are many of the latter. James achieves basic phenomenological insights which derive the meaningfulness of thought from the meaningfulness of the appearing world, a world he is often able to grasp *just* as it appears —no small accomplishment. Phenomenology has been called an exercise in seeing.

Yet it might be objected that if what is seen are just phenomena, just appearances, then phenomenology is much ado about nothing. It might be said that real knowledge of phenomena cannot be gained, but that this deficiency is unimportant because appearances are not reality, or it might be said that it is easy to know what appears to be the case, but hard to know what really is so; either way no discipline concerned with appearances is called for. But phenomenology rejects any such sweeping bifurcation of appearance and reality and maintains that grasping the phenomenon in its purity is difficult and requires a method.

Although James does not call his method phenomenological, his actual practice points in the direction of what Husserl later explicated. We are deceived about phenomena, James says, both by our practical concerns as men and by our theoretical concerns as scientists. Both concerns prompt us to pick out, before we know it, in the twinkling of an eye, what particular physical things *cause* the phenomenon. As men we are prompted for reasons of personal survival, as scientists for reasons of our theoretical projects. This produces the deception, James says. We then name or specify the phenomenon in terms of the single thing that causes it (for example, "an odor of violets," "a cheesy taste") and mask out the whole phenomenal field—the sense of the world's presence—in which the phenomenon is embedded, and for which, in its wholeness, the

Why a phenomenological psychology? 7

phenomenon should be named if it is to be specified adequately. Since we specify our thoughts in terms of the phenomena which are their objects, this also amounts to deception concerning thoughts.

Husserl took James's insight and formulated it thus: all judgments concerning physical things and causation are to be bracketed or suspended—not denied or ignored, but suspended, i.e., viewed within the environing context of meaningfulness which makes them possible as meaningful judgments, regardless of whether they be true or false. The seeing, which is phenomenological seeing, is difficult because what must be seen all at once is the total context of related phenomena, which render any particular phenomenon meaningful, a context which includes phenomena related not only to other phenomena but to ourselves as centers of consciousness. As phenomenology developed in the hands of Husserl, it became increasingly clear that the whole lived world (*Lebenswelt*) as the founding level of meaning is even more basic than the internal relationship of thought to thought's object (intentionality), since the specification of thought is parasitical on the specification of thought's object (phenomenon), and the specification of the latter is in turn parasitical on the sense of the whole lived world in which the particular phenomenon is embedded. James's thought anticipates in some ways this development.

The tradition in America has been to construe James's psychology as "functionalist." Unfortunately, like too much Jamesian scholarship, this construction conceals more than it reveals. It is all very well to say that James believed that mind performed a biological function in adjusting the organism to the environment; but if it is not added that he also believed that the function of mind cannot be rendered exclusively in biological terms, but requires irreducibly mentalistic ones expressing the way the environment appears to an organism conscious of its ends as its own, then more is concealed than revealed. Moreover, it must be added that James's conception of mentalistic terms is very different from that of an introspectionist. He is neither a pure functionalist, nor an introspectionist, nor a behaviorist; *if* he is any single thing, he is a pioneering phenomenologist.

John Watson, the founder of behaviorism, claimed that James's alleged functionalism was really subjectivistic and introspectionist.[4] But both allegations are wrong, and showing how they are wrong throws added light on James's actual position. Watson and the intellectual communities in England and America were so ignorant of Husserl and of Continental thought that they usually lumped any talk about mental states or acts of thought in the category of introspective psychology: i.e., a psychology which attempted to develop a special vocabulary for the description of special nonphysical entities called thoughts or sensations, and which armed itself with its own units and modes of measurement so as to be adequate to "the other realm" of mind.

But a central doctrine of phenomenology is that mental states are intrinsically referential and worldly, that they cannot be specified in isolation as elements of another "realm," and that what they are as nonphysical entities (assuming this makes any sense at all) is at best a peripheral matter. For phenomenology, introspectionism is a displaced and misguided empiricism—and a disguised mimic of natural science—which is blissfully unaware of its own confusion. As E. G. Boring has pointed out, James's *radical* empiricism might have served as a basis for an American school of phenomenology, but it was simply never integrated into American psychology.[5]

What distinguishes James's protophenomenology from functionalism, behaviorism, and introspectionism, is the idea of the intrinsic referentialness of mind, which snowballs in the *Principles* and turns that book in mid-course toward new intellectual horizons. Functionalism eschews the point of view of the conscious organism itself; behaviorism avoids reference to consciousness and *intentional* behavior; introspectionism does not ground itself on the intentional mind-world relation.

The chief value of phenomenology, I think, is that it raises a challenge to dominant modes of psychology and supplies an alternative mode of thought that keeps open vast reaches of western civilization which are in danger of being sealed off by contemporary science. The phenomenologist maintains that any psychology which limits itself to an examination of organisms' contingent responses to contingent stimuli imposes a gratuitous limitation on its own development as a science. He maintains as well that human behavior can be adequately understood only when its *meaning* is understood; and this meaning can no more be understood as externally or contingently related to the world meant than can the meaning of a symbol be understood as externally related to the symbolized. The "meant" is part of what we mean by the meaning, and behavior *is* what it means.

For example, no analysis of the mere movements of a speaker's mouth, no matter how finely they are correlated empirically to contingent events in the speaker's organism or environment, can elucidate the meaning of what he is saying, a fortiori no such analysis can elucidate the meaning of what he is doing. The phenomenologist maintains that, owing to the very concepts involved, mind is not reducible to an isolated, nor even contingently correlated, event, but that it must be understood to be internally related to the world. The language as well as the whole symbolizing and evaluational life of the person, together with his brute awareness of the world, must be understood. But to do this, psychology must at some point acknowledge that it is an inherently humanistic discipline, since we understand a person's language and evaluations only when we understand what the world has meant to all men in the course of civilization. The relation of mind to world is internal *and* communal. The value of phenomenology, then, is that it prompts us to reconsider the scientific and cultural value of what has always seemed to be the core of our existence: that relational and referential opening onto the world—that pervading sense of *what the world means to us.*

ONE

James's dualistic program for a natural scientific psychology and its failure

I

My purpose is to chart the movement toward phenomenology in the psychology of William James. Phenomenology appears on the horizon at that point where James's natural scientific program for psychology encounters a fundamental philosophical difficulty. His avowed aim in his *Principles of Psychology* is to divorce psychology from first-philosophy or metaphysics and to establish it as a natural science. Yet at the conclusion of his psychological studies, in the last chapter of the abridgment of the *Principles*, he confesses that a "scientific psychology" is one into which "the waters of metaphysical criticism leak at every joint."[1]

It is likely, I think, that the difficulties are endemic to any natural scientific psychology which presumes to thoroughness and that phenomenology must play an intrinsic, reinforcing role; thus, as I have said, psychology is at some point a humanistic discipline. Hence it appears that the significance of the phenomenological breakthrough in the thought of James is more than merely historical: it contributes to our understanding of current problems in

Program for a natural scientific psychology

philosophical psychology, and it shakes up our deepest preconceptions concerning the nature of culture and existence.

What did James mean when he declared in the preface of the *Principles* that psychology was to be a natural science? He explains it in few words and with seeming clarity:

> Psychology, the science of finite individual minds, assumes as its data (1) *thoughts and feelings*, and (2) *a physical world* in time and space with which they coexist and which (3) *they know*. Of course these data themselves are discussable; but the discussion of them (as of other elements) is called metaphysics and falls outside the province of this book. This book, assuming that thoughts and feelings exist and are vehicles of knowledge, thereupon contends that psychology when she has ascertained the empirical correlation of the various sorts of thought or feeling with definite conditions of the brain, can go no farther—can go no farther, that is, as a natural science. If she goes farther she becomes metaphysical.[2]

Thus James's program for a natural scientific psychology is dualistic. There are two kinds of stuff: thoughts on the one hand and physical things in space and time on the other. It is a programmatic dualism adopted for the purpose of scientific research—one in which both sets of data are taken to be equally clear and equally well established.

Some physical things are brains, and James maintains that the objective of a natural scientific psychology is to discover the empirical correlation of thoughts or mental states with physical states of a brain. Later he uses the word "correspondence," and this suggests either a parallelistic or an interactionist theory of the mind-brain relationship, not an identity theory. In the early and predominantly physiological portions of the *Principles* the alternatives are narrowed to one, for he talks of "what happens when to a physical state a mental state corresponds," and this is construed as a causal happening. He speaks of "forces" and "dampenings" of nerves caused by mental states; thus he is advancing an interactionist theory of the mind-brain relationship. The point of establishing correlations is to determine causal laws of functional covariation.

There is a relationship other than the causal into which mental states can enter: it is the cognitive relationship. Mental states are related to physical things when they know these things; these things are seldom brains, and more rarely still the brain that corresponds causally to the mental states in question. All that James says about this cognitive relationship is that it is one of knowing, and that to say anything more about it is to be metaphysical and metaphysical is what he chooses not to be. Later in the *Principles* he repeats his statement of his natural scientific program and reiterates his refusal to specify the cognitive relationship more exactly:

> *The psychologist's attitude towards cognition* will be so important in the sequel that we must not leave it until it is made perfectly clear. It is a *thoroughgoing dualism*. It supposes two elements, mind knowing and thing known, and treats them as irreducible. Neither gets out of itself or into the other, neither in any way *is* the other, neither *makes* the other. They just stand face to face in a common world, and one simply knows, or is known unto, its counterpart. This singular relation is not to be expressed in any lower terms, or translated into any more intelligible name.[3]

Despite James's refusal to specify the cognitive relationship more exactly, his words do tell us something about it, if only negatively and by implication. He seems to be saying that the relationship is not internal; i.e., the fact that the mental state enters into a cognitive relationship to the thing known in no way determines what the mental state, as a term in the relationship, is. The mental state is utterly distinct from the thing known by it. Thus the relationship is external: it could be anything whatever (e.g., a relationship of truth or one of falsity), and the nature of the terms related would be unaltered. Thus, though he speaks of the relationship as "singular," he would seem to imply that it is an external relationship like the causal except that it lacks the ingredient of causal interaction.

This reading of James's conception of the cognitive relationship is strengthened by other passages in the *Principles*:[4] The psychologist simply reads off the empirical facts and decides when the mental state and its cognitive object are in phase (the cognitive relationship is veridical) and when they are not (the relationship is nonveridical, e.g., the psychologist shows a pink blanket to the subject who reports a pink woman). The psychologist's "real work" begins only when he attempts to discover which brain states correspond to these true or false mental states, e.g., alcohol in the brain. His real work begins with the causal relationship.

So James's program for a natural scientific psychology is a

Program for a natural scientific psychology

double dualism, as it were. There are thoughts and there are physical things in space and time; the thoughts are related both causally and cognitively to the physical things. In the case of the causal relationship of thought and brain the relationship is definitely empirical and external; in the case of the cognitive relationship of thought and what thought knows (thought's object) the relationship *seems* to be empirical and external. The grand objective of a natural scientific psychology, according to James, is to discover the causal relationship of thought and brain; the determination of the cognitive relationship appears to be a peripheral matter.

II

In view of the avowed intentions and implicit expectations of James's natural scientific program, the actual results achieved by it are disappointing, if not embarrassing. His objective was the causal correlation of brain states and mental states. In the last chapter of the abridgment of the *Principles* James looks back and attempts to assess the significance of his psychological discoveries. The chapter has a confessional quality. His last confession is a telling one: mental states, he says, are not verifiable facts.[5] He cannot establish causal laws of correlation between mental states and physical states of the brain because, as he writes, "We don't even know the terms between which the elementary laws would obtain if we had them. This is no science, it is only the hope of a science."[6] An embarrassing admission, for it is absurd to attempt to discover laws of correlation without first being able to specify the terms which could enter into the correlation; e.g., it is absurd to attempt to correlate physical and mental states without being able to specify what could possibly count as a mental state.

What had gone wrong with James's specification of mental states? Since this is necessary for their correlation to brain states, and since the correlation is necessary for the realization of his natural scientific program for psychology, the question is tantamount to asking what had gone wrong with James's natural scientific program. He himself suggests what seems to be an answer.

Almost immediately before his final assessment of the unhappy state of his theory concerning the causal correlation of mental states and brain states, he offers another assessment. This time it pertains to the other relationship into which mental states can enter: the cognitive relationship between thought and what thought knows—thought's object. Again his words have a confessional quality:

> From the common-sense point of view (which is that of all the natural sciences) knowledge is an ultimate relation between two mutually external entities, the knower and the known. The world first exists, and then the states of mind; and these gain a cognizance of the world which gets gradually more and more complete. But it is hard to carry through this simple dualism, for idealistic reflections intrude.[7]

James here admits that he has regarded the cognitive relationship as external; what is more, he admits that this has caused him trouble. It is not immediately clear how it has, however.

This statement in the abridgment is immediately followed by James's summary assertion of his metaphysics of radical empiricism, which he did not introduce explicitly as metaphysics until twelve years later (1904). This then is part of what he means when he says that a scientific psychology is one into which "the waters of metaphysical criticism leak at every joint." One of the joints into which metaphysical criticism leaks is the cognitive relationship regarded as external. But why does he equate this with the intrusion of idealistic reflections? Because in James's metaphysics mind is simply a different organization of the very same specific natures or pure experiences which comprise matter: he described his metaphysics as a "comminuted *Identitätsphilosophie*" (a modified identity-philosophy; viz., the idealists' doctrine of the identity of subject and object, of thought and thought's object).[8] He writes in 1892:

> The fact is that such an experience as *blue*, as it is immediately given, can only be called by some such neutral name as that of *phenomenon*. It does not *come* to us *immediately* as a relation between two realities, one mental and one physical. It is only when, still thinking of it as the *same* blue, we trace relations between it and other things, that it doubles itself, so to speak, and develops in two directions; and taken in connection with some associates figures as a physical quality, whilst with others it figures as a feeling in the mind.[9]

Program for a natural scientific psychology

This is a radical turnabout from his program for a natural scientific psychology, i.e., his dualism of two utterly distinct entities: mind and matter, thought and thought's object. He has come to the point of saying that thought and thought's object are in some fundamental way *identical*. The turn of events is pregnant with implications: If the phenomenon is identical to both thought and thought's object then a single specification would apply to both terms in the cognitive relationship; being a term in the relationship would be part of what we *mean* by the terms, therefore the relationship would be internal. Moreover, if it takes a metaphysics to assess this internal relationship, then the autonomy of psychology as a natural science is surely destroyed.

By "internal" we mean a necessary, noncontingent relationship —"a relation of ideas," to use Hume's phrase but not his metaphysics—one in which the denial of it is necessarily false or self-contradictory. To use a banal example, rectangles are related internally to figures; to deny the assertion "rectangles are figures" is to contradict oneself, for part of what is *meant* by the subject of the assertion is just that they are figures. Thus we mean a relationship which is necessarily true and which can neither be verified nor falsified by empirical investigations of fact, because the very concept of one element related involves qua concept the concept of the other. There can be no falsifying evidence because to turn up a nonfigure is to turn up what could not possibly be imagined to be a rectangle.

On the other hand, what do we mean by an external or contingent relationship? It is at least that the things related can be specified independently of each other: water is related externally to plants, i.e., what we mean by water can be defined or specified without any mention at all of plants. It is part of what we mean by such relationships that there are some means of specifying (in the sense of identifying) each thing related without including a specification of the other.

If James is saying that the cognitive relationship is internal, then the connection between the inquiry into the causal thought-brain relationship and the inquiry into the cognitive thought-thought's object relationship is close indeed and disruptive of his natural scientific program. For if the relationship between the elements in the cognitive relationship is an internal one, then the adequate specification of thought necessarily involves the specification of its object. Their conceptions would involve each other qua conceptions.

The connection between the two inquiries becomes clear in the light of the following inferences: If thoughts cannot be causally correlated to brain state unless they are first specified (which condition certainly is the case), and if thoughts cannot be specified unless the relationship of thought and thought's object is specified before this (which condition seems to be the case), then the inquiries are intimately connected. If the latter condition is the case, then the specification of the cognitive relationship would have to be achieved *before* the attempt to determine the causal relationship could even begin, that is, profitably begin. Not only would it be impossible for James to leave the relationship of thought and thought's object unspecified, or regarded as external, while he pursues through empirical investigations causal laws correlating thought and brain, as he wishes to do, but he would have to regard the cognitive relationship as internal before he embarks on the causal pursuit. This would throw the natural scientific program itself from a logically prior to a logically posterior position in investigations of psychology.

III

I think that such a sweeping philosophical reversal does take place in James's *Principles*. I also think, however, that it is a blessing, once it is properly understood. Only when we grasp the extent of the reversal can we appreciate the significance of the phenomenological breakthrough.

Nearly everything in the two volumes of *The Principles of Psychology* gets turned around. But the work makes sense as it never did before. Reading through the *Principles* again, armed with the understanding that phenomenology is that which "leaks in at every joint," we see why James can never really get started in his natural scientific program, and why he must always do something else before he can do what he planned to do next. It is as if he started a race at the middle and could get to the starting line only by going back over the track he wants to run. But he seems to be in doubt as to where the starting line might be, so he runs backward in order to keep the goal always in view. Of course, he cannot see clearly where he is going, but he is making an amazing effort to locate the starting line. He is trying to finish a race without having ever properly begun it.

No doubt phenomenology has been called a transcendental inquiry, and thus a study of a priori truths; therefore my assertion that James exhibits similarities to such a movement of thought will grate harshly on the ears of those who are accustomed to thinking of the James of the *Principles* as merely an empirical scientist. I am advancing just such a contention, however.

Repeatedly we observe James's strange mode of progression in the *Principles:* he cannot sustain his forward pace because he must always go back to uncover the foundation of his own presuppositions. He gets ahead of himself; but ahead of himself in an odd kind of way: he cannot run backward fast enough to keep up with himself. But when it occurs to us that he has unintentionally involved himself in a transcendental investigation there is instruction in his effort; we begin to see the supreme importance of such investigations.

The point of a transcendental investigation is to expose necessary truths which must be presupposed if that which is actual (e.g., in the way of phenomena) is to be shown to be possible, that is, intelligible. For phenomenology a fundamental presupposition is the necessary truth which expresses the cognitive relationship: the very concept of a mental state involves the concept of its object; without this presupposition neither term in the relationship is intelligible.* This is the doctrine of intentionality.

Now James is able to render the concept of mental state intelligible only by tacitly relying on the doctrinal presupposition in question. But his realization of this reliance is delayed; thus the massive inversions and disorganizations of his *Principles*.

In the end he is carried a great distance from his original

---

* My argument requires only that I take intentionality to mean that the cognitive relationship is internal in the "direction" of thought to thought's object; that the first internally involves the second, but not necessarily conversely. I do not wish to become embroiled in this interesting controversy between the "realist" and "idealist" wings of phenomenology. A book should be written about this point alone; see Harmon Chapman's illuminating article, "Realism and Phenomenology," in *The Return to Reason*, edited by John Wild; reprinted in *Essays in Phenomenology*, edited by Maurice Natanson.

program for an empirical psychology replete with external, contingent, and, at its core, causal relationships between mental states and brain states. The ostensible core is displaced to one side. Notice: Since James's actual analyses and discoveries imply that some of the necessary conditions for applying the concept of a thought (which we abbreviate as A) are the very conditions for applying the concept of its object (which we abbreviate as A'), then it is the case that A presupposes A'. Also, since this is the case, the statement (S_1): "Thought A is thought of A'" must be a necessary truth, and the relation between A and A' an internal one, for the concept of A would involve qua concept the concept of A'. That is, the conditions for applying A (the specification of A) include the conditions for applying A' (the specification of A'). If A' could not be applied, then A could not be either. So at no time can A be applied unless A' is also applicable. But if A cannot ever be applied unless A' is at least applicable, then we cannot imagine a situation in which A is applicable and A' is not. But if we cannot imagine such a situation, we cannot imagine that S_1 will ever be false. S_1 is, then, a necessary truth.

James's *de facto* tendency to specify mental states in terms of their cognitive objects has significant repercussions. I believe that this tendency—or latent strand as I call it—can be profitably discussed within the conceptual framework of the phenomenological concept of intentionality. I use the word "strand" instead of "thesis" because the latter suggests that the thinker consciously and methodically takes a position; this is just what James does not do.

More than this, however, I believe that the latent strand in James's *Principles* can be discussed profitably within the conceptual framework of the phenomenological doctrine of the lived world or *Lebenswelt*. There are these reasons: He specifies the mental state in terms of its cognitive object, but he does not specify the latter exclusively in terms of an isolated particular, e.g., he specifies it as something occupying a place in space and having relationships to other things in space; indeed, he declares that part of what we *mean* by the known thing is that it occupies a place in space. At times James talks in terms of a connection of meanings determined by "the world of practical realities," which is much like a phenomenological approach.

James is close to *Lebenswelt* conceived as founding level of meaning. He cannot correlate brain states with mental states unless he specifies mental states; he cannot specify them unless he specifies their objects; he cannot specify the latter unless he specifies them as part and parcel of the whole lived world of practical realities. This is his tendency which points to the lived world as the foundation of all inquiry and all meaning. And if it is such a foundation, then it is the foundation of psychology as well.

My textual analysis of the *Principles* attempts to show how James's program for the specification of thought as an externally related entity breaks down, and how it is joined by a strong phenomenological strand which in time becomes irruptive. The *Principles* is a vivid illustration of the power of the concepts of intentionality and *Lebenswelt*. Over and over, as he attempts to push through his program, he fails; over and over, in spite of his strongest intentions, he is thrown out into the world; his thought must draw on objects known within the world for its meaning.

But it is not my purpose merely to pile up verification for my thesis. I believe that a prolonged and intensive account of the *Principles* is required to display fully the *meaning* of the thesis I advanced. The concept of the worldliness of thought is not subject to instant elucidation. I want to show just how it happens—and indeed how it must happen—that James's metaphysics in the form of the worldliness of thought "leaks into" his program "at every joint." Although at times we will be following the sequence of James's text, somewhat like a commentary, nevertheless there is a structure in the argument, because it moves toward psychological themes that are ever more and more enmeshed with the *Lebenswelt*.

If my reading of James is correct, much traditional Jamesian scholarship is faulty: Far too much emphasis has been placed on his later popular philosophy of pragmatism and his occasional pieces in oracular metaphysics, and not enough on his early theory of meaning and on his systematic metaphysics which emerges directly from his conception in the *Principles* of the world of practical realities as a founding level of meaning.

TWO

The puzzling opening of "the principles of psychology"

I

In view of the fact that James's programmatic sketch in the Preface to the *Principles* is but three pages long and that he neither offers definitions of his key terms (e.g., "mental state") nor a statement of the mode of procedure which he intends to follow in the work, there is some reason to conclude that he intends the first numbered chapter, the one following the Preface, to serve as an additional, *de facto* introduction to the work. First, there is the title of the chapter, "The Scope of Psychology," which suggests an overview of the subject matter; second, there is included an apparent definition of "mind" or "mentality" (or at least the "marks of Mind's presence").

But this chapter raises problems. Granted, the Preface has told us precious little about mental states, yet it has contrasted them emphatically with physical things in space and time. The apparent definition of mind found in this following chapter may make the reader wonder why mental states themselves are not characterized as physical events. It is almost as if James's manifest program of dualism had broken down immediately, and reduced itself to a

The puzzling opening

one-leveled behaviorism. Let us see how this disruption in our expectations comes about.

He begins the chapter by defining psychology as the science of the mental life, "both of its phenomena and their conditions."[1] The phenomena, he says, are feelings, desires, cognitions, reasonings, decisions, and so on; but aside from reading off this list he tells us nothing more about them. Their (causal) conditions are physiological states, and these interest him more. Whether the mental states are distinct psychical existents correlatable to the conditioning physiological states, he does not say. Neither does he say whether they are observable only by the person possessing them (i.e., by introspection). Nor does his initial attack on faculty psychology and association psychology throw any light on this matter, since he does not focus his attack on their modes of specifying mental phenomena. Such a focus might have illuminated what he himself thinks about the matter. He simply attacks the ability of these psychologies to account properly for the physiological conditions of the mental phenomena (e.g., the effect on the phenomena of reasoning caused by chemical injections into the organism). Manifestly, he is centrally concerned with physiology, and this strikes us as rather odd in a chapter which presumes to some generality in a book which is supposedly dualistic.

What is more, James expands the meaning of "mental" to include patently physiological states. Thus he asserts that not only do causally conditioning physiological states precede and accompany mental states (whatever they might be), but that they also follow them as their consequences.[2] And any such caused or consequential motor phenomena which indicate directedness toward an end or goal he chooses to call mental.[3]

Now there is an implication in this that there *is* something which is preceded, accompanied, and followed by physiological states, presumably the mental state, and this implication fits in exactly with our expectations formed in the Preface, that James will develop a dualistic interactionism. But he does not develop the implication—not at all. In fact, he goes on to say that since even machinelike reflex movements attain ends for the organism, we should not shrink from calling them mental.[4] "The boundary line of the mental is certainly vague," he writes.[5] Of course, such movements are not the effects of mental states, nor need they be accompanied by them. While he does not comment directly on this, he does, however, proceed to qualify a "mental motor phenomena" as one of *several possible* means to an end—thus not strictly machinelike. But he does not consider the possibility that even these might not involve mental states in the usual sense of *consciousness*.

The process of digestion, say, in animals brings about a definite end, but no variable means for the attainment of this are possible, so it does not meet James's criterion of mentality. The teleology here is merely "outward," to use his word, as when an outside observer says: If so and so is considered the end, then that process is an effective means of achieving it. But with animals like frogs and dogs which employ variable means to escape dangerous or unusual situations James seems willing to grant that some future end is being "pursued" or even "chosen," and that their behavior thereby meets the criterion for mentality. He does not here consider the possibility that the teleology in these cases may also be merely "outward."

The fact is that the word "mental" is used so broadly that we do not really know what James means by it. Does he mean awareness or consciousness, or at least that some motor phenomena are accompanied in some way by consciousness? But this question itself hardly helps us, for pertaining to the "variable means" criterion of mentality James writes:

> The physiologist does not confidently assert conscious intelligence in the frog's spinal cord until he has shown that the useful result which the nervous machinery brings forth under a given irritation *remains the same when the machinery is altered*. If . . . the right knee of a headless frog be irritated with acid, the right foot will wipe it off. When, however, this foot is amputated, the animal will often raise the *left* to the spot and wipe the offending material away.[6]

The point is that if the physiologist does "confidently assert conscious intelligence in the [headless] frog's spinal cord," then James is sanctioning a use of the words "conscious intelligence" or "consciousness" which is so broad and so far removed from the ordinary use that we cannot be sure what he means by the words.

James's criterion of mentality in this first chapter of the *Principles*,

> *The pursuance of future ends and the choice of means for their attainment are thus the mark and criterion of the presence of mentality* in a phenomenon,[7]

The puzzling opening

is sufficiently broad to render unnecessary, it might seem, any reference at all to mental states. As he uses "end," it has little to do with our common locutions, "having an end in mind" or "in view." An observer, it might seem, would be able to determine if publicly observable behavioral phenomena met the criterion without ever having to assume that the organism observed was conscious—in our ordinary use of the term "conscious." In the ordinary use, it is true to say that when I close my eyes I experience a change which is more than any observer can see by *just* looking at my organism.

It might be argued that James's natural scientific and dualistic program breaks down right here in the first chapter of the *Principles*. Or—most disturbing to our thesis—it might be argued that this is not a breakdown of the manifest program but really a refining and an expediting of it. The manifest program is being expedited, it might be said, because James is actually supplying us with a feasible, operationally testable definition of "mental state." Instead of meaning by this term private states of consciousness which are not publicly observable and controllable, he is substituting for it certain publicly observable behaviors. The natural scientific program is expedited because all that is really meant by "the correlation of mental states and brain states" is the correlation of certain publicly observable behaviors with certain publicly observable physiological conditions of the brain. "The unscientific, unverifiable dross of mentalistic terms is skimmed away leaving the pure ore of scientific terms exposed and accessible beneath"—such an argument might go.

What really breaks down, this argument might continue, is not James's manifest thesis but the thesis of this present study which states that his manifest thesis does break down. Our thesis is wrong, because it is impossible that James's specification of mental states should involve him in a nonnatural scientific use of terms which involve necessary, nonempirical truths about the relationship of thought to thought's object. For all he really means by a mental state is an empirically testable, contingent, factual bit of publicly observable behavior which could not possibly have a noncontingent, internal relationship to anything else whatsoever. The observing psychologist is assumed to have consciousness in the ordinary loose sense, but this assumption is irrelevant to the specification of the scientific situation; for what the psychologist's consciousness reveals, with a calculable but usually negligible margin of error, are objective facts which can be specified without reference to anything, a fortiori *any* consciousness.

But does such an argument speak for James? Is this what he really means by "mental state"? If it is, then why does he talk about a mental state which is "preceded, accompanied and followed" by motor behaviors which the above argument asserts are *equated* by him with mental states? It might be conceded that as James expresses himself in this chapter, these nonmotor-behavior mental states are irrelevant to his purposes. But the question that bothers us is just what his purposes are in this chapter. Is it an introduction to the work as a whole or is it simply the first part of "the physiological preliminaries" which he speaks of in the first sentence of Chapter Seven ("The Methods and Snares of Psychology") as "now finished"?

The possibility that it is only a part of the physiological preliminaries is strengthened when one scrutinizes James's teleological criterion of mentality. He does not really say that he is offering a definition but only "the mark and criterion of the presence of mentality." He may mean this to be understood as a definition, but we cannot tell. Any assertion that we can would be based on the assumption that James is a strict behaviorist, that he believes that mind can be reduced to a set of publicly observable, contingent behaviors; but this is just to assume the point which needs to be proved. That a man is kneeling in a church may be the criterion for the assertion that he is praying; it is some evidence for the assertion. But is his praying nothing but the kneeling, or at least nothing but all similar evidence? James's position on the question is not decidable strictly on the basis of the text so far covered, but in view of his later chapter on "The Stream of Thought," in which he attempts to describe teleology from *within*, the provisional answer must be that he denies that mind is nothing but a set of factual and contingent behaviors observable from without.

The behaviorist view cannot be accepted both because of James's mention of nonmotor-behavior mental states and the indefiniteness of his teleological criterion of mentality. He does not tell us enough about the opposite of teleology-judged-from-without, that is, teleology-judged-from-within, or the agent's point of view. Because he has a great deal to tell us about this later in the book (and because only a fifth of the book is devoted to experimental psychology, as R. B. Perry has observed[8]), we can conclude that he is not advancing behaviorism.

II

But I cannot accept the view that the chapter is *merely* a part of the physiological preliminaries. Aside from his mention of nonmotor-behavior mental states, the chapter is too general in its scope to fit in neatly with such preliminaries. It is significant that in Chapter One of the *Principles* the only criterion of mentality offered features as its central stipulation the directedness of mind toward ends. It is significant as well that mental states, while maintained, are not spoken of as discrete psychical existents. In his statement of program in the Preface he mentioned that mental states are utterly distinct from their cognitive objects in the world of space and time, and that their relationship to their objects would not be discussed. Yet to say that mind is directed toward ends *is* to say something about the relationship, and this suggests that his program is already being modified. The central point is that James here conceives of mind as referring to the world. True, we do not know what the reference means in this preliminary Jamesian context, and we do not know how cognitive objects are ends. But the fact remains that he may be amending his manifest program in the direction I maintain.

For instance, let us note a passage in this puzzling first chapter that bears directly on the thesis I am advancing:

> We may . . . try to explain our memory's failures and blunders by secondary causes. But its *successes* can invoke no factors save the existence of certain objective things to be remembered on the one hand, and of our faculty of memory on the other. When . . . I recall my graduation-day, and drag all its incidents and emotions up from death's dateless night, no mechanical cause can explain this process, nor can any analysis reduce it to lower terms . . .[9]

He writes of the mysteriousness of the cognitive relationship and the fact that psychology can only (not just will only) assume it as an ultimate datum before any psychologizing takes place.[10] From this he draws the above quoted and notable corollary: He speaks of the mode of cognition called memory, and though he is referring explicitly to faculty psychology, the fact that his own natural scientific psychology also assumes the cognitive relationship to be irreducible makes his words applicable to his own as well.

First it must be noted, and remembered throughout this study, that James in nearly all instances uses the word "cognition" as a generic term which has as its species "successful cognition" (truth) and "unsuccessful cognition" (error).[11] By cognition in general he seems to mean simply meaning or intention. Now what he says in the passage above amounts to a severe limitation put on physiological psychology. For he is saying that such a psychology, since it deals only with factors of the organism, can give an explanation only of the failures of cognition, not the successes: e.g., the patient failed to perceive the nurse because he was chloroformed. After all, accounting for the successes of cognition requires more than a knowledge of what goes on in the organism, no matter how accurate such knowledge may be; it requires a knowledge that what is referred to by the thought is "out there" in reality.

This early admission by James is an anticipation of one of the fundamental poles of his thought. The pole, which I maintain is fundamentally distinct from his search for causal relationships between mind and brain, is erected in the course of his thinking about the referentialness of thought—the cognitive relationship. This observation stems, I think, from his growing awareness that thought can be specified only in terms of what it is *of;* in this particular case it can be specified as successful or true only if what it refers to is really there.

The opposite pole of James's thought is plain to see: In one passage, for example, in which he insists that the laws of successful thinking are totally different from the laws of actual thinking (as different as ethics is from history), he nevertheless also insists that the laws of actual thinking, expressed ultimately in physiological terms, can give a "sufficient explanation" of *all* our thinking.[12] This is in blatant contradiction to the passage cited above, and it spreads before our eyes in synoptic fashion the lineaments of tension to be found in the *Principles*. It is only a glimpse, however, and it does not reveal the full depth of the problem posed by James's treatise.

Let us ponder for a moment what a sufficient explanation of a successful cognition would involve. If we could find all the neces-

The puzzling opening

sary conditions, this would amount to a sufficient condition, so the citing of them would be a sufficient explanation of the successful cognition. That the thing referred to really be there is certainly one of the necessary conditions. But how do we know what kind of thing is referred to? We seem to have uncovered another necessary condition. Not only would we have to know *that* it is really there, we would have to know first *what kind of thing* to start looking for; i.e., we would have to know what the cognition *meant*. (Note that successful cognition for James is only a species of cognition in general.) Surely James must agree that determination of meaning is logically prior to determination of truth: we cannot even begin to tell whether a thought, statement, or gesture is true (the thing referred to being really there) unless we already know what it means. Meaning and knowledge of meaning (e.g., "I know what you mean") is a necessary condition for successful cognition or truth. There may be other such conditions still, but at least there must be these two.

We begin to sense the peculiar centrality for psychology of the knowledge of meaning. We must know what the agent is intending, meaning, and/or referring to in the world before we can determine if his cognition has the specific characteristic of being successful or unsuccessful, true or false. We must know the intended relationship to the world—i.e., the cognitive relationship. The problem which this raises for an exclusively physiological psychology is obvious: If the psychology is concerned only with the organism (at best only one term in the relationship), it is impossible to see how it could ever determine the relationship itself. But a subtle form of the problem seems to be raised for any natural scientific psychology, even one which considers the environment, e.g., behaviorism. Since an onlooking psychologist is presumably interested in only the actual facts of the behavioral situation, and since he can check these facts and tell if the agent's cognition is successful or unsuccessful only if he already knows what the agent's utterance or overt action (say, a gesture) means, then this would seem to suggest that he must already know to what *possible* facts the utterance or gesture has reference. But how can this be reconciled with the limitation of holding to the actual facts of the situation? If it is said that the utterance or gesture itself is an actual fact, not a possible fact, then we reply that it is an actual fact of a very peculiar sort for natural science, and simply to say that it is an actual fact is to speak loosely and to beg the whole question which this study raises. For presumably it is a *meaningful* utterance or gesture we are talking about, not a mere noise or movement, and good arguments can be advanced for concluding that meaning is a noncontingent relationship between utterance or gesture and the world. If it is noncontingent, then it is necessary and subject to description through necessary truths. And if it is such, the question which inevitably arises is: Can a natural scientific psychology, which is presumably empirical and concerned only with contingent and actual relationships, ever hope to include such an investigation within the purview of its project? Since such a psychology must presuppose meaning, and since the study of meaning requires an investigation which is prior to the natural scientific project, the question arises as to whether a natural scientific psychology can possibly be autonomous, as James wishes it to be.

Now we have a fuller account of the problem posed by James's *Principles of Psychology*. It is our concern to delineate his attempts at coping with it. We face the difficulty that he himself never formulates the problem in a perfectly explicit way.

III

Let us recapitulate. We find that Chapter One is problematical. Whether James intended it to be an adequate introduction to the work as a whole is not clear, and yet it is so general, so sweeping, and gives rise to so many ambiguities that it implants the suspicion that the manifest program of the work will not unroll smoothly. Not only does it leave the nature of mental states very much in doubt and unspecified, but it says very little about them. Enough is said, however, to render doubtful the contention that James is only expounding a behaviorism which reduces the notion of mental states to publicly observable, contingent facts. The thesis of this study is also unconfirmed, but nothing has been found which could make its confirmation impossible. On the contrary, what has been found gives it some slight probability. First, the manifest program gets little initial support, thus rendering a latent strand possible. Second, James's own observations on the cognitive relationship and the conditions for determining successful cognition imply that the cognitive relationship is the meaning relationship, or act of mean-

The puzzling opening

ing, and that this must first be specified if his natural scientific program is to get under way. James himself does not draw out the implications to this conclusion. Thus we can only say that a problem has been generated in the *Principles* itself which may lead him to advance a latent strand of thought.

It should be observed that if the thesis of this study is correct, if James advances a latent strand to the effect that thought cannot be specified without specifying thought's object, this would not preclude his consistent consideration of natural scientific, biological, and environmental factors in his philosophy of mind. For to say that natural science does not play a logically prior role in investigations of mind is not to say that it plays no role, or an unimportant role. Thus, for example, James's tribute to Herbert Spencer in Chapter One, based on Spencer's formula for mind ("the adjustment of inner to outer relations"), is explicable even in the light of James's epithet that it is "vagueness incarnate," since he can at the same time appreciate Spencer's contention that minds interact with environments and are not merely "detached existents," while he denies that Spencer's philosophy of mind as "correspondence" is an adequate philosophy.[13] And indeed he does deny this.[14]

We now proceed to examine James's attempts to specify mental states as contingent psychical entities which causally interact with brain states. We will observe the pitfalls to these attempts which he himself uncovers. We will also observe how the attempt to impute causal properties to mental states dies away after the physiological preliminaries of the *Principles*, although the attempt to regard them as contingent entities is still maintained, albeit with notable inconsistencies. It is to the physiological preliminaries that we now turn.

THREE

Initial difficulties of
psychophysical dualism:
inadequacy of causal theory
for the specification of
mental states

I

In contrast to the very broad use of "mental" in Chapter One of the *Principles*, James narrows its use in the subsequent five chapters on the "physiological preliminaries" to "mental states," and he is obviously concerned with consciousness. Though he is thus dualistic, we will observe that he wishes to avoid a direct confrontation with the problem of the specification of mental states. We will observe the difficulties into which this procrastination throws him. After all, if someone says that a golliwog corresponds to a state of the brain, we will not know how to go about verifying his statement unless we already know what "golliwog" and "corresponds" mean. Before the connection of mental states and brain states can be explained, it must at least be *stated*. Not until Chapter Six does James acknowledge openly the priority of the need for an initial specification of terms:

> [The] formula which is so unobjectionable if taken vaguely, positivistically, or scientifically, as a mere empirical law of concomitance between our thoughts and our brain, tumbles to pieces entirely if we

Initial difficulties of psychophysical dualism 31

assume to represent anything more intimate or ultimate by it. The ultimate of ultimate problems, of course, in the study of the relations of thought and brain, is to understand why and how such disparate things are connected at all. But before that problem is solved (if it ever is solved) there is a less ultimate problem which must first be settled. Before the connection of thought and brain can be explained, it must at least be *stated* in an elementary form; and there are great difficulties about so stating it. To state it in elementary form one must reduce it to its lowest terms and know which mental fact and which cerebral fact are, so to speak, in immediate juxtaposition. We must find the minimal mental fact whose being reposes directly on a brain-fact; and we must similarly find the minimal brain-event which will have a mental counterpart at all. Between the mental and the physical minima thus found there will be an immediate relation, the expression of which, if we had it, would be the elementary psychophysic law.[1]

Earlier than Chapter Six he begins to glimpse the dangers of postponing explicit specification of mental states. He recognizes, as he says, the danger of "what Aristotle calls 'slipping into another kind.'"[2] Specifically, he begins to see the dangers of confusing what we know about physical states (i.e., brain states) with what we know about mental states—and conversely. He points out some obvious confusions. For instance, one of the characteristics of the brain's functioning is that it secretes chemical substances into the bloodstream. This led some psychologists to maintain that the brain secretes thought in a similar manner. James contends that the analogy is baseless: the similarities between a stream of thought and a stream of chemicals is superficial, to say the least.[3] Or, again, he notes that one of the characteristics of the nervous system is that the time it requires to react to stimuli is measurable. But he contends that reaction time is not necessarily thought time.[4]

However, James's failure to offer exact criteria for the identification of mental states soon involves him in difficulties which are suspiciously like category mistakes or "slipping into another kind." Take his account of an instance of learning: a child that has already learned to avoid a flame. James begins his account from the mental "side" of the child's experience: his perceptions of present occurrences and his memories of past ones. James assumes that the child's perception of the flame has become associated with remembered ideas of grasping, of pain, and of avoidance. The question for James becomes: How do the physiological processes which correspond to these mental processes become organized in the brain?⁵

He then advances a hypothesis about how this happens. In the child's first exposure to flame, sensory and motor processes (physiological ones on the physical "side," of course), originally of a reflex type, are projected physiologically into the brain and there leave traces (a physiological unit) which, through combination with other future traces, can become efficacious in the modification of reflex action; learning will have taken place. To each of these physiological units in the brain there corresponds a mental unit or state, James maintains. Now, in the child's first exposure to flame, in his condition of ignorance, the hypothetical process of learning is this: The organism's initial sensory process is consciously experienced by it (on the mental "side" now) as perception of this novel thing, the flame; this perception triggers the motor process of grasping; the grasping in turn causally involves the second sensory process, experienced this time consciously as pain; the pain in turn causally triggers the second reflex motor process of recoil of the hand. This sequence of reflex actions leaves a connected series of four physiological units connected in the fibers of the brain by neural pathways of such a sort that when the flame is seen again, the last implanted trace (from the recoil) is sufficiently strong to shunt out and prevent the grasping. Learning has occurred.

We might suppose that James wishes to assert that this occurs within the physiological autonomy of the physiological states alone. But he says that all the brain traces are experienced in *idea* before the motor action of grasping can occur in fact,⁶ and that the idea causally prevents the motor grasping.⁷

To this, of course, a critic might reply that James is mixing his levels of discourse, slipping into another kind, confusing the logic of his terms in spite of his own warning. The critic might continue that a mental state or idea is not the kind of thing that we can coherently assert to have any kind of relation to a physical state, a fortiori, not a causal one. James himself imagines such a critic and offers to mollify him by allowing him to speak of "ideational process" (physiological process) as the cause instead of idea or mental state.⁸ For James supposes a one-for-one correlation between the four brain states and the four mental ones. According to him, if we map the cognitive apparatus with X's for units and with

Initial difficulties of psychophysical dualism

lines connecting them, then the X's can stand indifferently for physical states of the brain or for mental states. The lines connecting them can stand indifferently for nerve fibers or for associations between ideas.[9]

It is questionable, however, if such a neat correlation of mental and physical terms would mollify such a critic at all. He would object that this very correlation presupposes that one can legitimately slip from one "kind" to another; it assumes that there is sufficient similarity between the mental and the physical to enable one to establish a point of contact or correlation between them, and this is precisely what should be proved, not assumed.

Moreover, it assumes something even simpler and more fundamental: that the mental state can itself be specified. For James begins on the mental "side" of the dualism with "idea," and then proceeds to say that this term can be used interchangeably with "ideational process" (the physical "side"). He wants to say that the "idea" *or* "ideational process" of pain shunts out the grasping reflex and causally prevents it. But his fundamental specification of "idea" relies on a tacit acceptance of the traditional associationist theory of mental states, and we find that his own investigations of thought lead him to criticize this theory. We find him saying that we do not associate ideas; rather we associate things known, but then only for a single idea or awareness.[10] Thus we do not have a discrete idea of pain linked with other discrete ideas in a temporal sequence, and thus we cannot map them against a sequence of discrete physiological "ideational processes" in which the causal connections take place.

It can be seen that James's attempt to accommodate the critic by allowing him to say that the physiological "ideational process" does the causal work gets him nowhere. For such a physiological state is specified only on the basis of similarity to a mental state, and the specification of the mental state as a discrete existent which copies the discrete object known by it is then discarded. Moreover, James later concludes that the classical theory of the association of ideas, if it has any merit at all, is a disguised physical hypothesis about brain states, and not a valid theory of mind at all.[11] The confusion of mental states and brain states has come full circle.

Note the unhappy symbiosis of concepts which obtains between "idea" and "ideational process." It is as if two parasites were parasitical on one another—something which cannot happen for long in nature, but which, unfortunately for thinkers, can plague their thought forever. First, since by his own admission his analysis of mental states is mixed up at the outset with physical considerations, he is prevented from seeing what role mind might distinctively play if it were understood in its distinctiveness. Second, since by his own admission the theory of association of ideas is really a disguised physical hypothesis, James is prevented from open-mindedly examining the physiological processes as well; he is prevented from seeing what role physiological processes might distinctively play if they were understood in their distinctiveness. In sum, the validity of the theory of association qua physical hypothesis is not established, and as an unestablished mental hypothesis it prejudges both the mental states and the physiological states by an initially dubious location and specification of "physiological traces" through their supposed correlation and similarity to allegedly and dubiously associated mental states. The concepts of the physical and the mental attempt to borrow from each other, but neither has any cash, so to speak.

To this confusion a behaviorist critic might retort: Eliminate all reference to these publicly unobservable mental states. Not only are they an unnecessary admixture in the analysis and explanation of learning, but they are an endlessly confusing one as well. Employ only theories that rely on the data of publicly observable events.

Yet there is the possibility that this retort is as confused in its own way as the position it rejects. The rejection of a fallacy is not in itself any guarantee that it will be replaced by a truth. Particularly, it can be asked if the data of psychology are actually understandable as publicly observable events shorn of all reference to a subject's consciousness. The question remains, What is consciousness *properly* understood? A state? A causally efficacious event?

James calls the position of this hypothetical behaviorist critic an "unreal abstraction." Two distinct grounds for his stand are to be found in the *Principles*. The first is a dualistic and causal ground, consonant with his manifest program, which we have already begun to expound. We shall shortly see how it develops internal difficulties and begins to collapse within the physiological preliminaries themselves. The second ground is the latent phenomenological strand which begins to emerge clearly with Chapter Six. Ac-

Initial difficulties of psychophysical dualism

cording to this latter ground, the behavioristic position is an unreal abstraction not because it fails to do justice to mental states as a nonphysical kind of existent which is causally efficacious vis à vis the brain (somehow), but because it fails to do justice to the kind of analysis which is appropriate to mind. It is a difference between kinds of entities and kinds of analyses. This difference in kinds of analyses—which I take to be crucially important—will be dealt with later.

II

James's first ground for objecting to the behaviorist is undercut from several different directions. On the one hand, there is his growing conviction that if a physiological analysis of mind is to be attempted at all, it must be conducted in exclusively physiological terms. On the other hand, there is his growing awareness that an incompleteness in such an account cannot be remedied by the postulation of mental entities with causal powers.

We use the phrase "growing conviction" deliberately. It is not until over a hundred pages later that James explicitly refers to the danger of mixing physiological and mentalistic terms in his account of the child's learning to avoid a flame. He uses the words "a short way back" (104 pages) in an elastic way:

> In describing the functions of the hemispheres a short way back, we used language derived from both the bodily and the mental life, saying now that the animal made indeterminate and unforeseeable reactions, and anon that he was swayed by considerations of future good and evil; treating his hemispheres sometimes as the seat of memory and ideas in the psychic sense, and sometimes talking of them as simply a complicated addition to his reflex machinery. This sort of vacillation in the point of view is a fatal incident of all ordinary talk about these questions; but I must now settle my scores with those readers to whom I already dropped a word in passing (see page 24, note) and who have probably been dissatisfied with my conduct ever since.[12]

James realizes that one way to eliminate this confusing mixture of terms is not to use any mentalistic ones at all. It is fair to say that the possibility of a thoroughgoing materialism both attracts and repels him throughout the *Principles*. At times he is greatly impressed with how far one can get in philosophy of mind through the use of physiological terms exclusively, and at these times he wishes to push such an attempt to its limits.

Let us examine James's physiological treatment of habit, since he thinks that such a treatment is fruitful, and since he thinks that habit is a fundamental topic. He thinks it is fundamental because the central phenomena of attention and effort are dependent on the laws of habit and the habituated brain:

> The strongest reason for believing that [attention and effort] . . . depend on brain processes . . . and are not pure acts of the spirit . . . [is] that they seem in some degree subject to the law of habit, which is a material law.[13]

If attention is subject to a "material law," then most of the mental life must be also, since attention is central for James: for example, ". . . the turnings of our attention form the nucleus of our inner self."[14] If attention is subject to a material law, then the all-important matter of the will must be subject also, or so it would seem, since for James we will to do only that to which we attend (and consent: "be thou the reality for me,"[15] but more of this matter of consent, belief, and reality later). Obviously, if mind is teleological (directed on ends), then attention, effort, and will are fundamental; and if they all depend on habit, then habit must be utterly basic.

James writes, "The moment one tries to define what habit is, one is led to the fundamental properties of matter."[16] If a piece of paper just happens to be folded once along a certain line, then it has already acquired the habit of folding along that line. The tissue of the nervous system behaves in a comparable way, he believes. The question arises for him: Might not the changing physiological structure of the brain be itself a matter of evolving habit, and might not habit therefore be completely understandable in physiological terms? Might not consciousness and the feeling of choice be a mere derivative—an epiphenomenon? A particular behavior which "directs" the organism in its environment may be no more than a function of a modification of the "highly unstable" brain tissue which first chanced to change on a certain sort of occasion and then fell into that same way on subsequent similar occasions. A specific change in the same sort of occasion will produce a change in the means used to attain the goal, but each means is a product of

Initial difficulties of psychophysical dualism

trial-and-error behavior and habituation of the brain, just as much as the more constant end or goal is. A feeling of attention, decision, and voluntary action may be no more than a mere epiphenomenal effect in consciousness, derivative from the incipient discharge of one of several opposing motor pathways, laid down in advance, the prevailing one's being, after a deceptive "struggle of decision," no more than the one most habituated, given the circumstances. Might not the study of the brain offer the key to the study of the mental life? This is the question which James seriously considers.

He never quite brings himself to an affirmative answer. Thoroughgoing materialism remains for him an "unreal abstraction." The reasons for his stand which he gives in the physiological preliminaries are largely causal ones. This is so despite his awareness that one cannot explain a causal correlation unless one first states it, and one cannot state it without at least specifying what is meant by "mental state." Despite his admission that "we can form no positive image of the *modus operandi* of a volition or other thought affecting the cerebral molecules,"[17] he writes nevertheless:

> It is to my mind quite inconceivable that consciousness should have *nothing to do* with a business which it so faithfully attends. And the question, 'What has it to do?' is one which psychology has no right to 'surmount,' for it is her plain duty to consider it. The fact is that the whole question of interaction and influence between things is a metaphysical question, and cannot be discussed at all by those who are unwilling to go into matters thoroughly.[18]

James will indeed step into metaphysics, which is startling in view of his statement in the Preface that he will avoid it. He admits that Chapter Six is "exclusively metaphysical."[19] But in the passages wherein he maintains that consciousness is a causal force he takes refuge in a kind of metaphysical agnosticism. How, he asks, can a materialist be so sure that there is no causation between consciousness and brain when causation between physical entities is itself such a mystery? How can a materialist be so sure that a mental idea does not have something causally to do with "the distance two molecules stand apart" (in the brain)? The materialist dogmatizes about physical causation "as if Hume, Kant and Lotze had never been born."[20]

Of course, it might be noted that James cannot even specify what he means by "mental state," while a materialist can specify "physical state." James does not consider such a criticism, however. At this point he argues as follows: Although the repertory of possible actions is set by the habituated structure of the brain, consciousness can act causally to the extent of determining which one of several possible and equally impelling lines of action will be pursued. Its causal force is limited, but in those seesawing cases where its influence is decisive an approach employing only physiological terms will be unable to predict the outcome. Such a physiological approach, James implies, will be able to account for the action only after it is accomplished; but because of this, and because it can account for any action equally well, we can conclude that it has mistaken proximate and invariable physiological effects for causes; it has unrealistically abstracted from the causal mental states, and it is consequently irrelevant to the adequate explanation of such actions.

James then alludes to the theory of evolution. Consciousness has evolved, and only that which is useful evolves. If it is useful, it must be considered causal.[21] Pursuant to this argument he advances a hypothesis on the functioning of the brain. On the basis of minimal physiological evidence, he hypothesizes that the human brain by itself is so unstable that incoming neural impulses will lay down lines of incipient habit which have no more than an accidental or chance organization—like throwing dice. But our behavior is not like this, James observes; it is directed, intelligent. Only because of this do we survive and evolve. The dice, then, must be "loaded."[22] With this hypothesis about the unstable brain we can suppose, says he, that it is consciousness that loads the dice. All we need to do is allow consciousness to be what it seems to be (uniquely causal), and there is a place awaiting it in our theoretical structure.

How does consciousness exert causal influence on the unstable brain? We cannot suppose that it creates new electrical energy and introduces it into the physiological system for this would violate the law of conservation of energy, says James. So consciousness can only be said to "strengthen" or "dampen" what energy is already there:

> The nerve currents, coursing through the cells and fibers, must in this case be supposed strengthened by the fact of their awaking one consciousness and dampened by awakening another.[23]

But what is this except an evasion? Instead of saying that consciousness "dampens" a neural impulse, why does he not say that it slams into it and knocks it down? The logical difficulty is as great in either case. There can be no dampening without an exchange of energy, just as there can be no slamming and knocking. James's formulation is a bit like saying that one only commits a little bit of murder. At this point, however, he refuses to discuss the matter further because he says that it would be metaphysical to do so.[24] This is an amazing statement in view of the very next sentence in his text: "The reader who found himself swamped with too much metaphysics in the last chapter will have a still worse time of it in this one, which is exclusively metaphysical."[25] He cannot have it both ways: metaphysical when it suits him, and nonmetaphysical when it does not.

It is surely significant, I believe, that there is only one other place in the *Principles* (as far as I can determine) in which James speaks of consciousness as having causal characteristics. It is found in Volume I in his chapter on attention. James is impressed by the fact that we often attend to things which stimulate us only faintly (he would use units of physics to measure strength of stimulation), and that we do this in the presence of things which stimulate us much more strongly; we pick out quiet little things from a buzzing and teeming background. He concludes that we must be "pre-sensitized" to what we attend to—that we "pre-perceive it." He first speaks of this sensitizing, anticipatory preparation as the work of apparently physiological processes, the "ideational centers."[26] But the equivocation between "idea" and "ideational process," between mentalistic and physicalistic terms, which we have already noted, recurs: What is the meaning of "ideational centers"? He specifies the brain processes on the basis of mental states to which they supposedly correspond, so he must first specify mental states. He begins to do this by saying that they are what apprehend the characteristics of things, the ones "that have been labelled for us and the labels stamped into our mind."[27]

It seems that he is about to specify mental states in terms of language about their objects, which might be consistent and appropriate, but instead he speaks of attention as a causally initiating "spiritual force."[28] Force, of course, would be specifiable only in terms of physics or physiology (e.g., "foot-pounds"); but when he qualifies it with the word "spiritual" we do not know what he means by the combination, and can only conclude that the equivocation has recurred in the form of a pointless deadlock.

Although he continues to speak of the correlation of mental and physical states throughout most of the *Principles*, his talk about mental states causally affecting brain states ceases after the chapter on attention in the first volume. It is conspicuously absent from his long chapter on the will in the second. We say "conspicuously" because James would be tempted to invoke consciousness as a causally initiating force in view of his frankly expressed bias in favor of free will. He does not invoke it.

III

Although early in the *Principles* James ceases to predicate causal powers of mental states, still there are a number of passages sprinkled throughout the text in which he continues his attempt to specify mental states within the confines of causal theory; he attempts to specify them in terms of the physiological systems which allegedly cause *them*. A tacit epiphenomenalism, a one-sided interactionism, occasionally crops up. We shall see how unsuccessful are all of these attempts to specify mental states in terms of causal theory.

James writes:

> The mental states usually distinguished as feelings are the *emotions*, and the *sensations* we get from skin, muscle, viscus, eye, ear, nose and palate. The 'thoughts,' as recognized in popular parlance, are the *conceptions* and *judgments*.[29]

And again:

> The brain is so made that all currents in it run one way. Consciousness of some sort goes with all the currents, but it is only when new currents are entering that it has the sensational *tang*. And it is only then that consciousness directly *encounters* (to use a word of Mr. Bradley's) a reality outside itself. The difference between such encounter and all conceptual knowledge is very great. A blind man may know all *about* the sky's blueness, and I may know all about your toothache, conceptually . . . But so long as he has not felt blueness, nor I the toothache, our knowledge, wide as it is, of these realities will be hollow and inadequate. Somebody must *feel* blueness, somebody must *have* toothache, to make human knowledge of these matters real . . .[30]

Initial difficulties of psychophysical dualism

Though it is not a certainty, James seems to be attempting to distinguish mental states which are sensations from those which are not, on the basis of a difference in physiological, causal ground.

The crucial issue is this: Certainly he does believe that sensations are caused by "nerve currents coming in from the periphery," while conceptual thoughts are not.[31] He believes that such physiological events comprise some of the causal conditions of sensations, and he is certainly right. But does he believe that these conditions are identical with the *logical conditions* of "sensation"? That is, he believes that sensations are caused by such physiological events, but does he believe that these events are the *criteria* for what we *mean* when we talk about sensations? Does he believe that we must think that these causal conditions do occur before we can meaningfully apply the term "sensation"?

There is a radical difference between causal conditions and logical conditions, and they must be determined by radically different inquiries. For example, if we point out to a child a cat asleep in a shop window, and if the child then asks why the cat is sleeping, we will not know how to answer him unless we understand his question, and we will not understand it unless we understand what is being asked for. Is he asking, in effect, for causal conditions or for criteria of application for the term "sleeping" (logical conditions)? If he is asking for causal conditions, we will answer that the cat is tired;[32] or, if he is a bright and advanced child, we will make reference to such causal conditions as the chemical state of the cat's brain. If he is asking for logical conditions, we will give him an answer which includes a reference to the conditions which must be met before we apply the term "sleeping" to the animal, and *these* conditions need have nothing to do with the physiological conditions we speak of in our first answer. We do not recognize the cat to be a sleeping cat by noting the chemical state of the cat's brain. Indeed, we can profitably note the causal properties of the chemical state of its brain only after we have recognized that the cat is sleeping.

The point is that the child may only want to know why we say the cat is sleeping and not dead, and if we cite the chemical state of its brain before he is sure that it is sleeping, he may think that the cited chemical conditions make the difference between the cat's being asleep and its being dead, and they most assuredly do not.

They make the difference between the cat's being asleep and being awake.

In the case of sensation, if the nerve currents's coming into the brain from the peripheral nervous system is one of the logical conditions for speaking of or specifying sensations, then we cannot speak at all meaningfully of sensations unless we think that such currents are actually coming in. If so, a philosopher like Aristotle, who believed that the brain was merely an organ for cooling the blood, would not be able to speak meaningfully about sensations, since in not knowing the causal conditions of nerve currents for sensations he would literally not know what is meant by the term "sensation." But this does not sound right, for Aristotle speaks of sensations more meaningfully in some ways than most of us moderns do.

Is James saying, then, that part of what we *mean* by "sensation" is that nerve currents are coming in from the periphery, and that part of what we *mean* by "conceptual thought" is that they are not? Certainly he would say that what we mean by "sensation" must be *consistent* with what we know its causal conditions to be. But is he saying that these causal conditions comprise in whole or in part the logical criteria for the application of the term? If he is saying this, then he might be tempted to say that part of what we mean by "sensation" is that it is something which occurs in a private, perfectly mentalistic world;[33] for nerve currents are particular events, and the currents in your nervous system are cut off from those in mine. Hence if sensations are correlated one to one with nerve currents, and the nerve currents are separate and individual, then the sensations would be separate and individual as well. That there are two thoughts of the constellation of stars called Orion and only one Orion would mark not only a sundering of nervous systems, but a sundering of thoughts as well. The problem would be how we could know that we are thinking of the same thing, or even that there is a same thing. But if mental states are specified in terms of what they are *of*—if the logical conditions are in part set by the object—then there well may be two thoughts *of* the same thing, and insofar as this is true they are insofar-forth the same thought. But then a new problem arises: how could they be different in *any* way? One is yours, one is mine. The problem is crucial.

Initial difficulties of psychophysical dualism 43

In view of James's sharp criticism of the practice in psychological literature of using the term "sensation" as if it meant one and the same thing as "the physical impression either in the terminal organs or the centers," it would seem that he would be reluctant to say that the causal conditions constitute the logical conditions of "sensation." It would seem that he would repudiate the practice of the contemporary psychologist D. O. Hebb, for example, who uses the term synonymously with galvinometrically measurable impulses of electricity in the receptors and neural tracts.[34]

With great emphasis James writes:

> The word Sensation . . . is constantly, in psychological literature, used as if it meant one and the same thing with the *physical impression* either in the terminal organs or in the centres, which is its antecedent condition, and this notwithstanding that by sensation we mean a mental, not a physical, fact. But those who expressly mean by it a mental fact still leave to it a physical *place*, still think of it as objectively inhabiting the very neural tracts which occasion its appearance when they are excited; and then (going a step further) they think it must *place itself* where they *place* it, or be subjectively sensible of that place as its habitat in the first instance, and afterwards have to be *moved* so as to appear elsewhere.
>
> All this seems highly confused and unintelligible. Consciousness . . . cannot properly be said to *inhabit* any place. It has dynamic relations with the brain, and cognitive relations with everything and anything . . . But the supposition that a sensation primitively *feels either itself or its object to be in the same place with the brain* is absolutely groundless . . .[35]

James says that it is confusing and unintelligible to assert that a sensation inhabits the neural tracts which causally occasion its appearance because it is absurd to say that it inhabits any place.

But he goes on to say that the psychologist, who adopts a (presumably) causal point of view, may, "if he wishes," assume that the sensation is "in the same place with the brain."[36] Now, even with the qualifications this seems to relapse into the very confusion which he inveighs against. He has removed the sensation from the neural tracts of the sense organs only to deposit it in another physical place, the brain.

Yet he has eased the confusion somewhat, if only by delineating the ever-central problem he comes up against. Just how does the psychologist go about an intelligent adoption of the causal point of view? How can the psychologist conceive the sensation as being in the same place as the brain? And with this the logically prior problem is forced on our attention: How is it possible to conceive the sensation at all? How is it possible to achieve that initial specification without which empirical inquiry of any sort is impossible? It is like this: If someone says that a golliwog is in a brain we are speechless unless we know what "golliwog" means. We are powerless to agree or disagree or to add or subtract information about its causal relations to the brain.

That James is also speechless is clear: he simply lets the problem of the spatial and causal relations of sensations to the brain drop out of the account and leave no trace. Still, though he does not speak about his speechlessness, he does do something which may be germane to its alleviation. He begins to deal with what the sensation primitively feels its object to be.[37] He calls this "the original cognitive function of our sensibility." He treats of the object.

However, there is a not-to-be-ignored blurring in James's account which suggests that he thinks there is an overlapping of causal and logical conditions. This blurring appears unmistakably in his talk of sensations as "bodily sensations." For example, he asserts that a bodily sensation can never be twice the same because a sensation has to occur in a brain which must have been modified by the previous sensation.[38] Since all feelings are bodily sensations in *some* way (all caused by the body), all the distinct types of feeling get lumped together in the gross phrase "bodily sensation."

Nowhere is the ambiguity of James's account of sensation more apparent than in the ambiguity of "bodily sensation." Does he mean a sensation *of* one's own body, like a sensation of pain in the big toe? We shall call this the "cognitive *of*" because the sensation is spoken of as if it were a cognitive object. Or does he mean a sensation of one's own body in the sense that all sensations are *caused* by one's own bodily processes? We shall call this the "causal *of*." He seems to mean the latter, since he does not speak just of aches and pains felt in one's body, but of sensations of sounds of pianos and of the color of grass. But his use of the equivocal "bodily sensation" is badly misleading, for at the same time that it suggests sensations like aches and pains in the body which may very well be successfully specified in terms of their

Initial difficulties of psychophysical dualism

cognitive object (e.g., one's toe or one's tooth), it also suggests that they are caused by this bodily part, which in turn suggests that we specify sensations in terms of our knowledge of their different organic causes. But this is precisely the point to be proved, not to be assumed in a phrase like "bodily sensation." The phrase tends to be question-begging.

Let us now repeat our basic question, this time with a fuller knowledge of the difficulties which James puts in his own path. Can he, in the light of his own findings, specify a sensation by its causal source and without involving himself in talk about its object? I think that he cannot.

Note carefully the following key passage in which he equates "bodily sensation" with "real sensational effect." He has finally nailed down the real being of a mental state, or thinks that he has:

> Does not the same piano-key, struck with the same force, make us hear in the same way? Does not the same grass give us the same feeling of green . . . ? It seems a piece of metaphysical sophistry to suggest that we do not; and yet a close attention to the matter shows that *there is no proof that the same bodily sensation is ever got by us twice. What is got twice is the same OBJECT.* We hear the same note over and over again; we see the same quality of green . . . The grass out of the window now looks to me of the same green in the sun as in the shade, and yet a painter would have to paint one part of it dark brown, another part bright yellow, to give its real sensational effect. We take no heed, as a rule, of the different way in which the same things look and sound and smell at different distances and under different circumstances. The sameness of the *things* is what we are concerned to ascertain; and any sensations that assure us of that will probably be considered in a rough way to be the same with each other. This is what makes off-hand testimony about the subjective identity of different sensations well nigh worthless as a proof of the fact.[39]

So "there is no proof that the same bodily sensation is ever got by us twice."[40] But let us reverse the onus: What proof does James offer us that each bodily sensation is different from every other? That is, what conditions does he employ to mean them or specify them and thus to show that they are all different? I think that he employs causal conditions at times and that they fail to do the job he wishes.

James says that the grass looks the same green to him whether it lies in the sun or the shade. Yet to give the "real sensational effect" of the color of the shaded part we would have to paint it a dark brown and the sunlit part a bright yellow. This "real sensational effect" is the very "being" of the sensation, and he calls it a "bodily sensation." Now how does he mean that the "real sensational effect," say of the dark brown of the grass seen in the shade, is never twice the same? We have already cited his allusion to brain facts. He cites other facts.

He declares that "the absolute quality or quantity" of a sensation in many cases cannot be "sensibly learned," and he gives an example of our sensibility being blunted and deceived:

> What appeals to our attention far more than the absolute quality of a given sensation is its *ratio* to whatever other sensations we may have at the same time. When everything is dark a somewhat less dark sensation makes us see an object white. Helmholtz calculates that the white marble painted in a picture representing an architectural view by moonlight is, when seen by daylight, from ten to twenty thousand times brighter than the real moonlit marble would be.[41]

This, James declares, "could never have been *sensibly* learned; it had to be inferred from a series of indirect considerations."[42] He then adduces facts which take their places in such inferences. He writes:

> The eye's sensibility to light is at its maximum when the eye is first exposed, and blunts itself with surprising rapidity. A long nights' sleep will make it see things twice as brightly on wakening.[43]

Nowhere, however, does James adduce any facts which would make us believe that seeing things twice as brightly can be inferred from only the changed causal conditions of the physiological organ, the eye. Nowhere does he adduce any facts which would make us believe that the experimenter can do anything but rely on the subject's report concerning his own sensibility (or on behavior which involves that sensibility), or that the experimenter can do anything but determine this *first*. On the basis of what James himself tells us, he should not have said that certain differences in sensations can *never* be sensibly learned, but only that the subject must be taught to exercise his sensibility more keenly, and in situations more highly structured than usual. It would seem that the experimenter can profitably note the changed causal conditions

Initial difficulties of psychophysical dualism

in the eye only after he has learned from the subject about the subject's changed sensibility. Although if a mapping were ever set up which *began* with the subject's report, or with the meaning of his behavior as established by internal relations between organism and environment, then it might be inferred that to a physiological condition there corresponded in some way a condition of sensibility. Thus James gives us no good reason to believe that differences in sensations can be specified on any grounds other than that of sensibility itself; and this ground need include no references whatsoever to physiological causal conditions. This is precisely what we should have expected in any case. For are we to say that a Greek, for example, who knew nothing of neural impulses or retinal rods and cones was incapable of speaking meaningfully about vision and things seen visually?

We find James using disconcerting locutions. He speaks of "the eye's sensibility to light" and of the eye's seeing things twice as brightly on awakening. We are tempted to ask what he has told us that would justify our saying that an *eye* has a *sensibility* or that an eye *sees* anything. Is it not, instead, persons who see things and have sensibilities? Should not we talk rather of the eye's *sensitivity?* That could be specified and measured in physiological units *after* something about sensibility had been determined. Of course, the experimenter may be interested in just the eye and in just physiological units. But then he is a physiologist, not a psychologist.

James also writes:

> The difference of the sensibility is shown best by the difference of our emotion about the things from one age to another, or when we are in different organic moods.[44]

Recall that James referred to emotions as feelings (see page 40). This is another sense of the word "feeling": the emotions. It is identical to the ordinary use of the term. We say, "I feel sad," or "I feel happy." We do not ordinarily say, "I feel a sensation of red," when we see a red cube. But in neither case am I referring to my body, even though I may at the same time feel something happening in my body; I am referring to something in the world which is red or which I am sad or happy about. The phrase "bodily sensation" confuses the distinction between causal and logical conditions. Certainly, a disturbance in my body may cause me to have a different sensation, and in the case of emotion at least *may* even be *part* of what we mean by the words "I feel sad," but the disturbance cannot supply the whole specification.

Suffice to say at this point that James does not prove through a citation of causal facts that no two emotions or sensations are ever the same. If it is the case, he does not establish it through causal reasoning. We are left with our sensibility, and it certainly seems that we are sensible of something—the cognitive *of*—which is the same as what we were sensible of before, and that for this reason we feel the same way again.

Now let us examine more closely James's citation of brain facts: a later sensation must happen in a brain modified by an earlier one, and so must be different. Notice a difference between this fact and the others he adduces. Since on the basis of his own causal theory there is no *direct* correspondence between physiological changes in the eye, say, and visual sensations (that being limited to such changes in the brain), there should have been no temptation to attempt to specify visual sensations and their changes in the causal terms appropriate to the specification of the visual organ. That he does nevertheless attempt this only underscores the strength of the temptation.

Let us narrow our investigation to this last fact. On his own terms, the brain is the only proximate cause of mental states; and if mental states are not to be specified in terms of this causal ground, there is no good reason to think that they are to be specified in terms of any causal ground (e.g., the eyeball and retina). James reasons thus: No neural event in the brain can be twice the same, because the fact that it happened the first time modifies the brain, therefore no mental state can be twice the same. There is an all-important omitted premise, however: "to every brain-modification, however small, must correspond a change of equal amount in the feeling which the brain subserves."[45]

This premise is not acceptable even as a presumption. For James does not offer us any independent criterion for the specification and identification of a minute change of feeling. By his own admission the agent may not even notice the minute change of feeling; and if he does notice it, James tells us nothing which leads us to believe that he notices it *as*—or in terms of—a minute brain

Initial difficulties of psychophysical dualism

change. Moreover, he tells us nothing to make us believe that the experimenter can detect it without the report of the agent. In effect, then, James is only renaming the feelings "feelings of brain modifications"; thus he is not only advancing a criterion for the meaning of "feeling" which employs specious logical conditions, but he is also robbing his causal theory of whatever explanatory force it might have had *as* a causal theory.

Both causal theory and logical theory (theory of meaning) are disrupted when they are mixed together. For causal connections are not discovered through tracing, or in this case generating, a priori connections of meaning; we do not discover them through a process of renaming things. Given James's conceptual framework, if the experimenter should detect a minute change in the brain, he could only specify it as "a brain modification felt by the subject." But without a criterion for minute brain change, which is itself independent of the criterion for minute change of feeling, we again have on our hands a pointless treadmill of words.

We now turn to the analysis and specification of mental states which is the more convincing one in the *Principles,* and in terms of which the same sensation—in some real sense of the phrase same sensation—*can* be had twice. Numerically they are all different, we grant this; but James in places seems to want to say more than this. We shall note how in one passage he himself criticizes associationist psychology for confusing logical and causal conditions.

IV

James refers to the first six chapters of his *Principles* as "physiological preliminaries."[46] But as early as Chapter Five he is dealing with matters that bear on the all-important subject of specification of mental states, and this is of particular significance precisely because it cannot be construed as part of a physiological (and causal) analysis. James maintains in Chapter Five that terms like "interest" and "end" are inapplicable to the physical organism as such, and it is only when the biological scientist's "commenting intelligence" is projected unwittingly into his data that he makes the mistake of so applying them.

Now this is a crucial point. Recall James's "criterion of mentality" introduced in the puzzling first chapter of his work: "The pursuance of future ends and the choice of means for their attainment are thus the mark and criterion of the presence of mentality . . ." If the concept of "end" is not applicable to the physical organism as such, then it would follow that mind is not specifiable in exclusively physiological terms. In Chapter Five James begins a specification of mental states in terms of ends; but it has a nonintrospective cast. The upshot of this is to throw doubt on his basic programmatic dichotomy of the psychical and the physical, and to raise the suspicion that the role of mind must be more subtly conceived. One suspects that mentalistic terms—which are yet not part of the introspectionist's vocabulary—simply cannot be kept out of the account when the worldly ends, goals, and objects (the full range of behavior) of a being like man are under discussion. This suspicion helps to clear up the puzzling opening chapter of the *Principles* which was more, but unaccountably more, than physiological. One suspects that the physical and mental "compartments" are not airtight, and that a criterion of mind must be introduced before either the purely physiological or purely psychological (if such exist) can be distinguished. When we deal with what James wants to call the purely psychical ("the stream of consciousness") we shall see that he can no more keep the worldly out of the mental than he can keep the mental out of the worldly. But as early as Chapter Five the latent strand begins to emerge: the stress on the cognitive relationship over the causal and the need to solve the cognitive problem before the specification of mental states is possible.

Notice what James says in his critique of evolutionism about the irreducibility of consciousness to nonmental terms. What emerges is his most potent argument against behaviorism, which, recall, he termed "an unreal abstraction." What begins to appear is an argument for the irreducibility of consciousness which is much better than, and totally different from, the argument that consciousness has strange causal properties. He suggests cryptically that the difference between mind and matter is not a difference of entities at all, but of analyses.

James maintains that when consciousness emerges, it is a unique and unprecedented affair. Consciousness creates its own interests which were not there before: ideals, standards, decrees, goals.[47] He is concerned with exposing what he takes to be "an irresponsible mode of darwinizing" which consists in an irresponsible mode of

Initial difficulties of psychophysical dualism 51

speaking. It is to speak as if the mere body which "owns" the brain had interests. But interest and the ends of interest are not terms to be predicated of the organism qua organism. He writes:

> We speak about the utilities of its various organs and how they help or hinder the body's survival; and we treat the survival as if it were an absolute end, existing as such in the physical world, a sort of actual *should-be* . . . We forget that in the absence of some such superadded commenting intelligence (whether it be that of the animal itself, or only ours or Mr. Darwin's), the reactions cannot be properly talked of as 'useful' or 'hurtful' at all. Considered merely physically, all that can be said of them is that *if* they occur . . . survival will as a matter of fact prove to be the incidental consequence. . . . But the moment you bring a consciousness into the midst, survival ceases to be a mere hypothesis. No longer is it, '*if* survival is to occur, then so and so brain and other organs work.' It has now become an imperative decree: 'Survival *shall* occur, therefore organs *must* so work!' *Real* ends appear for the first time on the world's stage.[48]

This treatment of consciousness as *sui generis* plays a basic role in James's philosophy of mind; it is not true to say he believes consciousness is *sui generis* merely because it has a *sui generis* causal characteristic. James is here broaching his broad position that terms which are applicable to consciousness (e.g., interest) are not applicable on the physiological level. It is an attempt to heed Aristotle's warning against "falling into the other kind," and it has the broadest repercussions.

This line of thought in James antedates the *Principles;* it is developed in the *Principles,* but not initiated there. It goes back to his early attack on Spencer, his brilliant article of 1878 (the year he began to write the *Principles*), "Remarks on Spencer's Definition of Mind as Correspondence."[49] In this he was already concerned with criticizing what he took to be Spencer's naïve conception of the cognitive relationship, what Spencer called "correspondence." (Note: correspondence between the mind and the environment, the mind and its object—not mind and brain.) In criticizing this conception of the cognitive relationship as correspondence James, in effect, is criticizing his own programmatic conception of the cognitive relationship as an external one.

Let us see how this tacit self-criticism takes shape. James addresses himself to Spencer's notion that mind is to be defined as a correspondence of internal relations to the external relations of the environment. (What is meant by "internal" is left quite undefined by Spencer; thoughts are just "in" the mind somehow.) James contends that Spencer's word "correspondence" is ambiguous, but that on neither of its senses can a sound philosophy of mind be based. If "correspondence" is taken to mean survival of the organism in its environment, then a moth which has some cognition of a flame and flies into it and dies will be said to have no mind, while another moth which has no cognition of the flame and does not fly into it and thus survives will be said to have a mind—an absurdity. What follows from this for James's own theory of the cognitive relationship? At least this much: Successful cognition cannot be construed in terms of the survival of the organism. Here as elsewhere, James maintains, Spencer is led into absurdities because he forgets the role that his own "commenting intelligence" plays in his observations. He is led to believe that there are "actual should-be's" which can be predicated of the physical world qua physical. Spencer forgets that the notions of interest and goal and norm are imposed by his own commenting intelligence. In forgetting the role that his own mind plays he thus falsifies the role that any mind plays. Well then, how must James construe the phenomenon of cognition in the light of his criticism that Spencer has forgotten his own commenting intelligence, i.e., that he has misconstrued cognition?

Part of an answer emerges in James's criticism of the second sense of Spencer's word "correspondence." Sometimes it is taken to mean "point for point cognitive registering of the environment," and when it means this James asks how Spencer *knows* what is *really there* in the environment to be corresponded to by mind. Spencer begins with what he knows but forgets that he can do this only because of the structure of his own knowing. Let us investigate this primal knowing when we philosophize about mind, James maintains. Spencer again forgets the role that his own commenting intelligence plays; in so doing he misconstrues mind.

Now this criticism is congruent with James's observation in Chapter One of the *Principles* that a condition for determining successful cognition is that the thing cognized really be there. We went on to note in our commentary that another condition seems to be that what is cognized in general (meant, intended) be also

Initial difficulties of psychophysical dualism 53

known. With this James touches on the fundamental problem of the *Principles:* What is the nature of the cognitive relationship in the broadest sense of meaning and intending? It is our task to adumbrate his developing conception of this.

James's treatment at least suggests that it is bootless to begin a philosophy of mind with either thought (the "internal") or thing known (the "external") and try to build up the cognitive relation between them from there; bootless to begin with a thought on the one hand and a thing on the other and think that a thought can be found to correspond to a thing in any way similar to the manner in which a thing corresponds to another thing (e.g., a disk corresponds to a slot). The suggestion is that thought and thing are oddly interdependent, and that thought cannot be specified independently of its object as a disk can be specified independently of a slot. The suggestion is that we must begin with the cognitive relationship, not end with it.

We must comment on another aspect of this passage which deals with irresponsible darwinizing, for it bears directly on our observations concerning the problematical Chapter One and indirectly on our general thesis. Notice James's remark that survival "considered merely physically" can only be regarded as an hypothesis: If certain movements of the organs occur ". . . survival will as a matter of fact prove to be the incidental consequence . . . But the moment you bring consciousness into the midst, survival ceases to be a mere hypothesis." He characterizes this physical point of view on teleology as teleology-judged-from-without, and contrasts it with teleology-judged-from-within. The exclusive presence of the first point of view in Chapter One underlines the incongruous nature of the chapter: it is both very general and very limited, at one time an introduction to the work as a whole and at other times merely a segment of the physiological preliminaries. For it is certain that James regards teleology-judged-from-without as very limited, and he simply fails to apply it to his abiding topic of interest: human consciousness, specifically his own.

In the case of teleology-judged-from-without, an outside observer hypothesizes, "If that activity is considered the end, then this behavior is an effective and variable means to that end, and so it is intelligent." But James wrote that as soon as the animal "consciously realizes" his own interest or end (teleology-judged-from-within), there occurs something "absolutely new . . . intelligent intelligence."[50] With consciousness there comes a "reservoir of possibilities." Consciousness then "seems both to supply the means and the standard by which they are measured. It not only *serves* a final purpose, but *brings* a final purpose—posits, declares it." This positing is like a command: this *shall* be the goal and standard. "*Real* ends appear for the first time on the world's stage," he writes, and he finds these ends and standards irreducible: "It seems hopelessly impossible to formulate anything of this sort in non-mental terms."[51]

When James speaks of interests, purposes, standards, and goals as being irreducible, he is not speaking merely of the volitional sector but of mind in general. To be "selective," as he puts it, to be interested in one thing or property over another, is one of the characteristics of cognition and mental life in general.[52] More specifically, with regard to standards, norms, and goals James maintains that we cognize things in terms of what we expect to experience under conditions which we consider the norm or standard. What we expect to experience under normal conditions are definite characteristics of the thing cognized; these characteristics form the very essence of the thing; they are what it really is.[53] Thus the essence of things cannot be divorced from their most important characteristics, and the concept of importance involves the concept of an interested mind as well as the concept of a norm fulfilled. The essence of a thing and the intention of a mind are deeply intertwined for James, and our task will involve the explication of this relationship; but now we merely note that his criterion of mentality (the pursuance of future ends, etc.) is not to be construed exclusively in a volitional or narrowly practical sense. For he conceives of "ends" very broadly; as the expected satisfactions of experiential standards they figure in *all* cognition no matter how detached, scientific, or even contemplative. We cite as consonant with this warning Roderick Chisholm's observation that James's idea of satisfaction has been badly misunderstood, particularly in England and America. James did *not* think that a cognition or intention is satisfied in the same sense that a hungry belly or an empty pocketbook is satisfied.[54] Finally, we note that he conceives of teleology in the pregnant sense as teleology-judged-from-within: the ends he talks about as real ends are ends which the agent himself is aware

Initial difficulties of psychophysical dualism   55

of and holds as his own, not merely ends which are imputed to him by an observer.

The essence of a thing and the intention of a mind in regard to the thing are deeply connected for James. This is just another way of saying that the cognitive relationship of mental state to thing cognized emerges as a fundamental topic. But in the "physiological preliminaries" and also, for example, in Chapter Eleven on attention (a chapter we regard as regressing to dualism and the manifest program of the *Principles*) it is not easy to see what James could mean by the cognitive relationship. In arguing for the possibility that all our thoughts are determined, James writes, "dynamically" (causally) considered, attention might be an inexorable function of the object attended to, its interest; the object attended to would not be determined by a fiat-like attention. The "ordinary laws of attention and interest" would force the object on us; we would have to attend to the one which was most interesting.[55]

But is this the time for "dynamical" (causal) considerations? What is the *meaning* of saying that a thought is a "function" of its object? Is it a causal function? Is thought a function of its object in any sense comparable to that in which the penetration of a steel casing is a causal function of the foot-pounds of force per unit area impinging on it? James speaks of the mind's brain as being "struck by the object," and this is clear enough: the object emits packets of energy which trigger electrical impulses in the nerves which do strike the brain in a definite way. But he does not make it clear how the mind or a mental state is struck by the object it cognizes, and thus he does not make it clear how *thought* is a function of its object.

We must learn much more about the cognitive relation between thought and its object. Simply being told that we preperceive and then attend to those objects whose characteristics have been "labeled" by language and these labels "stamped" into our minds tells us nothing new, unless the sense of "stamped" is made clear, which it is not.

And why is it that one object is more "interesting" or "exciting" than another? First, does an object have properties like interest and excitement in the same sense that it has lumens, decibels, foot-pounds, and inches? Second, is an object the most interesting and exciting one because it bombards our sense organs with the most intense stimulation? The answer to the latter question is no, James is quick to assure us.[56] The Greek geometrician "lost in his circles" simply does not hear the barbarians beating on his door. To the former, more general question, however, James does not give a firm answer; he merely leaves the problem.

At this point in the *Principles* it is only the shape of the problem and the few hints dropped about language and "labels" which can guide interpretation. Presumably an object is interesting and exciting because of what its characteristics mean to a conscious agent. Can characteristics meant be talked about in physicalistic terms? This involves the relationship of thought and thought's object, and as a relationship, it would certainly seem to be no more adequately treatable by allusion to physiological events within the envelope of the agent's skin (nor perhaps purely psychical events, if such there are) than it is adequately treatable by allusion to the purely contingent physical properties of the physical things which lie outside the envelope. Such a juxtaposition of physical properties within the organism to those outside would not give us the cognitive *relationship* between organism and environment. The question of the interestingness of an object involves the question of the status of the relationship between thought and thought's object, and particularly whether this relationship is understandable causally, externally, and dualistically. We need to know whether a mental state is specifiable at all in isolation from its object. Can we have an interesting thought without thinking *about* something interesting?

V

The problem of the specification of mental states comes more to the fore in Chapter Six, "The Mind Stuff Theory," and the cognitive relation does likewise. We find the beginnings of James's explicit attempts to specify mental states, and along with this signs of the connection of this attempt with the specification of their objects. It is a glaring fact that he cannot keep talk of the psychical out of his "physiological preliminaries" (Chapter Six being the last of them); the value of the dichotomy of psychical and physical is thrown into question.

It is revealing as well that James here attempts to clarify what is meant by "metaphysics." At some points, as in the Preface, he vehemently eschews metaphysics, and at others, as in Chapter Six

Initial difficulties of psychophysical dualism

itself, he admits that he has become involved in it. This vacillation and confusion are egregiously plain at the close of Chapter Five and the beginning of Chapter Six. After writing at the close of the fifth chapter that ("pending metaphysical reconstructions not yet successfully achieved") he will use the nonmetaphysical language of natural science and common sense *throughout* the book, there appears the following, suggesting that his vacillation is due to a fundamental ambiguity in the word "metaphysics":

> The reader who found himself swamped with too much metaphysics in the last chapter will have a still worse time of it in this one, which is exclusively metaphysical. Metaphysics means nothing but an unusually obstinate attempt to think clearly. The fundamental conceptions of psychology are practically very clear to us, but theoretically they are very confused, and one easily makes the obscurest assumptions in this science without realizing, until challenged, what internal difficulties they involve. When these assumptions have once established themselves (as they have a way of doing in our very descriptions of the phenomenal facts) it is almost impossible to get rid of them afterwards . . .[57]

He admits that he will be "metaphysical" in the sense that he will attempt to think clearly about the fundamental conceptions and assumptions of psychology. Moreover, he tells us that these assumptions establish themselves "in our very descriptions of the phenomenal facts." He will be metaphysical, then, in the sense that he will attempt to clarify and rectify fundamental concepts and assumptions of psychology in the light of a proper description of the phenomenal facts.

Now clearly this is a different sense of the word "metaphysics" from that which he used in the Preface, i.e., a search for transempirical entities or transempirical causal forces (e.g., a soul—a search he eschews). We find the first of a series of fundamental ambiguities in the *Principles* which we must unravel. He will be metaphysical in the sense that he will engage in a fundamental *description* of the phenomenal facts; he will not be metaphysical in the sense that he will not engage in a transphenomenal *explanation* of these phenomenal facts. Already we see that he is on his way to his own metaphysics of radical empiricism: that which takes as its point of departure the fundamental observation that the basis for the description or specification of both mind and matter is the single phenomenon which is neutral between them and which immediately presents itself for description.

Recall I contend that there is a latent strand in the *Principles* which leads directly to the phenomenal monism of the metaphysics of radical empiricism. I think that all the talk through the decades of James's "pluralism" has tended to obscure the demise of dualism in the *Principles* and the emergence of phenomenal monism and incipient phenomenology. The talk arose from viewing James in only one limited historical context: his attack on the peculiar monism of the absolute idealists. It is an example of being confined to the closet of contemporaneity.

The purpose of James's endeavor is to focus the specification of mental states on the purely descriptive as opposed to the explanatory level, and to weed out all explanatory assumptions that have no place there. He characterizes the mind-stuff theory as that which claims our mental states are made up of smaller states conjoined. It is one of those explanatory assumptions which slips into our description of the phenomenal facts, and he proposes to examine it critically, since we must first describe before we can explain.

James observes that the assumption derives originally from British associationism and evolutionism. Associationists require fundamental mental units to supply the elements in their explanatory theories. Evolutionists make the assumption in an attempt to preserve their doctrine of continuity of development in the face of the apparent *sui generis* nature of consciousness. James writes:

> But with the dawn of consciousness an entirely new nature seems to slip in, something whereof the potency was *not* given in the mere outward atoms of the original chaos. . . . *Everyone* admits the entire incommensurability of feeling as such with material motion as such.[58]

Evolutionists can maintain their doctrine of continuity of development only by supposing that mind was present in some form from the first, i.e., in rudimentary forms of life or even in the "atoms of the nebula." Mind's form must be equally rudimentary: particles of it, bits of mind-dust which sum themselves and cluster into ever larger wholes and which only then become readily identifiable as consciousness. Spencer is a proponent of the theory, and consistent with this he analyzes present human consciousness into minute "sensations."[59] As with the connection between a musical note and its outward cause, we find the heard note simple while the cause (the sound waves, overtones, and so on) is multiple and discrete. A summing up must take place, and Spencer assumes that it takes place (somehow) on the mental "side."

James first attacks this on physiological grounds. Usually many neural impulses are required to impinge on a cell before its threshold is reached and a single impulse is emitted. Thus the summing can occur on the physical "side," and only an irreducible whole of consciousness (what he later calls a "field") would correspond to a whole brain state.

What seems to me more significant, however, is the attack he launches on what he calls "logical grounds."[60] James appears to ask, What do we mean by "combined" or "summed"? He maintains that something is combined only for something else.[61] What is this other "something else" for which things known are combined? He replies that it can only be the mental state itself. From this it follows that that which is combined (at least in nonreflective or first-intention consciousness) is not mental states but rather that which mental states are *of*, i.e., their objects. James maintains that associationists and evolutionists lump together and confuse the mental state and that which it is *of*. Because of this fundamental confusion they are drawn into the error, for example, of thinking that the idea of *A* followed by (or plus the) idea of *B* is the same as the idea of *A plus B*. But James observes that in the first case we merely have a succession of two ideas; nothing is summed up and no combination is achieved; it is not the same as the idea of *A plus B*.[62] The point of his critique is that we must keep our eye fixed on the *object* of the idea if we would keep our description of the idea itself pure and clear.

This critical approach is developed in his later attacks on associationism. James concedes that there is some value in associationism.[63] After all, we do think things together which are similar, which are considered to cause one another, etc. But James says he is attempting to formulate association more definitely and more clearly ". . . to escape the usual confusion between causal agencies and relations merely known . . ."[64] This confusion of causal and descriptive analyses plagues associationism, because it causes mental states to be misdescribed and misspecified. He declares that the ingenuity of the associationists' formulation in their mechanical language of struggle and inhibition between mental elements is of doubtful merit when the elements associated are artificial.[65]

How, according to James, have the mental states been misdescribed? They have been so because that which is immediately presented to consciousness has been so. What is immediately presented is not the mental state itself but what the mental state is *of*. We do not associate mental states at all; we associate the things thought about:

> *Associationism,* so far as the word stands for an *effect,* is *between* THINGS THOUGHT OF—*it is* THINGS, *not ideas, which are associated in the mind.* We ought to talk of association of *objects*, not of the association of *ideas*. And so far as association stands for a *cause,* it is between *processes in the brain*—it is these which, by being associated in certain ways, determine what successive objects shall be thought.[66]

This is a grave charge. Its point is that associationist psychologists have lost the psychical, that they have unwittingly confused physiological and psychological considerations; they have left the mental out of mind.

James continues to weed out causal explanations in an attempt to purify description and grasp the object which is immediately given to thought:

> But ordinary writers talk as if the similarity of the objects were itself an agent, co-ordinate with habit, and independent of it, and like it able to push objects before the mind. This is quite unintelligible. The similarity of two things does not exist till both things are there —it is meaningless to talk of it as an *agent of production* of anything, whether in the physical or the psychical realms. It is a relation which the mind perceives after the fact . . .[67]

He claims that it is meaningless to think that an actual similarity either of the things thought about or of the thoughts about them is an agent of production "able to push objects before the mind," because the objects (things thought about) are perceived as similar only after they are already there before the mind.

In the realm of thought or feeling (here James uses the words interchangeably) *esse* is *sentiri;* "as a psychic existent feels, so it must be."[68] Replying to the mind-stuff theorists' contention that a feeling of a thousand things is a summation of a thousand feelings,

Initial difficulties of psychophysical dualism 61

James writes, "If the one feeling feels like no one of the thousand, in what sense can it be said to *be* the thousand?"[69] His point is simply that, described as immediately presented and shorn of explanatory interpolations, the multiplicity is thought or felt *in the objects*, and it is thought or felt that way *for* a single thought or feeling, because ideas are not summed up, but only the objects of ideas. All summing up is done for another, and that other can only be a single idea or mental state.

Only when we ponder his attack on psychophysics can we appreciate his attack on the theory that mind is a kind of stuff which is lumped together or divided. We cannot think of mind as a set of units which are summed, says James, because perception of the growing intensity of a light, say, requires judgment; and the *meaning* of the judgment—which is central in *some* way to what the judgment *is*—simply cannot be elucidated in terms of "units of sensation." We perceive a light bulb increasing in brightness here in the room. But in what sense does the "mental stuff" "inside" us increase in size? The "mental stuff" which composes a judgment of greater intensity or largeness is not itself larger than the "mental stuff" involved in a judgment of lesser intensity or smallness. In fact, James observes trenchantly, if by the ambiguous phrase "units of sensation" one means the mental effort or eyestrain involved in making judgments, then judgments about little magnitudes and minute differences involve more "units of sensation" than judgments about large magnitudes and great differences. The moral of the story is that a thought must not be confused with what the thought is *of* (its object, its meaning), and *yet* the thought is intimately connected to what it is *of*. James states emphatically, "A thought neither is what it knows (its object) nor knows what it is." The problem which drops on James, and on ourselves as well as we attempt to follow him, is simply statable, then, but maddeningly difficult: What *is* the thought itself?

VI

That thoughts or feelings have objects, i.e., are referential, is a doctrine that runs through all of James's *Principles of Psychology*. He calls it "the omni-presence of cognition."[70] It is the doctrine around which our commentary comes to pivot. We ask what implications for the specification of mental states follow from it. The doctrine implies, of course, along with a close relation between thought and its object, some kind of distinction between them. But what kind—and what kind of relation?

James uses the distinction between them to attack not only the mind-stuff theory and associationist psychology, but soul-psychology as well. Both schools suppose that states of mind are composed of discrete, simple mental elements. They diverge in supposing different agencies for their composition: the one maintains that the agency is psychological "laws" of association, the other that it is the transempirical soul. James uses the doctrine of the omnipresence of cognition to undermine both: they have mistaken the multiplicity in the object of the mental state for a multiplicity in the mental state itself, and they have done so because they have blurred the distinction between mental state and its object.[71] Mental states are not composite in structure, James maintains, therefore any theory about the agency involved in their composition must be wrong.

He goes to some lengths in his attack.[72] For example, both schools have used their theory of abstract ideas to further their own ends. The associationists maintain that there really cannot be any abstract ideas, for all ideas are particular existents, thus no ideas are abstractions or generalities. The soul-psychologists, on the other hand, maintain that there are abstractions and universals, but then they infer that they must be nonparticular and nonempirical mental existents, and there must also be a nonempirical organizing agent which combines them and in which they inhere. Both schools are wrong, says James, because they both confuse idea and object. From the fact that the object of an idea is a universal we cannot infer that the idea itself must be a strange sort of universal-particular existent. It is possible to have that which both schools deny: particular mental states or particular psychical existents which nevertheless are *of* universals.

However, James's doctrine that there is some kind of distinction between thought and the object of thought develops difficulties. Let us see how they arise in the context of his attack on the mind-stuff theory. He attacks what he takes to be a corollary of this theory: the notion that if two successive ideas refer to the same external reality, one after the other, they must really be a single idea

Initial difficulties of psychophysical dualism 63

"published in two editions." This involves two consequences which James rejects. First, under the theory beliefs about unconscious ideas must be introduced, because this is the only way of explaining the differences in "the second edition" which have accrued through memory, shifts of attention, and learning, i.e., all that which is manifest in the second appearance of the idea must have actually been present in the first, but unconsciously:

> The distinction is that *between the unconscious and conscious being of the mental state*. It is the sovereign means for believing what one likes in psychology, and of turning what might become a science into a tumbling-ground for whimsies.[73]

Second, James points out that if it were really the case that two ideas of the same external reality, one following the other, were really the same idea in "two editions," we could never know that the second idea was the second, i.e., occurred *after* the first. For the second would be simply a reversion to the first state. We would lapse into timelessness and ignorance. The second mental state, then, must be distinct from the first. Later he writes that it is "logically impossible"[74] that the same object should be known by the same mental state (i.e., a mental state which is only numerically distinct from its first appearance).

Problems immediately emerge from this treatment of thought and its object which James does not deal with in Chapter Six. Talk of consciousness leaks into the physiological preliminaries—we think inevitably—but in quite inadequate doses. If thought is constantly changing, if no two thoughts are ever really the same thought, if thought is an ever-changing "stream," to use James's now famous metaphor, then what makes it possible for us to say meaningfully, as we do say, that we have the same thought today as we had yesterday? James nowhere denies that this is possible. Certainly, when I think on Tuesday and again on Wednesday that "the apple in the bowl is rotten," there must be *something* identical on Wednesday to what I thought on Tuesday, or I would not even be able to think "I thought of that before." Moreover, the problem is compounded by the fact that James is the first to admit that the brute existence of a selfsame rotten apple "out there" in the bowl is ". . . not a sufficient cause for our knowing it: it must strike the brain in some way, as well as be there, to be known. But the brain being struck, the knowledge is constituted by a new construction that occurs altogether *in* the mind."[75]

Something is missing in the argument. If the knowledge of sameness must be present before we can detect the distinctness of Wednesday's thought as against Tuesday's, and if this knowledge of sameness cannot be accounted for by reference to the brute physical existence of the selfsame object "out there," and furthermore, if as a psychical existent the second thought is utterly distinct from the first, then James has left something out of his account of the knowledge of sameness. According to his account the sameness can be located neither in the psychical existent itself, the mental state, nor in the physical existent itself, the apparent object of the thought. Where is it then? The something which has been left out must be utterly prior and basic to inquiries both about mind and about physical things, for we cannot specify mental states without it (even as to their distinctness), and we cannot talk about physical objects without it, since we cannot talk about physical objects at all unless we know that what we are talking about is the *same* thing that we *keep* talking about. Indeed, this is a most important gap, and later we find James referring to the sense of sameness as "the keel of the mind."[76] So far, then, in his voyage of psychological discovery he has left out the keel.

The nature of the problem itself indicates something about that which could prove to be its solution, if it has one. The problem calls for some prior go-between, some relationship between mental state qua psychical existent and object qua physical existent which must be known before either existent can be known, and yet this connection must occur entirely *in* thought (in some sense of the word "in").

In fact, later in the *Principles* we find James introducing a second sense of the word "object" in the phrase "thought's object," a sense other than mere physical object as referent of the thought; it is a sense which can, it seems, fill the relational gap. It is the sense of the phrase "thought's object" around which much of our study will revolve; we contend that James is forced to specify this sense before he can specify the thought itself. We contend that he is forced to the conclusion that thought itself is merely an aspect of "thought's object"—i.e., that thought itself as a psychical existent is a mere conceptual appendage to "thought's object."

VII

Let us review. In this chapter we have seen how James's plan of treating the physiological and causal conditions of thought first, while simply assuming the existence of thought as a psychical existent and letting its specification go until later, generates problems. First we saw the confusing mixture of physicalistic and mentalistic terms, and the unhappy symbiosis of concepts: James specifies physical states of the brain partly on the basis of a similarity to the mental states to which they supposedly correspond; but he turns around and specifies mental states on the basis of the physical. He seems to realize that he has "fallen into the other kind"; at least he realizes it to the extent of finally desisting from predicating causal attributes of mental states.

We also observed, however, that James does not accept the materialist position which would reduce mentalistic terms or eliminate them altogether. In his critique of evolutionism he maintained that some terms essential to philosophy of mind (such as "interest" and "real end") are not predicable of the physiological organism as such. Even after the cessation of the attempt to predicate causal attributes to mental states, then, the problem remains of how to specify mental states in their own proper terms and of how to correlate them, once specified, with the physiological states of the brain—physiological states which must be predicated in their own very different terms.

We then observed how this problem begins to be focused when he talks about the cognitive relationship and thought's object. In his critique of associationism James maintains that reference to the causation of ideas must be relegated to talk about the brain. To specify mental states one must operate on the level of a purely descriptive analysis of what is immediately presented to consciousness. But when we do this, we find that it is thought's objects we are specifying, not thought itself. We can only assume that thought is that *for which* objects are objects. But all that James can tell us about thought as a presumably "psychical existent" is that it must be different each time we have one. We have observed that he can accomplish even this little bit of specification only because he presupposes a sense of sameness which he does not acknowledge and for which he does not make theoretical room. He leaves a gap which only a further specification of thought's *object* can fill.

The question now arises how James could otherwise specify the thought itself without relying on a specification of thought's object. All that is immediately given is the object itself. Presumably the thought itself would be accessible to study only through reflection. But James has told us nothing about reflection, and we wonder how he could even begin to reflect unless he already knew what he was reflectively to look for. On the basis of what he has so far told us we can only conclude that this prereflective knowledge consists in the assumption that there is a seamless psychical something *for which* all things known in thought's object *are* things known. Notice, however, that we have used the singular in "thought's object," and that this raises the possibility that the singularity or wholeness might be localizable in the *object*. The settling of this matter must await James's further attempts to specify the thought-thought's object relationship.

Already, however, we notice a salient peculiarity in James's text: in an italicized passage he confuses talk about thought's object ("the immediately known thing," "the phenomenon") with talk about "the state of consciousness," presumably the psychical existent. This is after he has explicitly made the distinction between thought and thought's object, so we believe the confusion to be most significant. We think it springs inevitably from two combined factors: the actual internality of the cognitive relation and James's presently inadequate conception of it.

> *The bare* PHENOMENON, *however, the* IMMEDIATELY KNOWN *thing which on the mental side is an apposition with the entire brain process is the state of consciousness* . . .[77]

This confusion is grievous, for James's fundamental doctrine of the omnipresence of cognition and his highly accented criticism of the mind-stuff theory require that thought and thought's object be first distinguished if they are ever to be properly related. When James speaks of "the single state of mind" for which objects in the environment *are* objects, we do not know whether he means thought or thought's object.

Worse yet, another confusion centers in the word "object." When we think of a particular man in his particularity, he is a single object of thought in the sense that he is a single object and thought is about him; but he alone is not the "single object of thought"—of which James makes so much—when, for example, we think of his being related to another man. Only the whole relational context thought about can qualify for this. In sum, he is not necessarily all we think about when we think about him.

Thus two fundamental distinctions must be made: between thought and thought's object and between thought's object in its two different senses. James attempts to make these two distinctions in the crucial chapter on "The Stream of Consciousness," which we shall now examine. He tries to overcome the crude dichotomy of his psychophysical dualism; a trichotomy of a strange sort appears. With this his dualism crumbles. A new interpretation of consciousness arises.

FOUR

Further difficulties of dualism:
the stream of thought

I

Chapter Seven of the *Principles*, "The Methods and Snares of Psychology," marks the beginning of what James calls study of "the mental states themselves whose cerebral conditions and concomitants we have been considering hitherto."[1] This is inaccurate in view of his limited study of mental states in Chapter Six. In any case, he claims it marks the end of the "physiological preliminaries" and the beginning of a new stage. But it is of such generality that it is as if he were beginning the book for the second time. He offers a detailed delineation of his program for psychology as a natural science.

He staunchly reaffirms his dualism. On the one hand, there are thoughts and, on the other, things. The psychologist as natural scientist is to assume that the cognitive dualism is ultimate and he has only to compare the thought with the thing in order to see if the thought is a truthful one. The psychologist says,

> . . . that under certain circumstances the color gray appears to him green, and calls the appearance an illusion. This implies that he compares two objects, a real color seen under certain conditions, and

Further difficulties of dualism 69

a mental perception which he believes to represent it, and that he declares the relation between them to be of a certain kind. In making this critical judgment, the psychologist stands as much outside of the perception which he criticises as he does of the color. Both are his objects. And if this is true of him when he reflects on his own conscious states, how much truer is it when he treats of those of others![2]

The psychologist "cannot but believe" that he knows the real color,[3] and he simply takes this knowledge for granted. He "stands outside" the real color and yet knows it. He also stands outside "the mental perception which he believes to represent it."

But James says nothing about the psychologist's belief that the latter mental perception represents the real color. Does he stand outside of this, too? How could he when the belief is his own? And how could the psychologist believe that the perception truly represents the real thing unless he already knew what it generically represents (to use the word "represents" for the moment)—i.e., unless he already knew what the perception *meant* or was *intended* to be of? We cannot believe that a perception of a color is true by comparing it to the pencil shavings on the floor, the stars in the sky, the sounds from the other room, or even every color. We must already know what to compare it to—i.e., *that* color. How can anybody stand outside this primordial knowledge of meaning?

Here James does not address himself to this urgent question. He simply goes on to say that the psychologist's main task consists in discovering which conditions (e.g., chemical) cause us to have truthful as opposed to illusory perceptions. But our question does not arise from a point of view totally foreign to the *Principles*. After all, James himself has already pointed out that a claim about reality or truth is a necessary condition for a claim about successful cognition; and we have observed that knowledge of meaning is logically prior to knowledge of truth and that thought's object is the meaning of the thought.

The inference seems to be that the psychologist must already know what the perception means—he must already know its object. James gives us no reason to think that only true thoughts have objects. On the contrary he speaks of the "omni-presence" of cognition: all mental states have objects of some sort. And this stands to reason. It is only because we know that the perception is of, or about, a gray color, that we can go on to determine that it is an untruthful perception of the real red color.

The contention of this section of our study is that James is forced to speak of the mental state's object when he proposes to speak of the mental state itself, and that he cannot construe thought's object exclusively in terms of particular physical existents. For what about nontruthful mental states? They still have objects, but they are not physical existents. Furthermore, I think the contention is corroborated by what actually transpires in James's text. It is a text full of surprises.

James *says* that he will be naïvely dualistic, and will not discuss at all the cognitive relationship of thought to what it is about.

> Now the *relation of knowing* is the most mysterious thing in the world. If we ask how one thing *can* know another we are led into the heart of *Erkentnisstheorie* and metaphysics. The psychologist for his part does not consider the matter so curiously as this. Finding a world before him which he cannot but believe that *he* knows, and setting himself to study his own past thoughts, or someone else's thoughts, of what he believes to be the same world, he cannot but conclude that those other thoughts know it after their fashion even as he knows it after his.[4]

But there is already a telltale phrase: the mental states studied by the psychologist are "of what he believes to be the same world," the same world which he believes his own true thoughts are of. It is this knowing in the generic sense of meaning or intending *of* a world common to all thinkers which is the basic but tacit assumption of James's natural scientific program. Only after it is assumed can he talk of thought and "external reality," as if they were external and independent of each other and as if the specific knowing of the latter by the former (truthfully or erroneously) were merely a matter of the contingent coincidence of two empirical entities or the lack of it. But James cannot leave his assumption untroubled and unquestioned. His text discloses that he must actually grapple with the generic or meaning relationship of thought to that which it is believed and intended to be about in the world before he can deal with the specific relationship of truth or falsity.

Right off, we find that when he spells out more exactly the assumptions of his psychology he does not follow his dualistic program and say merely that the psychologist compares two enti-

Further difficulties of dualism 71

ties, "a real color seen under certain conditions and a mental perception," *but that the psychologist has before him three entities*. They are "the thought studied," "the psychologist's reality" (the "real world"), *and* "the thought's object." Our investigation shows that the third element wreaks havoc with his dualism. It will not fit into either the mental or the physical "side," and in trying to force it into the mental "half" James breaks down his dualistic structure.

Take careful note of the following diagram which is intended by James to express the ultimate and independent data of a natural scientific psychology. It is his intended conceptual framework, and we shall be referring to it throughout this study; sometimes we refer to the classifications of data by number alone:

1. The Psychologist	2. The Thought Studied	3. The Thought's Object	4. The Psychologist's Reality (the real world)

James writes:

> These four squares contain the irreducible data of psychology. No. 1, the psychologist, believes Nos. 2, 3, and 4, which together form *his* total object, to be realities, and reports them and their mutual relations as truly as he can without troubling himself with the puzzle of how he can report them at all. About such *ultimate* puzzles he in the main need trouble himself no more than the geometer, the chemist, or the botanist do, who make precisely the same assumptions as he.[5]

But though he is constrained to include thought's object in the inventory, he declares that the natural scientific program demands that all three of the data be treated as coequal and independent entities, and that the cognitive relationship between No. 2 and No. 3 be treated as "ultimate" and not discussed. It is assumed that the relationship *need* not be discussed since it is assumed that each related entity can be specified independently of each other one. That is, it is assumed that the relationship between them is external.

II

We find this assumption to be questionable in the light of James's own text. If the ultimate data of his conceptual framework for psychology are related externally, then they are specifiable independently of each other. If they are specifiable independently of each other, then it is reasonable to expect that they should actually be specified that way. But our reasonable expectation is not realized: the data do not get sorted out into separate piles.

Even after James has distinguished thought from thought's object (No. 2 and No. 3), we find the distinction blurred and concealed in his writing. Take his very summons to inquiry itself, in which he proclaims that no one can doubt that introspection directly and plainly reveals the nature of thought. Consider also that James becomes his own psychologist, that he does not rely on reports of introspection from another person, and that this practice, if anything, should plainly reveal the structure of thoughts themselves.[6] But in the following passage we do not know whether he is speaking of thought or thought's object. Nor do we know if he is speaking of thought's object or real object (No. 4). Datum No. 3 blurs in two directions at once, toward No. 2 and No. 4:

> *Introspective observation is what we have to rely on first and foremost and always.* The word introspection need hardly be defined—it means, of course, the looking into our own minds and reporting what we there discover. *Every one agrees that we there discover states of consciousness.* So far as I know, the existence of such states has never been doubted by any critic, however sceptical in other respects he may have been. That we have *cogitations* of some sort is the *inconcussum* in a world most of whose other facts have at some time tottered in the breath of philosophic doubt. All people unhesitatingly believe that they feel themselves thinking, and that they distinguish the mental state as an inward activity or passion, from all the objects with which it may cognitively deal. I regard this belief as the most fundamental of all the postulates of Psychology, and shall discard all curious inquiries about its certainty as too metaphysical for the scope of this book.[7]

But we find that he does not discard such "curious" inquiries, so let us see just how it comes about that he cannot avoid them.

He takes the mental state to be obviously distinct from the object which it is *of*. But "the object" is ambiguous on his own terms.

Further difficulties of dualism

Does he mean thought's object (No. 3), or the "external object" (No. 4)? He probably means the latter, for this is what has (most obviously at least) "tottered in the breath of philosophic doubt." But since this is so, we do not know to what James is referring when he talks of that which must be distinguished from the external object. That is, by "mental state" does he mean thought (No. 2) or thought's object (No. 3)? Moreover, this ambiguity affects the meaning of "introspection," a term which names the method by which mental states are discovered, but which he says "need hardly be defined." For if a distinction must be made within mental states, and if we must sort out thoughts from thought's objects because of their differences, then the possibility arises that two entities which are different require different methods for their discovery; thus the word "introspection" would be as ambiguous as "mental state."

James does, in effect, address himself to this problem, although he does not explicitly single it out. Congruously with his doctrine of the omnipresence of cognition, he contends that, "No subjective state, while present, is its own object; its object is always something else."[8] "What the thought sees is only its own object . . ."[9] That is, it only sees immediately, and is only immediately *of* its own object (No. 3). Only later, in reflection, can the psychologist apprehend the thought itself (No. 2). "What the thought sees is only its own object; what the reflecting psychologist sees is the thought's object, plus the thought itself, plus possibly all the rest of the world."[10]

Now what does James mean by "mental state," "cognitions," that which is "the *inconcussum* in a world most of whose other facts have at some time tottered in the breath of philosophic doubt"? He says that introspection plainly and directly reveals the nature of thought. But does introspection immediately apprehend what thought is immediately *of*, thought's object (No. 3), or does it through reflection apprehend thought itself (No. 2)? He speaks really affirmatively only of what is immediately apprehended (No. 3); thus mental states themselves are already tottering in the breath of philosophical doubt.

Recall in his critique of the mind-stuff theory his claim that the theory confuses mental states with their discrete objects in the world, and that it is really things which are composite while mental states are seamless wholes. But there is every reason at this point to think—given James's more sophisticated conceptual structure which distinguishes three sorts of data in addition to the psychologist—that James really means that the mental state's object (No. 3) is the seamless whole. In the first place, he never speaks of reflection but rather of getting straight on what is immediately presented to consciousness. Second, he says that the summing, combining, and relating of objects known to be discrete (like a man running after a child) is a new *object* in mind. Note the word "object" is singular. We have a thought of *A plus B* whose togetherness and wholeness is in the object of thought (No. 3). Even when we mention that the physical objects in the world are different and discrete, James maintains, as did Kant, that in order for them to be differentiated and separated they must first be *together* in the object of our thought.[11] Moreover, James maintains, as we shall see more exactly below, that a thought *of* succession is not a succession of thoughts.[12] Still further, James maintains that we have *feelings* of relation, that things *come* already related in our most fundamental mental life (for now we simply honor James's claim that he is using "feeling" and "thought" interchangeably).[13] Finally, there can be no valid objection to our using "object" in the phrase "thought's object" in a different sense from discrete "object" in the world, because we noted in our commentary on his critique of the mind-stuff theory that James must introduce a sense of "object" other than that of outright physical object if he would solve the problem of how we can think of the same thing at different times, and also because he himself *does* introduce another sense in compartment No. 3 of his conceptual framework. In terms of James's actual analysis, then, the wholeness is in thought's object (No. 3), and the assumption that there is a mental state qua psychical existent (No. 2) *for which* the wholeness is a wholeness, is just an assumption which is possibly quite gratuitous. While there must be something, it might be said, for which the objects in the world are objects, why cannot this something be the wholeness (thought's object) itself? Why must there be something for which the wholeness is a wholeness?

When we accept James's summons to inquire into the nature of mental states, we are immediately thrown into confusion. He does not clearly distinguish between mental states (No. 2) and their

Further difficulties of dualism 75

objects (No. 3), and the word "introspection" is ambiguous. One central point does emerge however: when he talks clearly and consistently about what he calls "mental states" he is really talking about the objects of mental states—the seamless totality of thought's object (No. 3)! All that he leaves us for mental states themselves (No. 2) is a pile of tag ends at which we must strain to make any sense. Take his adumbration of his principle *esse est sentiri* in the realm of mind. He seems to have adopted the position of Franz Brentano whom he quotes:

> The phenomena inwardly apprehended are true in themselves. As they appear—of this the evidence with which they are apprehended is a warrant—so they are in reality. Who, then, can deny that in this a great superiority of Psychology over the physical sciences comes to light.[14]

Yet James does not quote this with entire approval. He says that Brentano "takes high ground here and claims for (introspection) a sort of infallibility,"[15] a claim which James does not wish to make. How then can he assert that what immediately presents itself must be as it appears to be? The inconsistency is relieved when we realize exactly what James is objecting to: he does not doubt, evidently, that the "immediate feltness of a feeling" or that thought's awareness of its own object is infallible, he simply bridles at calling this introspection. However, he never clarifies his own use of "introspection"; usually he means the immediate awareness of thought's object, but at others he means a reflective awareness of the putative mental state itself; there is quite a difference. In the following passage the word is blurred beyond recognition:

> . . . we find ourselves in continual error and uncertainty so soon as we are called on to name and class, and not merely to feel. Who can be sure of the exact *order* of his feelings when they are excessively rapid? Who can be sure, in his sensible perception of a chair, how much comes from the eye and how much is supplied out of the previous knowledge of the mind? . . . . Who knows, of many actions, for what motive they were done, or if for any motive at all? Who can enumerate all the distinct ingredients of such a complicated feeling as *anger?* and who can tell off-hand whether or no a perception of distance be a compound or a simple state of mind. The whole mind-stuff controversy would stop if we could decide conclu-

sively by introspection that what seem to us elementary feelings are really elementary and not compound.[16]

This is surely an attempt to substantiate his natural scientific program with its implicit claim that the data are externally related and independently specifiable, since it suggests that mental states themselves (No. 2) can be specified ("named and classed") by an act of reflection on them which isolates them from their cognitive objects. But he tells us not at all how they can be reflectively "found" unless we already know what to look for; and since he himself claims that all that is presented immediately is the cognitive object, we can conclude that we already know what to look for only because of something about the cognitive *object* which we already know.

Furthermore, his examples of fallibility are suspicious for reasons which, in part, he himself provides. How do we know which feelings pass too rapidly to be accurately ordered as to sequence unless we already know something about them—e.g., unless we know which or what feelings they are and that they are indeed feelings? Also, he gives us no grounds for deciding what kind of difficulty is involved in knowing these rapidly passing feelings. Is it an essential difficulty having to do with the concepts we apply, or is it just an empirical one arising from the limitations of our powers of observation? His other examples of fallibility suggest that the assertion of fallibility and the assertion that it poses a problem arise only because of conceptual confusion. After his own critique of the mind-stuff theory how can he still genuinely wonder whether "a perception of distance be a compound or a simple state of mind"? On the basis of his own critique one can reasonably conclude that in James's judgment there are no compound states of mind at all. Things in the world are the kinds of things that are compounded and have parts; mental states do not have parts. And how can he genuinely wonder how much of his sensible perception of a chair "comes from" the eye and how much is "supplied out of the previous knowledge of the mind"? This is suspiciously similar to what he inveighs against: the treating of mind as some kind of stuff which can be cut up, constructed, and baled at will. More than this, it seems to be a confusing mixture of causal inquiries with descriptive ones, e.g., how much of the sensible perception comes from the eye? This is the very thing he inveighed against in his critique of

Further difficulties of dualism

associationism; according to James himself we must get a pure description before we can hope for an explanation.

The upshot of this internal conflict in James's text is to make us wonder if he expresses any clear meaning in "thoughts themselves" (No. 2). The only clear specification of mind which we have received so far is a *de facto* specification stated exclusively in terms of thought's object (No. 3). And when James attempts to specify thought independently of its object, he produces the confusions which we have just noted. Along with this flows a deeper unsettling question: In what sense can it be said that thought's object (No. 3) is an object qua substance, let alone a psychical substance?

III

James becomes centrally concerned with the problem of description. Mind must be specified in a primordial sense if it is ever to be correlated with the brain. He maintains that the chief snare for the psychologist is for him to confuse what he knows about the world, usually his knowledge of physics and physiology, with what the *thought* immediately knows,[17] i.e., thought's object (No. 3). Thus James's concern with the problem of the description and specification of mind centers on and fastens on *thought's object*, and not the thought itself (No. 2) at all. We take this to be a vastly significant fact about James's *Principles of Psychology*.

One might think, he writes, that the proper isolation of datum No. 3—thought's object—is an easy matter. But this is to deceive oneself. To grasp thought's object in its wholeness and fullness and "just as thought thinks it" is difficult, even though he admits that thought's object is the "immediate feltness of a feeling," and even though he talks about infallibility in terms of our apprehension of it (though he is not clear about the scope of this infallibility). This requires an explanation, and James offers one.

What he calls the "psychologist's fallacy" consists in the onlooking psychologist's confusing what *he* knows with what the *thought* knows (No. 3). That is, through his theorizing about causes, the psychologist knows the physical structure of the thought's referent in the world (No. 4), and likewise the physical structure of the subject's brain (also No. 4). In addition, through introspection, namely, reflection, the psychologist presumably knows the thought itself (No. 2) as well. The fallacy consists in introducing these data into that which the *thought* immediately knows (No. 3).

James asserts that the structure of our language conspires to produce this error. Since it is largely a physical-object language, we name our thoughts after the discrete physical objects to which they refer, or from which they are causally derived:

> Language was originally made by men who were not psychologists, and most men today employ almost exclusively the vocabulary of outward things . . . we have to describe a large number of sensations by the name of the object from which they have most frequently been got. An orange color, an odor of violets, a cheesy taste, a thundrous sound, a fiery smart, etc., will recall what I mean. This absence of a special vocabulary for subjective facts hinders the study of all but the very coarsest of them.[18]

He goes on:

> Empiricist writers are very fond of emphasizing one great set of delusions which language inflicts on the mind. Whenever we have made a word, they say, to denote a certain group of phenomena, we are prone to suppose a substantive entity existing beyond the phenomena, of which the word shall be the name. But the *lack* of a word quite as often leads to the directly opposite error. We are then prone to suppose that no entity can be there; and so we come to overlook phenomena whose existence would be patent to us all, had we only grown up to hear it familiarly recognized in speech.[19]

But for the attainment of what goal is our vocabulary lacking? When and where do we feel the lack of words? James says that the lack causes us to overlook "phenomena" and to miss all but the coarsest of "subjective facts." In view of his avowed and reaffirmed dualistic program we might naturally think that these "subjective facts" are mental entities of some sort, i.e., thoughts themselves (No. 2). But when James comes to give us an actual example of a lack in vocabulary that causes us to overlook "phenomena," he cites the fact that when we name the thought after the single thing to which it refers we miss the whole context of the presented phenomena in which the thing is embedded; but the whole context is just the whole object of thought (No. 3), not the thought itself (No. 2). He writes:

> Here . . . language works against our perception of the truth. We name our thoughts simply, each after its thing, as if each knew its

Further difficulties of dualism

own thing and nothing else. What each really knows is clearly the thing it is named for, with dimly perhaps a thousand other things. It ought to be named after all of them, but it never is. Some of them are always things known a moment ago more clearly; others are things to be known more clearly a moment hence. Our own bodily position, attitude, condition, is one of the things of which *some* awareness, however, inattentive, invariably accompanies the knowledge of whatever we know.[20]

No mention is made here of phenomena qua mental realities (No. 2) which are overlooked.[21]

Let us take another example of his exposure of the psychologist's fallacy, which exposure rectifies and throws light on thought's object, not on thought itself. A psychologist, James says, may be led to suppose that the thought which knows the physical thing knows it in the same way as he, qua natural scientist, knows it. If the physical thing has three detachable parts, he may suppose that the thought he is studying has three parts. Or the composite structure of the subject's brain may also lead him erroneously to suppose this. The seamless wholeness of thought is sacrificed

> . . . and in its place an atomism . . . is preached, for the existence of which no good introspective grounds can be brought forward, and out of which presently grow all sorts of paradoxes and contradictions, the heritage of woe of students of the mind.
>
> These words are meant to impeach the entire English psychology derived from Locke and Hume . . . so far as [it] treat[s] 'ideas' as separate subjective entities that come and go.[22]

But the wholeness to which James actually draws our attention is in the object of thought (No. 3).

IV

Of course, as James points out, thought is constantly flowing and changing; consciousness is like a stream which rushes forward—one thought twists and melts and flows into another.[23] The things in the world are not always thought to be changing, so it might be supposed that it is thought "itself" (No. 2) which is changing. But as we shall see more particularly below, and most emphatically in the section on the self, James's conception of the object of thought (No. 3) is broad and rich enough to include within itself an account of this constant change. It is this: the thing known (or meant) to be changeless in the world must nevertheless be known as being in a constantly changing relationship to ourselves, if only for the fact that we know it at different times.

This problem of knowing the same thing at different times comes up in James's exposure of that version of the psychologist's fallacy which lies implicit in associationism's theory that "the thought of the object's (physical thing's) recurrent identity is the identity of the recurrent thought."[24] James reports,

> A permanently existing 'idea' or 'Vorstellung' which makes its appearance before the footlights of consciousness at periodical intervals, is as mythological an entity as the Jack of Spades.[25]

When the psychologist falls into this trap he does so because

> . . . he ordinarily has no other way of naming (the thought) than as the thought, percept, etc., *of that object*. He himself, meanwhile, knowing the self-same object in *his* way, gets easily led to suppose that the thought, which is of it, knows it in the same way in which he knows it, although this is often far from being the case.[26]

James contends that thought is not a sequence of recurrent, self-identical mental bits; what is got twice is the same thing in the world cognized as being the same, not the same thought.[27] This, however, only tells us something negative: thought is not a sequence of self-identical mental bits. What is it—positively? James is remarkably slow in supplying an answer. He gives us metaphors which are not clear; e.g., thoughts "melt" into each other like "dissolving views," and thought is like a "stream." One thing is clear, however. His talk about the changing of thought (No. 2) involves him in some way in talk about the changing phenomenal structure of thought's object (No. 3). It is the elucidation of this which concerns us. The problem with which James grapples is central to his whole project: How can things in the world whose brute physical identity cannot explain how they come to be known as the same, nevertheless be so known, while mind (in some sense of the word) is constantly changing?

Intending to tell us something about thought itself, James succeeds in clearly telling us only something about thought's object. And the more he tells us, the more he needs to tell us. A whole new area of study is opened up through the introduction of the topic of thought's object, and it is an area which eventually overruns the limits James initially set for it in his conceptual framework for a natural scientific psychology (i.e., compartment No. 3). In fact, I believe that it breaks down all the other compartments.

Heretofore I have indicated how James is deflected from his intention of specifying thought itself and ends by specifying thought's object instead. It might be maintained, however, that he is still being true to his basic dualism, and that he is merely enriching his specification of thought by talking about its object. It is still *its* object, it might be maintained. The object must be distinguished from thought itself, to be sure, but the object is still mental, perhaps no more than thought's "content," and James is still operating on the mental "side."

But the word "content" suggests that thought contains its object as a container contains its contents, which suggestion is just what James's specification of thought's object militates against. He has become his own psychologist (No. 1), and when he talks about the "psychologist's reality" (the real physical world—No. 4) it is in nearly all cases impossible to distinguish this talk from his talk about thought's object (No. 3), that which is immediately presented to him. Of course, he acknowledges that his percepts may be wrong but he assumes that they are usually right, and when he does so he simply assumes that the real world is just as it presents itself, i.e., as it presents itself in his thought's object. He certainly is not standing outside of thought's object, and this means, if we are correct, that he is not standing outside of anything else either. In effect, compartment No. 3 encompasses all the others.

James does not maintain that thought's object is mental, and neither does he maintain that it presents itself as being so. It is simply not contained in thought as its content, and in the following passage he deals a blow to his own dualism:

> In some manner our consciousness is 'present' to everything with which it is in relation. I am *cognitively* present to Orion whenever I perceive that constellation, but I am not *dynamically* present there, I work no effects. To my brain however, I am dynamically present, inasmuch as my thoughts and feelings seem to react upon the processes thereof.[28]

If thought is never "out of itself," as he said in his statement of the dualistic program, then how can it be *cognitively present* to Orion? Quite obviously James is disrupting his own program.

With this the problematic of the *Principles* reaches its highest pitch: How can consciousness (or mental states) be causally correlated to the brain unless it is first specified, and how can it be specified in view of his constant allusions to thought's *object?* As we said, the more James tells us about thought's object the more he needs to tell; the topic grows under his hands faster than he can treat it. This is a prime example of a major point: James becomes involved in considerations pertaining to phenomenal presentations, the extent of which he does not at once comprehend, and the complications of which he cannot successfully handle. As we have already said, he cannot run backward fast enough to keep up with himself. He cannot expose his own presuppositions rapidly enough and clearly enough.

According to James, a major source of the psychologist's fallacy, as it turns out, is the failure to grasp thought's object in its wholeness and entirety. Recall that he said, "What each (thought) really knows is clearly the thing it is named for, with dimly perhaps a thousand other things. It ought to be named for them all, but it never is."[29] That is, the object of thought in its wholeness is not just the denoted thing itself, the referent, but the thing-in-relation. James is doing what he must do to solve the problem of how something can be known to be the same while the knowing occurs in a constantly changing mind; he is expanding his conception of thought's object (No. 3): it is not just the thing in the world known to be the same, but rather includes the latter in a larger network of relations. It even includes our own bodily position, attitude, and condition, no matter how inattentive awareness of these usually is.[30]

James speaks of thought's object as a "field." Notice the strikingly different metaphor for presentations to consciousness; stable, nonfluid characteristics are suggested. He speaks of that of which we have only inattentive awareness as the "margins" of this field. The margin is the nonfocal: what is in the "corner of the eye" when one is not thinking explicitly of it. For example, I need not look at my arms nor right *at* another's to know where they are. Just as the awareness of my body is marginal and inattentive, so the particular relation of a thing-in-relation, which is its relation to my body, must also be inattentive. That latter relation is not part, it would seem, of what we mean by the thing itself in the world.[31]

Further difficulties of dualism

Therefore that relation could change without our meaning that the thing in the world had changed, and thus James is laying the groundwork for a solution to his problem of how the same thing is known at different times. But he postpones his account of one's marginal knowing of his body and the relationship of other bodies to it until the chapter on the self.

The object of thought (No. 3) in its integrity and wholeness is so vast and complicated, as James sees it, that we find him narrowing it down in an evident effort to keep it intellectually manageable. The operation of narrowing down goes beyond a paring away of the inattentive awareness of one's body and includes other relations within the object of thought. Thus we find him soon abandoning the attempt to explicate the full object of thought when the thought is a sensuous perception. Notice the beginnings of this explication. The situation he chooses is our perception of a crack of thunder:

> The superficial introspective view is the overlooking, even when the things are contrasted with each other most violently, of the large amount of affinity that may still remain between the thoughts by whose means they are cognized. Into the awareness of the thunder itself the awareness of the previous silence creeps and continues; for what we hear when the thunder crashes is not thunder *pure*, but thunder-breaking-upon-silence-and-contrasting-with-it. Our feeling of the same objective thunder, coming in this way, is quite different from what it would be were the thunder a continuation of previous thunder. The thunder itself we believe to abolish and exclude the silence; but the *feeling* of the thunder is also a feeling of the silence as just gone.[32]

The point of this passage is clear: we should not confuse the object of thought of which we are immediately aware with what we know the thunder to be physically, i.e., an abrupt disturbance in the air which causes a disturbance in the brain accompanied presumably by a conscious experience which is the polar opposite of silence—noise. That it is the object of thought (No. 3) he wishes us to attend to and isolate seems clear, even though he uses the word "thought." Although the "things" (the thunder and the silence) are contrasted "violently," he says that there remains a large amount of affinity "between the thoughts by whose means they are cognized." But he is actually referring to what we immediately and actually hear, the object of thought. We do not hear a thought, but, as he says, "thunder-breaking-in-upon-silence-and-contrasting-with-it"; "the feeling of the thunder is also a feeling of the silence as just gone." Again, the continuity and the unity are in the object of thought (No. 3). He uses the word "introspection," but as it is here used it is not, apparently, a synonym for an act of reflection which grasps the thought itself a moment later (No. 2), for the whole intent and force of the passage are to direct us to what is immediately presented (No. 3).

Thought's object in this perceptual situation is still vastly complicated, even when the inattentive awareness of one's own body in the margin of the object is ignored. The question arises: Within the object of thought is the relation of the thunder to the silence which precedes it (but which continues with the thunder as "broken in upon") a part of what we mean by the thunder itself (in its being—as that kind of thing), or is it part of what we mean by mind, subjectivity, awareness? The point is that James cannot tell, and yet he will find this ambiguity startlingly pregnant with positive implications for philosophy of mind. That is, what we mean by the thunder itself is a matter of how it is "fringed" in our experience; and what we mean by the thought itself cannot be detached from the fringe and object, as we shall see. Thought's object is "neutral" between mind and world. But so far in Chapter Nine James has not sufficiently distinguished thought (No. 2), thought's object (No. 3), and physical thing (No. 4); he has yet to grasp the fundamental and pivotal role of thought's object in all its phenomenological repercussions.

James is far ahead of himself; he must go back. He abandons the attempt to explicate "thought's object" and "fringe" in the full perceptual situation and turns instead to the apparently simpler situation of baldly conceptual and judgmental thought. His discussion begins with another warning about the psychologist's fallacy: it is not the case that the thought is immediately aware of itself along with the object which it thinks. The psychologist thinks he knows the thought itself, and the danger is for him to confuse his putative knowledge with the thought's knowledge (No. 3). But then James ignores his insight into inattentive or marginal awareness, and this causes him to narrow thought's object unwarrentedly.

It is not the case, James says, that the thought need be immediately aware of the thinker, the psychologist; and the psychologist can also commit the fallacy by confusing his awareness of his own

Further difficulties of dualism

existence with what the thought is immediately aware of (No. 3).

> If, in addition to thinking O, I also think that I exist and that I know O, well and good; I then know one more thing, a fact about O, of which I previously was unmindful. That, however, does not prevent me from having already known it a good deal. O *per se*, or O *plus* P, are as good objects of knowledge as O *plus me* is.[33]

In his discussion of plainly judgmental thought James does not include the psychologist's inattentive awareness of his own body. Since he has said that some inattentive awareness of one's own body accompanies all else that one thinks every time one thinks, and since he will speak of the "fringe" and "margin" of thought's object in discussing the object of plainly judgmental thought, we are led to suspect that, for him, there are multiple nesting "spheres" in the object of thought—wheels within wheels—and that his attention is here narrowed to the more "internal" ones. He does not specifically state that he is employing an artificial simplicity, but if he is not he is inconsistent when he says that some awareness of the body accompanies all else of which one is aware.

It should be understandable that he fails to mention any narrowing of his treatment here, because as he conceives it, the object of thought is vast enough in its minimal form, and the more imminent danger is to destroy even a minimal object. Even so, what he broaches here is a conception of thought's object (No. 3) significantly more complex than a conception of physical object in the world; it is a conception pursuant to a solution of the problem of things cognized as being the same in the midst of phenomenal change:

> In popular parlance the word object is commonly taken without reference to the act of knowledge, and treated as synonymous with individual subject of existence. Thus if anyone ask what is the mind's object when you say 'Columbus discovered America in 1492,' most people will reply 'Columbus,' or 'America,' or, at most, 'discovery of America.' They will name a substantive kernel or nucleus of the consciousness, and say the thought is 'about' that,—as indeed it is,—and they will call that your thought's 'object.' Really that is usually only the grammatical object, or more likely the grammatical subject, of your sentence. It is at most your 'fractional object;' or you may call it the 'topic' of your thought . . . But the Object of your thought is really its entire content or deliverance . . . It is a vicious

use of speech to take out a substantive kernel from its content and call that its object . . .[34]

Here first explicitly appears a major distinction in James's *Principles of Psychology*—one whose necessity we anticipated at the close of our third chapter. There are two senses to the phrase "thought's object": There is the intended object (qua referent) in the world, and there is thought's intentional object in its entirety; the two are not divided by any epistemological chasm, since the particular object in the world is the "topic" or "kernel" of thought's object—it is a part of it. With this distinction arise two senses of the word "meaning," somewhat akin to Frege's famous distinction between "sense" and "reference,"[35] but more fundamentally akin to a distinction which arises in the work of Edmund Husserl.[36] With this distinction there arises also the possibility of a solution to the problem of how one can know at different times that things are the same: Things in the world as topics or referents can be judged to be the same even while they are cognized as falling into different relationships to the self (relationships which figure someway in the totality of thought's object).

Thought's Object in its entirety is the total "deliverance" of the thought: as we find James saying so often, "all that thought thinks exactly as thought thinks it"; it is that which thought is *about* in a primal way. Often he capitalizes this sense of the word—as we shall always in what follows—but sometimes he does not. It will be left to us to ascertain what he means when he speaks indiscriminately of "object." In one sense of the word "about," thought can be said to be "about" individual "objects" in the world. Then is this sense of "object" synonymous with "real thing" in the world (No. 4)? It would seem to be, at least as real things *meant* (topic or referent). No. 3 encircles No. 4.

The Object of thought—Object now, not just topic—is ". . . all that thought thinks, exactly as thought thinks it . . .":

> The object of my thought . . . is strictly speaking neither Columbus, nor America, nor its discovery. It is nothing short of the entire sentence, 'Columbus-discovered-America-in-1492.' And if we wish to speak of it substantively, we must make a substantive of it by writing it out thus with hyphens between all the words. Nothing but this can possibly name its delicate idiosyncrasy. And if we wish to

Further difficulties of dualism

feel that idiosyncrasy, we must reproduce the thought as it was uttered, with every word fringed and with the whole sentence bathed in that original halo of obscure relations, which, like an horizon, then spread about its meaning.[37]

Two questions arise. What does he mean by the "halo," "horizon," or "fringe" (all apparent synonyms) of "obscure relations" in which the sentence is "bathed"? What does he mean by saying that this fringe is "spread about its [the sentence's] meaning"?

James's analysis, which immediately follows, shows that he *equates* the fringe with the meaning of the sentence, and the meaning with the Object. This answers the first question and shows that the second cannot arise. It shows that his previous locution is loose: the fringe can neither be, nor not be, spread about the sentence's meaning, because the fringe *is* the meaning (in the primal sense of "meaning," that is Object):

> Now I believe that in all cases where the words are *understood*, the total idea may be and usually is present not only before and after the phrase has been spoken, but also whilst each separate word is uttered. It is the overtone, halo, or fringe of the word, *as spoken in that sentence*. It is never absent; no word in an understood sentence comes to consciousness as a mere noise. We feel its meaning as it passes; and although our object differs from one moment to another as to its verbal kernel or nucleus, yet it is similar throughout the entire segment of the stream.[38]

Now James's conception of meaning in the primal sense of Object is itself very broad, and some would say, no doubt, loose. This is why we said that it is *somewhat* akin to Frege's notion of "sense." James maintains that the only hope of repeating and recapturing all the meaning of a previous thought is to repeat the original sentence, with each word fringed in its original "delicate idiosyncrasy." The attempt can be only partially successful, he says, and psychologists who attempt to retrieve the thought through reflection only "garner the crumbs which fall from the feast." If a total meaning is not repeatable, then it would seem that what James means by "primal meaning" is not what Frege means by "sense," for as Frege treats this he seems to assume that it is repeatable: it would seem that we mean the same by "evening star," say, every time we say it, and that we mean it *all* each time.[39]

Evidently James includes in total or primal meaning all our associations (presumably free associations as well), and this would doubtless strike many philosophers as psychologistic.

But I do not wish to prejudge the status of primal meaning in James. The whole subject of meaning is itself far too delicate, and its study too much in a state of flux to be precipitous in our judgment. Few philosophers today are any longer willing to say, as many did a rather short time ago, that the meaning of a term is just all that can be deduced from it. Meanings in ordinary use are dazzlingly many-faceted and informal; this does not mean they are private or that they can be explicated only by psychology.

It is not at all certain that James is speaking about some sort of incommunic*able* meaning, and it seems likely to me that he merely intends to include the sense of the whole vast, variegated and shaded range of what we think and say, and that this does not mean that he intends to include something totally different from what Frege, say, means by "sense." He seems to mean a practical or actual inability to communicate totally, not an essential inability inherent in a "subjective structure" of thought itself. Moreover, Edmund Husserl maintained that James's attack on the problem of meaning helped him (Husserl) to *overcome* psychologism.[40] We shall have more to say about this below.

These are words of caution meant to safeguard the immediate inquiry. We should be careful not to conclude precipitously that James means something mentalistic or subjectivistic about primal meaning—Object. The greater portion of the text indicates that he does not, and if we do not see this we will forever be incapable of detecting what he *does* intend to tell us about the subjectivistic and mentalistic component of mind (No. 2) when he finally gets around to telling us. If we leaf forward to Chapter Twelve of the *Principles* we see that an Object or meaning passes before our minds; but that which passes does not itself change; nor is it "inside" the changing mind. Equating meanings and conceptions (note well the reference to Plato) James writes:

> Each conception thus eternally remains what it is, and never can become another. The mind may change its states, and its meanings, at different times; may drop one conception and take up another, but the dropped conception can in no intelligible sense be said to *change into* its successor. The paper, a moment ago white, I may now see to

have scorched black. But my conception 'white' does not change into my conception 'black.' On the contrary, it stays alongside of the objective blackness as a different meaning in my mind, and by so doing lets me judge the blackness as the paper's change. Unless it stayed, I should simply say 'blackness' and know no more. Thus, amid the flux of opinions and of physical things, the world of conceptions, or things intended to be thought about, stands stiff and immutable, like Plato's Realm of Ideas.[41]

It is only at a rather advanced point in Chapter Nine that James finally makes a reference to mental states which can be construed as a reference to mental states themselves (No. 2) instead of one to the cognitive object (No. 3). The fringe or horizon of a sentence is the meaning of it (Object), and the time intervals during which the meaning is present to thought are different ways of "feeling" the meaning, James says[42]:

> It takes time to utter the phrase . . . Now I say of these time-parts that we cannot take any one of them so short that it will not after some fashion or other be a thought of the whole object . . . They melt into each other like dissolving views, and no two of them feel the object just alike, but each feels the total object in a unitary, undivided way. This is what I mean by denying that in the thought any parts can be found corresponding to the object's parts.[43]

Note well this use of "feeling," for it has a different sense from his original use of the term which was actually that of a synonym for thought's object (No. 3). The original use is present even here: the total object (Object) is the changeless meaning which is *felt* in a "unitary, undivided way" and which is present as a whole and in a block throughout the change. Yet James says that each time-part is a different way of feeling this meaning. We cannot say that *this* use of "feeling" is synonymous with that of thought's Object or meaning, for if we did we would impute to James the obvious nonsense of saying that the different time-parts are different ways of feeling the same feeling. He is not saying this.

Nevertheless, he is saddling himself with the treacherously ambiguous word "feeling" which will plague his analysis. The ambiguity is the worst possible kind: it confuses No. 2 and No. 3.

But what does he want to mean by this second use of "feeling"? Recall he said that "our present (Object) differs from one moment to another as to its verbal kernel . . ."[44] It seems that he equates this second use of "feeling" with various kinds of passing "imagery," among which he includes "verbal imagery."[45] Take the sentence "Columbus discovered America in 1492." The verbal imagery involved at the point in time when we say "Columbus" differs from that at the time when we say "America," although the meaning or the Object remains constant. The brute sound of the terms (whatever this means exactly) is different.

Note, however: if thought "itself" (No. 2) is imagery and if different imagery is a different way of feeling (in the second sense) the same meaning, then how could we ever know what these different ways are unless we *already knew* what is felt differently in each case—the single meaning which remains the same (Object)? We could not.

This point is further corroborated by James's assertion that "the halo of relations" (the Object) can be the same "in very different systems of imagery."[46] In fact, James sets no limits to the kinds of imagery that can figure as different ways of feeling the same meaning. But if the imagery can be of *any* kind, then it would follow that there is nothing about the imagery per se which determines what kind of meaning it will have.

On another score, then, meaning would have to be known on its own merits and in its own self-sufficient terms, and the knowledge of the imagery involved would be a kind of conceptual dangler or trailer. This conceptual dependence would militate against James's programmatic assumption that the data of psychology are externally related and independently specifiable; it eclipses the smaller problem of how language can be conceived as "verbal imagery" at all. We find evidence from the text to show that the data are not independently specifiable, and that there is good reason for the fact that James can begin to talk intelligibly about mental states "themselves" (No. 2) only after he has talked about the objects of mental states (Object, No. 3). His talk about the data supposedly in compartment (No. 2) falls into a pile of tag ends within compartment No. 3.

The commanding position of datum No. 3—meaning Object, fringe of relations—in James's analysis of the stream of thought has not been clearly seen in much traditional Jamesian scholarship. For example, Professor R. B. Perry speaks of Object as the "internal object."[47] These are not James's words, however. It is not the case that even the suggestion of the internality of the Object is a

Further difficulties of dualism

consistent element in James's account; to speak of it as if it were is to beg the whole question which this study raises: Does James's dualism remain intact? It begs this question because it simply assumes that if James is not talking about a physical object in the world, he must be talking about a moving and changing psychical existent "inside" the "stream" of thought. But there is another alternative: that the Object of thought be explicated in its own uniquely proper terms (the third datum, No. 3). And James speaks of the Object as a changeless meaning; it is only sometimes that he speaks inconsistently of it as a changing psychical existent, as we shall see below. In terms of the strand of thought we have so far traced in James, it is nonsense to speak of the Object as if it pertained to, or in any way meant, a changing psychical state of the thinker. No, it means something about another person, Columbus, who lived hundreds of years ago. But neither does it pertain necessarily to an event which actually occurred in the world. Perhaps Columbus fabricated the story of discovering America; but we would still know what it meant to say or think "Columbus discovered America in 1492." Professor Perry writes:

> Over and above its present *meaningfulness*, consisting in the irradiation of the fringe within the circle of its horizon, there is also its *meant*, the non-present experience which is defined by the fringe's orientation. This ulterior and contingent experience consists, for example, of Columbus' experience of America in 1492, or, perhaps, his alibi.[48]

This is an interpolation, it seems to me. James does not say that the "meant," in any sense of the word, could be Columbus's alibi. And this stands to reason. If we say that Columbus discovered America, then we *mean* that he discovered it (whether he actually did is irrelevant), and we precisely do *not* mean that he did not but had an alibi instead.

Also Professor Perry asserts that for James the "meant" (qua topic or referent) is a *contingent* matter, but this is at variance with a considerable body of evidence which can be found in the *Principles*. Professor Perry makes these assertions, I believe, because he does not render James's distinction between Object and topic with entire accuracy. Perry asserts in another place that the topic is what the thought is "about," while the Object is what is thought about it.[49] But James asserts that thought is *also about* the

Object, that there are two senses of "about," just as there are two senses of "meaning." Perry's reading conflates data No. 2 and data No. 3 when thought's *Object* is the meaning in question (and why not say that Object can be the "meant"?). In so doing he blurs one of James's most intelligible references to thought itself (No. 2), i.e., as imagery. Moreover, in failing to distinguish what is thought about in the sense of Object (meaning), from what is thought about in the sense of topic (meaning), Perry fails to report James's contention that meaning in the sense of Object is primary. James speaks of the "mere" topic, and of the "ultimateness of the cognitive relation" qua Object[50] (how the cognitive relation is absorbed into the Object we shall see).

This is a major matter, for James is implying that we cannot even begin to isolate and identify a topic or referent meant to be in the world (let alone to verify an assertion of its existence) unless we have already thought it in relation to other things; i.e., unless it has already figured as, in James's terms, a topic *within* some Object of thought. If this is the case, a referent can be singled out only *through* a sense, and great repercussions for philosophy of mind follow. One repercussion is that the "meant" in the sense of topic or referent cannot be a contingent matter; there can be no two ways about it: we *have to* mean just *that* thing. In other words, James cannot start with data No. 4 and correlate contingently to data No. 2. He can get to No. 4 only through No. 3, and if No. 2 is not specifiable independently of No. 3, No. 2 is not specifiable independently of No. 4 either. He can get to both No. 2 and No. 4 only *through* No. 3. And as we shall see below, he can get to No. 1—his own self—likewise only through No. 3.

The elucidation of James's conception of the relationship of Object to topic depends on the elucidation of his conceptions of the temporal reference in the fringe and the satisfaction of such a reference. James contends that the cognized relations which comprise the fringe (or other synonyms for the Object, such as "halo of obscure relations") and which constitute the meaning of the thought (qua Object) are felt[51] relations of affinity to the topic of the thought.[52] These relations are of "harmony and discord, of furtherance or hindrance of the topic." As he says, there are no relations without terms related, and these relations are relations to the topic felt in the fringe.

Further difficulties of dualism

But how can these relations be such that they "further" or "hinder" the topic? The topic is that which we are thinking about in the sense of reference; it is that man, Columbus. Already we think him in relation: he belongs to that class of beings called men, but he is singled out from the rest. The topic is furthered when the relations felt in the fringe mesh with and further the relations already felt there. That is, to think of Columbus at all means that our expectations have been determined in a definite way.[53] We expect that he is the kind of being who could discover things which existed when he did, and when we think that he discovered America this furthers the topic. The topic is hindered when the relations felt in the fringe do not mesh with and further the topic because they are discordant with our expectations; e.g., if we should think that Columbus discovered something which we know did not exist when he did. This thinking of things in relation to Columbus is just what the Object of thought consists in. It *is* the "halo of obscure relations" (obscure at least in the sense that the thought feels that there is always more to be known about the topic than has already been thought; James does not mean that there are fringes only when we think obscurely). Even when there is a discord felt in the fringe, it is all in the fringe; i.e., the fringe qua Object of thought is a seamless totality. Moreover, nothing in the world need actually exist—nor need we necessarily think that it does—in order for us to have some kind of topic for our thought.

> The natural possibility or impossibility of the thing does not touch the question of its conceivability in this problematic way. 'Round square,' 'black-white-thing,' are absolutely definite conceptions; it is a mere accident, as far as conception goes, that they happen to stand for things which nature never lets us sensibly perceive.[54]

The Object, then, or fringe is an affinity of relations felt in respect to a topic; the relations are felt to obtain between the topic and other matters (they need not be other things, but classes of things, etc.).[55] This affinity of relations need not be felt as harmonious, but can be felt as discordant.[56] When they are felt as discordant, "we are dissatisfied," says James, and when they are felt as harmonious, we are satisfied.[57]

With the appearance of "satisfied" we sense the issue of James's pragmatism hovering on the horizon. I do not intend to deal with his later popularization of his theory of meaning, which he presented in conjunction with a theory of truth (the public lectures published as *Pragmatism*); nor will I deal with the flurry of criticisms it evoked, the main point being that James was guilty of championing a doctrine of wishful thinking. It is only the *Principles* which concerns us, and in this work when James says "we are dissatisfied," it would have been more in line with his own meaning if he had said that *the thought* is dissatisfied.

The real point James wishes to make is that the fringe of thought involves a reference to the future. To feel relations in the fringe is *ipso facto* to feel that certain definite other relations *will be* felt; the very thought itself involves this expectation for, as James says, the fringe is bone of its bone and flesh of its flesh. As early as his essay on Spencer, he had maintained that the thought of rain, for example, involves the expectation that a definite standard will be satisfied, e.g., the availability of sensations of water. For thoughts to be satisfied, standards must be satisfied, and this line of thought is continued in the *Principles*. Every kind of thought (or more accurately, each kind of Object—for that is what James is really telling us about) involves a reference to the future satisfaction of its appropriate standard (e.g., logic, empirical thought, and music are different kinds of thought, each with different standards). If I think, for example, that the teakettle is full, this involves as a present relation in the fringe the expectation that the teakettle will be heavy and not fly up in my face when I lift it.[58] The *teakettle* is thought of as fringed; the fringe is not a wraith floating somehow in psychical space. One of the definite relations in the teakettle's fringe is its relation to my body in a given set of circumstances—a set which need not be presently realized in fact. Now, without expecting it to be realized, I cannot, according to James, think the thought at all. So there must be this initial satisfaction in the fringe if the thought is to be thinkable. The thought is already satisfied to this degree. If I go over and pick up the teakettle with the expected amount of effort and it does not fly up in my face, then the thought is satisfied in still a further degree. It is now verified—true. But in neither case need anything but the thought qua Object be satisfied. Even in the latter case *I* may not be at all satisfied. On the contrary, I may be dissatisfied even though I did expect to find the teakettle full; e.g., "I really

Further difficulties of dualism

shouldn't have another cup of coffee." As Roderick Chisholm says of James:

> To say that a full teakettle would cause fulfillment or satisfaction, is merely to say that unlike an empty teakettle, it would not cause disruption or frustration. The kind of "satisfaction" we can attribute to successful expectation, then, is quite different from the kind we can attribute to successful strivings or springs of action.[59]

Chisholm adds the unhappy truth: "James's readers interpreted 'satisfy' in its more usual sense, in which it is applicable to strivings and desirings rather than believings."

Once James's conception of thought's object (Object) and fringe is introduced into his discussion it gains momentum and snowballs. It draws into itself the data on both sides of it which he had intended to keep separate (No. 2 and No. 4), and in so doing it disrupts his conceptual framework. Even when he narrows his attention from a perceptual to a conceptual situation (see the statement about Columbus), the primacy and inclusiveness of thought's Object is apparent. As his own psychologist, he contends that things known in the world (No. 4) are merely the kernel (topic) of an Object, and thoughts themselves as psychical existents or imagery (No. 2) are merely different ways of feeling the Object (in the second sense of "feeling") and are intrinsically unimportant to the Object (the primal meaning) felt. This demands further explication: The Object is a fringe of relations meant, and these relations are not necessarily subjectivistic or mentalistic at all. The Object embodies a temporal reference insofar as it involves an expectation of real possibilities and standards to be met; but the expectation is already present and already realized *as* an expectation, and there is no more movement in the Object itself than there is movement in a Platonic Idea. (See James's approving reference to Plato above.) The imagery involved in the Object moves, but not the Object.

James's introduction of thought's Object involves him in a *de facto* commitment to that which is not assimilable to his dualistic framework. His dilemma is, where does thought's Object belong? On the mental side or on the physical side? The answer is that there does not seem to be any room in James's dualistic framework for the Object. The framework must be destroyed. With this in mind a basic tension in his thought is understandable. There are passages, in line with his manifest program, in which he attempts to incorporate thought's Object into the constantly changing mental side, the stream of consciousness. The fringe is conceived as a rapidly moving psychical state. These passages are what Professor Perry seems to have drawn on exclusively in his account. We shall now see what disruption and what inconsistency they cause.

V

In certain passages James slurs over the distinction between thought itself qua imagery, including verbal imagery (No. 2), and thought's object qua Object (No. 3). The disastrously ambiguous word "feeling" is at work. Equating Object and Idea, he writes:

> The consciousness of the 'Idea' and that of the words are thus consubstantial. They are made of the same 'mind-stuff,' and form an unbroken stream.[60]

It is well that he put "mind-stuff" in shudder quotes, for he cannot mean this location literally. It is not so well that he put "Idea" in them.

James's conflations of No. 3 and No. 2 are abetted by a suppression of the primal sense of meaning (Object). In the passages in question he so accentuates meaning qua topic that meaning qua Object is eclipsed.

> *For the important thing about a train of thought is its conclusion.* That is the *meaning*, or as we say the topic of the thought.[61]

This might seem plausible. If I am walking down the street trying to remember the building on campus at which I am expected, the finally and clearly demarcated kernel in my Object of thought as finally defined by the fringes is my meaning qua topic or reference. The relations of affinity felt in the fringe are harmonized and satisfied. If I actually walk up to that building and enter it, then these fringes are further satisfied, and it might be said that that particular building is just what I meant (qua topic) all along. Now James wants to say that the imagery involved in this, whether it be tactile, visual, or verbal, is irrelevant to my meaning.[62] It merely leads to this sharply defined kernel, this topic, and since other imagery might have led to the same topic, the kind of imagery employed is irrelevant: ". . . that kind of mind-stuff which is

Further difficulties of dualism

handiest will be the best for the purpose." Though we do not know enough about what James means by "imagery" (presumably psychical existents, No. 2), still there is something plausible here.

But the rub is this: the imagery may be irrelevant to the leading to this topic, but is the *meaning* (qua Object) of the imagery irrelevant? Only if James succeeds in conflating imagery and Object and in convincing us that his *own* assertion, i.e., that the feeling of the meaning (Object) is different from the feeling of the imagery, is false.

In some passages he does attempt to conflate them and to throw the blanket term "mind-stuff" over them both. We find him speaking of the fringe as a transitive (or transitional) mental state in the stream of thought which has the function of leading to motionless substantive mental states, the topics.[63] James mixes his metaphors at this point and speaks of mental states not as a stream but as a bird's flight: consciousness is made up of an alternation of "flights and perchings," transitive and substantive states. This would certainly seem to be incompatible with his contention that the stream of thought is *constantly* changing. We find him hedging: the substantive states are periods of "comparative" rest.[64]

Less obviously, but more importantly, this is incompatible with what he tells us about meaning in the sense of fringe or Object. The fringe is an affinity of relations felt in respect to a topic. The total "shape" or deliverance of the fringe may alter rapidly and frequently as new ramifications appear and others drop away, as the topic becomes increasingly better described, related, and demarcated. In a loose sense we could say that the fringe expanded and contracted. But in a strict sense we would have to say that it was a new fringe, because it was a new *total* fringe each time (James described the Object as *all* that thought thinks exactly as thought thinks it). More than this, by James's own admission thought's Object or fringe is *already* present, cognitively, with the topic itself, even though the topic is as yet defined only vaguely. (Recall his example of thinking about Orion.) This stands to reason, since if it were not already present we would have no idea at all of what we are thinking vaguely about.

But James at some points writes of the fringe as if it were material on the move, so to speak, as if it took time to arrive at the topic or substantive states in the stream, the perchings. It is as if he were saying that the element of future reference already present in the fringe, the element of expectation, did not know what it was an expectation *of* until the course of experience reveals what actually happens. But the expectation that an expectation will be satisfied, which is all James need say concerning the fringe (and all he does say in many passages), is totally different from an expectation's *being* satisfied.

In short, in the light of James's observations at other points in the *Principles* he cannot consistently say that the fringe itself moves. This would be the same as saying that a meaning changes and yet remains the same, which is clearly at variance with his agreement with Plato. Total Objects of thought, total fringes, may be replaced rapidly by others, but no single fringe can move in the stream of consciousness. If an initial fringe contains a vaguely defined topic, then it contains it vaguely; it is simply a vague thought about it, and that, for the time being, finishes the matter. As James himself says of them:

> They may be faint and weak; they may be very vague cognizers of the same realities which other conscious states cognize and name exactly; they may be unconscious of much in the reality which the other states are conscious of. But that does not make them in *themselves* a whit dim or vague or unconscious. They *are* eternally as they feel when they exist, and can, neither actually nor potentially, be identified with anything else than their own faint selves.[65]

A vague thought about a topic is what we actually experience, and James pleads that we honor the integrity of this experience. But the immediate point is that we could not even know this much about the topic unless the thought (qua Object) were already cognitively present to it, not just approaching it temporally.[66] The passages in which James is inconsistent with himself are those in which his programmatic dualism remains intact. The inconsistency arises when he treats thought's Object as a psychical existent moving in the stream of consciousness.

More particularly, the inconsistency arises as follows: James maintains that traditional psychologies miss what he calls the movement of our thought. They attend only to the sharply defined topics and forget that topics emerge only as kernels within a dynamic whole. It is only because topics are defined by their fringes that they are topics at all, and he maintains that much of our thought is a movement toward topics not yet sharply defined. This movement is the heart of the creative process, and in its all-important initial stages it is the flickering first flash of insight which only vaguely prefigures a topic. He writes, "It is . . . the re-instatement of the vague to its proper place in our mental life that I am so anxious to press on attention."[67] He says this is missed by traditional psychologists because they commit the psychologist's fallacy. Instead of reporting what the thought itself immediately knows (No. 3), the psychologist substitutes what he qua natural scientist knows about the specific thing thought about in the world:

> All *dumb* or anonymous psychic states have, owing to this error, been coolly suppressed; or, if recognized at all, have been named after the substantive perception they led to, as thoughts 'about' this object or 'about' that, the stolid word *about* engulfing all their delicate idiosyncrasies in its monotonous sound.[68]

The psychologist gets his hands only on the tendencies of the agent which can be facts for an outside observer, while he misses the anticipatory tendencies of thought as they are actually experienced by the agent himself (teleology-judged-from-within); he misses the heart of thought.

> Tendencies exist, but they are facts for the outside psychologist rather than for the subject of the observation. The tendency is thus a *psychical* zero; only its *results* are felt.

> Now what I contend for, and accumulate examples to show, is that 'tendencies' are not only descriptions from without, but that they are among the *objects* of the stream, described as in very large measure constituted of *feelings* of tendency, often so vague that we are unable to name them at all.[69]

James is thus sharply critical of what we know today as behaviorism which misses these basic tendencies and is, therefore, a psychology which dispenses with the psyche; it is a self-satirizing science.

Yet James creates a glaring difficulty for himself. He says he wants to retrieve the anonymous psychic states of tendency which are vague and which cannot be named because their topic is not yet sufficiently defined. He says that psychic states must be disentangled from an eventually sharply defined kernel, a topic, which they are *about*, otherwise the seminally vague ones will be ignored. But he sometimes submerges the distinction which marks the other way in which a mental state can be *about* an object, and which marks the other sense of object, i.e., Object or fringe. Consequently we find a muddle when he writes:

> Now what I contend for, and accumulate examples to show, is that 'tendencies' are not only descriptions from without, but that they are among the *objects* of the stream, described as in very large measure constituted of *feelings* of tendency . . .[70]

What sense of "object," and what sense of "feeling"? The object must be Object, and not topic, since he is not talking about changing things in the world like rivers, cocoons, and blooming flowers. But if so, it is "feeling" in the first sense, not "feeling" in the sense of a psychical existent (No. 2).

Because he has failed to maintain his grip on the primal sense of "about" and "Object," and because of his remaining dualistic structure, he is led to infer that when we are not talking about a physical entity in the world, all else that remains (most notably Object or fringe) must be a changing and transitive psychical entity. But can a fringe change? Certainly, at the first moment in the creative process the fringe is loose and rapidly replaced, but the creative process is a sequence of Objects, of meanings, which are themselves changeless.

The impossibility of concluding that a fringe is a changing and transitive psychical state is demonstrable in James's own terms.[71] Take his contention that a fringe as a "feeling of relation" is what he calls in places a "swift consciousness."[72] Take also his example of the thunder's breaking in on the silence, for it is the best possible example of what he is trying to say. In some passages in Chapter Nine he wants to say that the transition from silence to noise is mirrored in consciousness by an equally rapid transition, a "transitive state." But this dualistic mirroring is egregiously inconsistent with what he elsewhere (although later!) says about the Object. For example:

> If asked why we perceive . . . the sound of an explosion, we reply, 'Because certain outer forces, ether-waves, or air-waves, smite upon the brain, awakening therein changes to which the conscious perception [of] . . . sound respond[s].' But we hasten to add that neither light nor sound *copy* or *mirror* the ether- or air-waves; they represent them only symbolically. The *only* case, says Helmholtz, in which

Further difficulties of dualism

such copying occurs, and in which 'our perceptions can truly correspond with outer reality, is that of *time-succession* of phenomena. Simultaneity, succession, and the regular return of simultaneity or succession, can obtain as well in sensations as in outer events . . .'

James comments on this:

> One experiences an almost instinctive impulse, in pursuing such reflections as these, to follow them to a sort of crude speculative conclusion, and to think that he has at least got the mystery of cognition where, to use a vulgar phrase, 'the wool is short.'. . . . The mental stream, feeling itself, must feel the time-relations of its own states. But as these are copies of the outward time-relations, so must it know them too. That is to say, these latter time-relations arouse their own cognition; or . . . the mere existence of time in those changes out of the mind which affect the mind is a sufficient cause why time is perceived by the mind.
>
> This philosophy is unfortunately too crude . . . *A succession of feelings, in and of itself, is not a feeling of succession.*[73]

With this in mind, then, when the thunder breaks in on the silence (or even when such a change is anticipated), what is immediately present to mind is a feeling of succession, not a succession of feelings. The awareness of the successive feelings supposedly comes later, in an act of reflective introspection. But James does *not* perform such an act, and he contents himself with inconclusive metaphors, e.g., feelings "blend" into each other like "dissolving views," which suggests nothing better than a running smear.

What is immediately presented then is an Object, not a pure psychic state. Of course, it is undeniably the case that changes in my way of feeling the succession go on also. At first I hear the succession fearfully, say, and then not fearfully. Later I remember the succession and this time perhaps happily. Can these senses of feeling be specified in terms of imagery, e.g., auditory imagery? The question is premature because James cannot expose the specific varieties of the second sense of feeling (passing imagery) until he exposes the second sense itself.

The important point here is that the psychic state is a subordinate matter. Object and fringe are primary. At some points he does not separate No. 2 and No. 3, and simply proceeds with programmatic dualism. As a result he thinks of Object-and-fringe as a transitive state. Whereas in the light of his own statements at other places, if the fringe were actually a transitive psychical state connecting two "comparatively stable" psychical states, no cognition of the phenomena of succession would be possible. This ironical conclusion follows from his own observations: If there is no single Object in which the succession can appear *as* succession nor in which it can be known in a fringe of relations, then the succession can never be known. But it is known, therefore there must be such an Object.

If an example other than the thunder had been chosen, the confusion of thought's Object and thought itself would have been more apparent. Suppose I turn around and as I do I see one man hitting another. If to the relation of one man's hand to another man's jaw there corresponds, mirror-like, a transitive state, a "swift consciousness" in my psyche, and if to the dazed man there corresponds a stable psychical state which persists somehow as I stand there, then I can never know what has happened between these persons. The end state of the event, the dazed and motionless man, would be mirrored in my mind by a perception of dazedness and motionlessness which replaced and crowded out all else, including the idea (memory) of the blow itself. There would be no way of distinguishing a transition in me from a transition in the rest of the world; I simply would not know what had taken place "out there." Thus that which begins as a simple dualism, with mind mirroring the world point for point, and with the intention of safeguarding both mind and world, ends, ironically, in the inability to know and distinguish either of them.

If still another example were chosen, this time a nontemporal relation in the world, say a man standing to the right of a woman, then the equation of fringe and transitive state loses even its initial shred of plausibility. James's choice of thunder as an example is unfortunate because it partially obscures the defectiveness of his interpretation of the fringe as a transitive state mirroring temporal relations.

His attempted incorporation of the fringe into the stream of thought was motivated by the desire to get his hands on psychical existents, but the confusion it produces is evident even further in his treatment of "feelings of tendency."

> Suppose three successive persons say to us: 'Wait!' 'Hark!' 'Look!' Our consciousness is thrown into three quite different attitudes of

Further difficulties of dualism

expectancy, although no definite object is before it in any one of the three cases.[74]

James then proceeds to elaborate on the fact that no definite object is before the mind. He says that there is a "gap" in our consciousness, an absence. But the feeling of an absence is not the absence of a feeling; indeed, the feeling of the absence is totally different in three different attitudes of expectancy cited, so it is not a case of having a mere nothing in each instance: zero = zero = zero.

> The ordinary way is to assume that they are all emptinesses of consciousness, and so the same state. But the feeling of an absence is *toto coelo* other than the absence of a feeling. It is an intense feeling.[75]

He then talks about these "singularly definite gaps" by way of another example: trying to remember a name. We do not know what the right name is, but the singularly definite gap "acts" emphatically to rule out all the wrong names that are proposed. He rejects the contention that, since the terms which might make the state of mind of trying to remember Spalding's name different from trying to remember Bowles's, have not, by hypothesis, arrived yet; therefore the states of mind cannot differ. True, says James, the psychologist cannot *completely* specify the difference, because the two states of mind can be so specified only in terms of the names not yet in mind. But this does not mean, he goes on, that the two states do not exist and do not exist as different from one another. They simply cannot be named. "But namelessness is compatible with existence," he says.[76] The observing psychologist can only take the subject's word for it, although the only words that the subject can utter are not the words which would identify the gap for the psychologist. Each mental state has

> . . . a nature of its own of the most positive sort, and yet what can we say about it without using words that belong to the later mental facts that replace it? The intention *to-say-so-and-so* is the only name it can receive. One may admit that a good third of our psychic life consists in these rapid premonitory perspective views of schemes of thought not yet articulate.[77]

The similarity in James's treatment of "feelings of tendency" and "transitive states" is evident. In both cases we are warned directly or indirectly against committing the psychologist's fallacy.

We must not confuse the mental state with what it is *about* (in the sense of No. 4); we must not conclude that since the specification of the referent or topic of the thought is not at present to be found, therefore a corresponding very definite mental state does not exist. It is still *about* an Object!

But in both cases James again fails to apply his own distinction. Just because it is a fact that what the mental state is about in the sense of topic cannot be specified, it does not follow that the mental state is about nothing, i.e., has no Object. On the contrary, it has its Object, which can certainly be specified to a great extent. Moreover, this is actually what James is specifying in his attempt to call our attention to the mental state in question. We are trying to remember the name of a *man*. We are not trying to remember the name of a dog, and we are not trying to remember how to tie a sheepshank knot. We *can* say this much, and this is quite a bit. In his own terms, there must be an Object and a great deal of fringe, even though it is incomplete as to its topic.

There are passages, however, in which he does not realize this and speaks again of Object as if it were a changing psychic existent. The consequences are momentous for philosophy of mind. In the first place he claims that we have a serious deficiency in our vocabulary for the description of psychic existents, whereas in the light of his own work he is only entitled to say that we have a difficulty in describing the Object of thought, and the real reason for this is not that it is hidden in a locked mental container or psychic pipe of some sort, but that it is very complex and sometimes incomplete. Men, dogs, and knots and their relationships in the world are not private mental entities.

In the second place all the difficulties connected with thinking of transitive states as moving psychic existents recur when we think of feelings of tendency and their fringes as such. The peculiarities of the fringe when we are trying to recall a man's name is described by James as a "singularly active" and "aching gap." "To fill it up is our thought's destiny . . . Each [thought] swims in a felt fringe of relations of which the aforesaid gap is the term."[78] We get a picture of the fringe as a quivering hole in a streaming sheet of psychical substance. But if the hole were in the knowing substance, we could never know it to be a hole. Yet we *do* know it to be a hole—a gap. This is the lesson of James's remark that a feeling of succession is not a succession of feelings; likewise, a feeling of absence ("feeling" in the first sense) is not an absence of feeling. The knower-known (subject-object) chasm cannot be bridged by a dualistically conceived, point-for-point sort of mirroring, and James himself helps teach us why.

VI

Let us review and then note James's admission of confusion. Unclarity arises in those passages in which he attempts to conflate No. 2 and No. 3. The attempt arises out of his residual dualism which stipulates the cognitive relationship to be an ultimate, undiscussable, and apparently external relationship which can be filled in after an independently specifiable mental state, on the one hand, and an independently specifiable physical thing, on the other, have received their specifications.[79]

So far he has not left himself room for the sort of analysis of thought's Object which his account at some places shows necessary. At times he lumps together No. 2 and No. 3 and attempts to correlate them as a unit with what is taken for granted, i.e., a physical particular in space and time, No. 4.

But the point to be elicited from his analysis is that James has become his own psychologist, and that the psychologist's realities, i.e., No. 4, are just topics *within his own Object* (No. 3). In other words, he already knows *rerum natura* in terms of the structure of his thought and language. He cannot say that *rerum natura* first exists in a self-evident way and is then mirrored by a stream of thought which is patterned after language. It is not proper to ask how we know which events in *rerum natura* are meant by which thoughts (or feeling in the first sense), nor to ask how the two become matched, because we are *already* talking about *rerum natura*, and talking is at least a part (and in James's actual analysis, a large part) of thinking.

If cognition in this very general sense of meaning is just a mirror-like representation, then how do we cognize (mean) that this representation itself is taking place? We could only cognize it with still another such cognition, and so on to infinity, without ever being able to ground cognition itself and locate its point of departure. But cognition *does* get going, and we do know what we mean, so it must have a point of departure. As James himself says, "We are masters of our meanings."[80]

There is a definite disparity between what he says he will do in the *Principles* and what he actually does do. He *says* that the natural scientific psychologist's conceptual framework is an unquestioned dualism. The psychologist deals with two entities only: a mental perception of color, say, and the real color.[81] His task is to discover the conditions (presumably causal) which prevail when the mental perception accurately represents the real color, when it is veridical, and those which prevail when it does not. The psychologist stands outside of both entities. Now how does he know which two entities to compare? Why does he not compare the mental perception to the square root of minus two instead of to a color? He does not pose this question in his statement of program, but some of its force must have been tacitly understood by him, because he adds that the psychologist believes that the mental perception is *of* a common world.

What does James *do?* Instead of dealing with only two entities, one of which (the psychical existent) either does or does not truly represent the other, we find him introducing a third: thought's object, and then subdividing this into Object (or fringe) and topic. His attempts to treat this third Object as a part of the original psychical existent conflict with his own analysis of it and its relationship to thought. He cannot consider it to be out of relationship to thought (it is *thought's* Object), but he cannot reduce it to thought itself (No. 2) without internal conflicts within his doctrine of cognition. Thus, instead of treating the cognitive relationship as an external one of which he need not speak—one which is characterized merely by true or false representation of one entity by another, and which is incidental to the correlation of the mental entity to its causal base in the brain—we find him actually subjecting it to a good deal of analysis and all the while regarding it as a relationship of meaning, not merely of truth or falsity. Thus, instead of simply assuming that the psychologist already knows what the mental perception is as a psychical existent, we find James treating its cognitive Object as if *it* were central, and leaving "the mental perception itself" (No. 2) in a strange state of neglect.

Further difficulties of dualism 107

In view of James's actual treatment of his material, the psychologist cannot stand outside of thought's Object: the Object is thought's and the thought is his. The psychologist always stands within his thought, but what is immediately given to thought is not thought itself, but rather thought's Object; so the psychologist always stands within the sense of, and within the reference to, the whole lived-world.

As James actually handles it, thought's Object envelops everything known, which includes the relationship of thought to what it is about. Since thought is never about itself, the Object cannot be specified as part of the thought itself. Since the Object includes this about-ness itself, the thought again is dependent. Yet at the dualistic points of the *Principles* James wishes to reverse the dependency: the Object and fringe are pictured as a rapidly moving psychical state.

This is a pivotal inconsistency, particularly in Chapter Nine; but the most revealing thing is that James admits it. He simply says that it is hard to make oneself clear in these matters, and then proceeds to repudiate outright the notion that the fringe is a rapidly moving psychical state which connects states of "comparative rest." This appears in a footnote to Chapter Nine, a chapter composed largely of material published in 1884 in article form, which had the benefit of criticism before its inclusion in the *Principles*. James complains that he has been misunderstood:

> . . . It is so hard to make one's self clear that I may advert to a misunderstanding of my views by the late Prof. Thos. Maguire of Dublin (Lectures on Philosophy, 1885). This author considers that by the 'fringe' I mean some sort of psychic material by which sensations in themselves separate are made to cohere together, and wittily says that I ought to "see that uniting sensations by their 'fringes' is more vague than to construct the universe out of oysters by platting their beards" (p. 211). But the fringe, as I use the word, means nothing like this; it is part of the *object cognized*—substantive *qualities* and *things* appearing to the mind in a *fringe of relations*.[82]

Ah, it is as it must be. The fringe is part of the *thing cognized*—meant, intended. But one can hardly blame Professor Maguire for misunderstanding. In the sentence to which the footnote is appended James speaks of the fringe as a "psychic overtone." Elsewhere he speaks of each passing image as fringed—instead of a single fringe for a single unit of meaning, a sentence say—and any reader could easily get the notion that the fringe is a moving psychical beard or gossamer set of tentacles which reaches out in time and fastens on the next discrete and "comparatively motionless" psychical image.

Another possible source of confusion is James's failure to compare explicity the meaning of "fringe" and that of "margin." He gives us a strong clue, however. "Fringe" is usually used in the plural ("fringes"), while "margin" is used in the singular. This is what we should expect. One can be thinking of many different things, each with its own fringe, but there is only one self doing the thinking, and therefore only a single field of consciousness with a single margin. The margin indicates the single "subjective pole" of experience, but we use this phrase in shudder quotes to remind us that the whole meaning of subjectivity is being overhauled by James. In some sense of the equally troublesome word "objective," everything, including the self, is objective, is "out there"; it is just that the self occupies a constant and peculiar sector of the total Object.

VII

A fundamental conclusion can now be drawn. In *The Principles of Psychology* William James gets ahead of himself in an odd kind of way: He cannot run backward fast enough to keep up with himself. He employs presuppositions which he only later acknowledges and clarifies—suppositions without which his account would be impossible. Inevitably his work must suffer.

The central presupposition is what he calls "the sense of the same." It is only because things in the world can be meant to be the same—known to be the same in the generic sense of "known"—that any other knowledge of anything else is possible. The self-sameness of the physical thing itself (No. 4) cannot account for its becoming known for what it is; neither can the allegedly constantly changing psychical existent (No. 2). Only one datum remains—thought's Object (No. 3) in its amazing entirety. Thought's Object, then, incorporates the sense of the same and is the central presupposition without which neither the sameness of the physical thing nor the changingness of the psychical existent can be understood.

Further difficulties of dualism 109

James calls the sense of the same "the keel of the mind"; but he does not deal with it explicitly until Chapter Twelve. So it follows that he attempts to navigate the "stream of thought" in Chapter Nine before he puts in place the keel of the mind. Indeed, it is only when we look back on Chapter Nine from the vantage point of Chapter Twelve that we can understand its wanderings, inconsistencies, and gaps.

Inevitably there was trouble in Chapter Nine. First, and most important, he was incapable of drawing the inference that the specification of thought is logically dependent on the specification of thought's Object, for the Object incorporates the meaning which remains the same, and it is just this which he could not yet analyze. James bids us say aloud, "Columbus discovered America in 1492." The sound when we say "Columbus" is different from the sound when we say "America"; different sounds, therefore different feelings or auditory imagery (No. 2), pass by in "the stream of consciousness." But, James observes, something also remains constant: the *meaning* of the whole utterance surrounds all the different sounds like a "fringe," permeates them all and is the *same* in all. This is thought's total Object; and it is only when the reader can look back on Chapter Nine from Chapter Twelve (or Chapter Fourteen), only after James has explicitly admitted that the detection of specific differences presupposes generic similarity, that the reader can see that the sound "Columbus" is detected as different from that of "America" only because they are comparable. And they are comparable only because they are known to be the *same* generically—that is, both sounds—or, specifically, both known to be sounds embedded in the *same* meaningful utterance. The implication is that we must grasp the single meaningful utterance before we can know the different sounds or "thoughts themselves"; the specification of thought independent of its object is impossible.

The impossibility is perfectly exemplified in James's treatment of visual imagery later in the *Principles*. Clearly, he is ever impressed with what we might call the raw feel of a sensation. There is a difference between seeing a bright red cube on a sunny day when one is "bright" and alert, and seeing the same cube on a dim day when one is tired. And there is a difference between both of these and a memory of the cube a week later. Or there is a difference between feeling a toothache and thinking about it later.

The difference seems to be a difference in feeling in the second sense—a difference of sensations and imagery. For what thought is *of* is the same in all instances. And the cube at least is the very same physical thing. So why not think that the difference consists in a change in a *mental* thing involved in the knowing? In his faltering attempt to find a verb which will take the place of "mental state" (he wants a verb), James writes:

> 'Thought' would be by far the best word to use if it could be made to cover sensations. It has no opprobrious connotation such as 'feeling' has, and it immediately suggests the omni-presence of cognition (or reference to an object other than the mental state itself), which we shall soon see to be the mental life's essence. But can the expression 'thought of a toothache' ever suggest to the reader the actual present pain itself? It is hardly possible; and we thus seem about to be forced back on a *pair* of terms like Hume's 'impression and idea' . . .[83]

James speaks of "the sensational tang" of a feeling as that which blind man lacks in the case of vision. He speaks of "the very being" of a sensation. He writes, "An idea neither is what it knows, nor knows what it is."[84] What *is* it then? I do not think he can give us a viable introspective account, only a worldly one.

Let us now refer to a key passage in which James thinks that he has finally nailed down the "real being" of a thought (No. 2):

> The grass out of the window now looks to me of the same green in the sun as in the shade, and yet a painter would have to paint one part of it dark brown, another part bright yellow, to give its real sensational effect. We take no heed, as a rule, of the different way in which the same things look and sound and smell at different distances and under different circumstances. The sameness of the *things* is what we are concerned to ascertain; and any sensations that assure us of that will probably be considered in a rough way to be the same with each other.[85]

Note that James says the painter must paint one part of the same green grass dark brown and the other bright yellow if he would give the real sensational effect of the grass, and he adds that we take no heed, as a rule, of how different the same things look under different circumstances. Now we see the green grass which lies in shadow under different circumstances from those in which we see the grass which lies in the sunlight. But James gives us no good reason to think that the artist must constantly keep changing the

Further difficulties of dualism

dark brown pigment on his palette in order to render accurately "the real sensational effect" of the grass in the shadows; nor must the artist try to paint something "mental." Let us assume a painter who wants perfect accuracy: it makes no difference. On the basis of what he himself tells us, it is difficult to know what he means when he refers to sensations in "their very being" as "subjective facts":

> . . . we shall see how inveterate is our habit of not attending to sensations as subjective facts, but of simply using them as stepping stones to pass over to the recognition of the realities whose presence they reveal.[86]

For James can effectively specify these sensations only in terms of the way the *thing* looks! This is the major point: The *grass* looks dark brown.

Of course, as he uses the term, the word "looks" is utterly ambiguous. And the only hope for unraveling what he is really telling us about the "mental" and the "subjective" seems to lie in unraveling what he means by "looks." The same grass which looks green also looks bright yellow and dark brown. How can this be?

There is a contradiction only if "looks" has a univocal sense—and for James it does not have. A thing can look two different ways if one uses two different ways of looking at it. In the ordinary way of looking at a thing (topic), i.e., when we are concerned with the "being" of the thing looked at, the thing looks *to be* green. In the extraordinary or peculiar way of looking at the thing, i.e., when we are concerned with what James calls the "being of the sensation" of the thing, the thing looks yellow or brown but need not look *to be* yellow or brown. What does James mean by the "being of the sensation"? It serves, he says, as a sign for revealing the being of the thing. It does this by signifying what the thing would look like under ordinary (normal) circumstances of vision (e.g., uniform illumination). That is—in terms with which we are already familiar—the sensation is fringed in such a way that it contains a reference to what we would see under normal circumstances. James says that it takes a peculiar or extraordinary way of looking before the fringes are cut away and the sensation itself in its very being is revealed. But in terms of what he actually tells us it is not revealed as a mental particle or image which floats somehow in a "psychical space." It is not a mental particle called a "looks." James writes:

> A man walking towards us does not usually seem to alter his size; but we can, by setting our attention in a peculiar way make him appear to do so. The whole education of the artist consists in his learning to see the presented signs as well as the represented things. No matter what the field of view *means*, he sees it also as it *feels*—that is, as a collection of patches of color bounded by lines—the whole forming an optical diagram of whose intrinsic proportions one who is not an artist has hardly a conscious inkling. The ordinary man's attention passes *over* them to their import; the artist's turns back and dwells *upon* them for their own sake. 'Don't draw the thing as it *is*, but as it *looks!*' is the endless advice of every teacher to his pupil; forgetting that what it 'is' is what it would also 'look,' provided it were placed in what we have called the 'normal' situation for vision. In this situation the sensation as 'sign' and the sensation as 'object' coalesce into one, and there is no contrast between them.[87]

James can only say that when we achieve this peculiar way of looking at the thing, we see *the thing* as it "feels." This is all that he can positively tell us about the being of the sensation. The only specification which he gives it is in terms of a thing known and a peculiar way of looking at it; and as we shall see in his treatment of the self, this odd way of looking is not independently specifiable as peculiarly mental; it is a matter of the position of one's body in the total Object. True, he calls a sensation a sign, and refers to it as that which is presented rather than represented, and speaks of "patches of color bounded by lines" which form an "optical diagram." But he does not use optical or physiological terms (e.g., the optics of the eye) to specify these patches of color; rather, they are the way the *thing* looks in the odd way of looking at it. The sensation as sign may be dark brown while the thing signified is green. But dark brown is a property which a thing, and only a thing presumably, *could* have, and it is the way *this* thing does look when looked at in this odd way.

Let us review the two senses of "looks": in the ordinary way of looking the thing looks *to be* so and so, while in the extraordinary way the thing looks so and so without looking *to be* so and so. Either way, however, it is still the way the *thing* looks. This analysis is supported by James's contention that all sensations are intrinsically spatial.[88] When he comes to specifying a sensation in

Further difficulties of dualism 113

its very being as imagery, he can only say that it is apprehended in terms of properties which some *thing could* have, not in terms either of a psychical entity (whatever that might be) or an epiphenomenal entity specified in its causal dependence on the brain.

James wishes to maintain that no two sensorial images are ever twice the same. Although he fails to demonstrate this sweeping assertion, still he shows convincingly that there are differences we might not have suspected. In one sense of "looks" the grass in the shade *does* look different from that in the sun.[89] But it all means the same thing to us observers—uniformly green grass—because the same cognitive or signifying function is involved; in other words, the imagery has the same fringe; what we mean as to the being of the thing remains constant. It is the same green lawn all over.

James maintains that there is no definite limit to the kinds of imagery which can be fringed in the same way. Presumably some images are not sensorial at all, for example, when the thing known is not known as being "an immediately present outward reality"—as in the case of a memory of a lawn. He also speaks of "verbal imagery" and of the "bare images of logical movement";[90] the latter are hardly images at all, and Professors Capek and McGilvary are quite right, I think, in contending that James occasionally alludes to "imageless thought."[91] In any case, he maintains that the fringe with its reference to the future is the salient thing.[92] The kind of imagery involved in getting to the expected or provisional conclusion of the thought is immaterial; what is important is only the "substantive conclusions, provisional or final, of the thought." And even this, evidently, applies only to very general kinds of conclusions, as when I think, There is a snake in the oven, some sort of visual imagery is present in the fringe in the form of an expectation.

> The reader sees by this time that it makes little or no difference in what sort of mind-stuff, in what quality of imagery, his thinking goes on. The only images intrinsically important are the halting places, the substantive conclusions, provisional or final, of the thought. Throughout all the rest of the stream, the feelings of relation are everything, and the terms related almost naught. These feelings of relation, these psychic overtones, halos, suffusions, or fringes about the terms, may be the same in very different systems of imagery.[93]

Now the conclusive inference is quite apparent, I think. If there is no definite limit set by imagery itself to the sort of images that can have the same fringe, then we can specify the actual images involved only *after* we have identified the Object or fringe. We cannot, in our specification, map from the imagery to the fringe, but only from the fringe to the imagery. Certainly an image we specify as dark brown is different from one we specify as bright yellow. But why do we specify and identify—why do we find—just these, and not, rather, a pink one, say, or an auditory one in E flat? The only answer would seem to be that no pink one and no E flat one is found fringed in the same way as the others. That is, *grass* is not the *kind of thing* which we think of as being pink or E flat, and when we think of it as being green, this sets some kind of limit—however broad—to the range of imagery involved.

When this point is coupled with the consideration that James has failed to supply us with any good reasons for believing that mental states can be specified in terms of their causal conditions in the organism, we are left with the conclusion that they can be specified only in dependence on the specification of what they are about—and this about-ness in the full sense is only the Object. This is the crucial point.

It is buttressed by James's analysis of apprehending the "real being" of a sensation. Apprehension is achieved only through a peculiar way of looking, he says. But this implies that we must already know what is peculiar about it, i.e., we must already know what *normal* looking is. This in turn implies that we must already know what is seen in normal looking: we must already know the *being* of the *thing* in the world.

In sum, we must already know that this is the *same* thing we have looked at before—long before we became artists. And, indeed, we might reflect that it was looked at long before we were born, in all likelihood, and its meaning built it into the body of civilization.

James's *Principles of Psychology* might be compared to a lens that burns as well as magnifies. We look for mind as a peculiarly psychical existent and it goes up in smoke before our eyes. As he himself says, sensation cannot be distinguished from perception in terms of different psychical material, but only in terms of differences in their Objects:

Further difficulties of dualism 115

They are therefore names for different cognitive *functions*, not for different sorts of mental *fact*. The nearer the object cognized comes to being a simple quality like 'hot,' 'cold,' 'red,' 'noise,' 'pain,' apprehended irrelatively to other things, the more the state of mind approaches pure sensation.[94]

"Sensation" is a kind of ideal—a limiting concept. If we could ever discriminate a single one of the world's characteristics in isolation from all others, then we would have a pure sensation.

Moreover, the conceptual dependence of the mental on the world-known is confirmed by James's treatment of his famous distinction between knowledge by acquaintance and knowledge by description.[95] Initially we are led to think that the first differs from the second because it is intrinsically private, subjective, psychical; that it can be attained only through one's own immediate, firsthand experience, with communication from one mind to another limited merely to indicating to the other the kind of experience one must strive to attain for one's self. Disregarding the whole cluster of problems which surrounds this distinction, we merely point out that James is forced to admit the distinction is only relative, not absolute, and that in minds able to talk (and he deals with no other —he does not attempt to discover the stream of consciousness, or lack of it, in a frog) there is some "knowledge-about" (knowledge by description), some knowledge of relations (fringe), in *every* cognition:

> In minds able to speak at all there is, it is true, *some* knowledge-about everything. Things can at least be classed and the times of their appearance told . . . The two kinds of knowledge are, therefore, as the human mind practically exerts them, relative terms.[96]

He seems to be admitting that we cannot even indicate to another the kind of sensational experience he must strive to attain for himself, unless we already tell him something *about* the thing to be experienced. And if we tell him something about it we will tell him that it is some *kind* of thing, and if we tell him that we will tell him that it is formally the *same* as some other possible thing and numerically the *same* as itself. The primary datum is the Object; the particular thing itself is the "mere topic."

What emerges in this latent strand of the *Principles* is the implication that we can talk about sensations qua images only to the degree that we can first talk about them as images *of* something, and we can talk about the latter only in terms of the total Object—the field of consciousness. Even an "afterimage" is specified as an image *of* something: the thing it is after. And we are struck by the words James chooses in order to describe what we "see" when we close our eyes and stare straight ahead: ". . . a curdling play of obscurest luminosity is always going on."[97] These words—"curdling," "play," "luminosity"—all derive their meaning from things and activities seen in the world: milk curdles, children play, the sun is luminous. There *is* something inadequate about much of our speech in this area. But does it derive from an essential incommunicability in the subject matter of sensations—or instead from the sheer amount of the subject matter and the particular limitations of our verbal skill? From what James actually discloses to us, it seems to be the latter. Furthermore, if an essential incommunicability is asserted, then how do we get any idea of what is asserted unless we do possess some sense of what is alleged to be missing? But if this is the case, it is not essentially incommunicable. Subjectivity and mind are not intrinsically private and cut off from the world.

It is only when we read through the *Principles* a second time that we can properly appreciate and interpret the pregnant first paragraph of Chapter Nine.

> We now begin our study of the mind from within. Most books start with sensations, as the simplest mental facts, and proceed synthetically, constructing each higher stage from those below it. But this is abandoning the empirical method of investigation. No one ever had a simple sensation by itself. Consciousness, from our natal day, is of a teeming multiplicity of objects and relations, and what we call simple sensations are results of discriminative attention, pushed often to a very high degree. It is astonishing what havoc is wrought in psychology by admitting at the outset apparently innocent suppositions, that nevertheless contain a flaw . . . The notion that sensations, being the simplest things, are the first things to take up in psychology is one of these suppositions.

Sensations are the *results* of discriminative attention: they are carved out from an enveloping world presented in the Object. It is just this sense of the whole enveloping world, and no less, which is presupposed in James's talk about sensations. Moreover, contrary to his words, "We now begin our study of the mind from within,"

Further difficulties of dualism

the study of the mind neither begins nor ends "from within." The moral of the *Principles* is that the psychologist is thrown out into the world at every turn, and that the distinction of within and without must be completely reformulated. When we confront our Self we confront a being that is "out there" with everything else—just strangely "sticky" and strangely "warm," as James would say.

His failure in Chapter Nine to expose and clarify his presupposition concerning the logical priority of the Object and the sense of the same prevents phenomenology from entering bodily there and then; it is that which knocks on the door. His idea of Object foretells the conception of *Lebenswelt*, and his notion of the sense of the same intimates intentionality.

James is prevented, for instance, from developing his interesting phenomenological observation on thunder in Chapter Nine. But how pregnant an observation it is. Recall his saying that we do not hear "thunder pure" but "thunder-breaking-in-upon-silence." Recall his saying also that we make the mistake of naming our thoughts simply, each after its own thing, but what each really knows is clearly the thing it is named for, with perhaps dimly a thousand other things (the fringe). It ought to be named for all of them; some of them are always things known a moment ago more clearly, while others are things to be known more clearly a moment hence. The point is that *thunder itself* is known as the kind of thing which, if it occurs, will appear to us as breaking in on silence—and then, presumably, giving way to silence once again. The relation between silence and thunder is not just a matter of relations between things in *rerum natura*, but is also a matter of relations in mind. We specify our thoughts in reference to relations in *rerum natura* known as a "fringe" surrounding particulars. The Object of thought, replete with networks of phenomenal relations, is the fundamentally ambiguous "place" where mind and matter meet; it is neutral between them—phenomenal. But for this abiding, half-hidden presupposition James could not even introduce his balky dualistic program.

Already we glimpse James's metaphysics of radical empiricism: the difference between mind and matter is just a difference between relationships of phenomena which are themselves neutral.

Already we glimpse an incipient phenomenology: There is no

gulf dividing reality and phenomena; indeed, knowledge of phenomena is the presupposition underlying knowledge of both mind and reality. Without knowledge of Object there is no knowledge either of thought itself or of physical particulars. His critique of the artist is telltale. The artist tells us to draw the thing as it *feels* and *looks*, not as it is known to *be*. But as James says, how a thing looks, in the normal situation for viewing, is just a revelation of its being. He can no more keep the worldly out of the mental than he could keep the mental out of the worldly. The relation of thought to its object is internal. His dualism collapses—only the rubble remains to clutter the seedbed of phenomenology.

FIVE

The phenomenological breakthrough
in James's psychology:
consciousness as field and
horizon as well as stream

At no point in *The Principles of Psychology* does James say, "Ah, now I am doing phenomenology," for this school of philosophy had not yet been founded by Edmund Husserl. Nor can the reader point to a single page and say that after that James is then doing phenomenology. Significant though it is, the breakthrough of phenomenology is a gradual and protracted and never quite completed turning in the general orientation of the *Principles*. The barrier is cracked open, but James never fully explores the territory.

It is relatively easy to describe the direction of this turning. It is away from psychology conceived as an empirical science which studies two orders of entities and toward a psychology which is dependent on a philosophical appraisal of the phenomenal world as a single foundation of all meaning. The swing is just as gradual as is the emergence of the stable, field-like Object of thought which forms in the *Principles* the unavoidable presupposition for knowledge of both changing mind and changing world.

Thought's Object is what is to be meant by "meaning" in its fundamental sense. James does not mean the particular thing which a subject takes to be real in the world. He means "all that thought thinks, just as thought thinks it." It becomes clear as he goes on that the ultimate Object is just the sense of the world's presence which pervades the outer fringes of our thoughts and which antedates all reflection and all science.

Husserl paid tribute to James early and late. In one of his last works he declared that James was the first to call attention to the phenomenon of the horizon (*Horizonphänomen*).[1] By "horizon" Husserl means substantially what James does by "fringe" (James on one occasion even uses the word): the relations and characteristics of the thing in the world as known or intended or meant. I know my room, for example, as that kind of place which I can escape from if need be—it is fringed that way—although my awareness of this fringe is usually nonfocal or marginal.[2] That is, it is only when my expectation, built into the fringe, is abruptly dissatisfied that I become aware of the fringe as such. It is only when I open the door and find a gaping abyss instead of stairs that I realize that I had all along known my room as that which has a place within a network of relations, e.g., relations of egress, ingress, having stairs, and so forth.

Husserl works out the implications implicit in James, that this is not just a psychological matter, but a philosophical and conceptual one. It belongs to the question of what we mean by "room" and, more important, to the question of what we mean when we say that such a meaning can be meant by consciousness. It is that which empirical psychology must presuppose, according to Husserl, and it is in a definite way a priori (see Chapter Seven). In contrast to Arnold Metzger's assertion that James's "psychologism and empiricism" bothered Husserl,[3] Husserl himself asserts in his *Logische Untersuchungen*:

> . . . how little James's observations—which have the status of genius (*geniale*) in the domain of the descriptive psychology of presentational experiences—force one into psychologism appears in the pages that lie before us. Because this seeker, whom I thank for his outstanding investigations in descriptive analysis, has only helped me break way from the psychologistic standpoint.[4]

Aron Gurwitsch points out further parallels between James's idea of fringe and/or thought's Object and the corresponding idea in Husserl. He also points out a parallel to James's idea of topic.

James's distinction between object and topic of thought coincides substantially with that [which] Husserl maintains between "object which is intended" and "object as it is intended" . . . In Husserl's later writings, the latter concept is denoted by noema.[5]

Professor Gurwitsch also writes:

> In *Ideen*, Husserl distinguishes "das Geurteilte" and "das Beurteilte." The *"Beurteilte"* corresponds to what James calls topic. As to the "Geurteilte," Husserl writes: ". . . *the total What as judged*— and moreover, taken precisely in the fashion . . . in which it is "consciously intended" in the mental process—makes up the *full noematic correlate*, the "sense" (in the broadest signification of the word) of the mental judgment-process." The "noema of judging" . . . described by Husserl, is precisely what James means by object of thought.[6]

I agree with this. However, Professor Gurwitsch denies that James extends the distinction of Object and topic beyond judgment to perception:

> . . . James introduces the distinction between object and topic of thought with reference to judgments formulated in propositions. However, it is possible and even indicated to generalize James' distinction and to extend it to perception as well.[7]

But James at least makes a beginning in applying the distinction to the perceptual situation of hearing thunder. Thunder-breaking-in-upon-silence is not the mere topic or the thunder itself; it is the perceptual Object. James's main point is that it is not judgmental but spreads into the margins of nonfocal awareness; it is perceptual and its presence can be detected only through an unusual mode of reflection. To *hear* thunder-breaking-in-upon-silence is not necessarily to *judge*, "Thunder breaks in upon silence."

We add, moreover, that Husserl conceives the grasp of the total Object to the *sine qua non* of phenomenology, "the principle of all principles" which he set forth in 1913: *"whatever presents itself . . . in primordial form . . . is simply to be accepted as it gives itself out to be, though only within the limits in which it then presents itself."*[8] This is strikingly similar to what James holds to be primordial: the Object conceived as "all that thought thinks, just as thought thinks it." It is similar as well to what James says here: "It is a vicious use of speech to take out a substantive kernel from its content and call that its object; and it is an equally vicious use of speech to add a substantive kernel not articulately included in its content, and to call that its object."[9]

Only when we understand the pivotal role of Object can we understand the major role played by teleology in James's analysis of consciousnes. A teakettle, for example, is seen within a horizon or known as fringed; its characteristics are apprehended in terms of expected satisfactions of present expectations. In other words, the teakettle's apprehended characteristics are the stable field, the total Object of the stream-like act of thought (more of this "act" later). One is now thinking that this is a teakettle full of water because he expects that it will not fly up in his face when he goes to pick it up—regardless of when or if he does. This is the sophisticated and pivotal role that teleology comes to assume in James's account. It is a far cry from consciousness supposed to exist in a decapitated frog's spinal column.

It is this global horizon of total meaning—on the margin of consciousness rather than in the focus—which is primordial for James; without it there would be no reference to particulars of any sort. We can "squint down" on the teakettle like an artist and get the sensory feel of its amazingly varied colors there in the corner only *after* we grasp this global meaning. A pure "sensation" or "feeling," according to James, is just a highly discriminated aspect of a thing known in the world—a final product, not a building block of knowledge. The whole is primordial, the part derivative, and James realizes that dissociation and not association first requires explanation.[10]

James implies that perceptual experience is impossible without conceptual framework—without expected satisfactions which fall in a set of channels of "senses of the same." Different colors are known as different, he says, when we have a "general purpose" (note well) like naming the tint.[11] I sit in my room not focally aware of anything outside it; but if I think of the room at all, I think of it fringed: as having relationships to other rooms, places, and persons, as having a chimney above it and as having stairs leading to and from it. It is that *general kind* of thing. It is only when the horizon or fringe determines expectations that are disappointed—only when I open the door and confront an abyss instead of stairs, or pick up the teakettle and it flies up in my face—that I become focally aware of what was always on the margin.

The phenomenological breakthrough 123

Well then, we live in a phenomenally presented world (*Lebenswelt*), and thoughts as well as things are identifiable only in conjunction with the meaning of this lived-world. It is the ultimate totality of thought's total object; it is the foundation that lies concealed under James's programmatic dualism of thoughts and things known in the world, and it is what makes the dualism possible, so far as it is possible.

We shall now turn to Chapter Ten of the *Principles*, "The Self," and observe how startled and discomfited James is when he begins to catch up with his own presuppositions.

SIX

James's conception of the self:
phenomenology in embryo

James's Chapter Ten on the self is dramatic. We see a thinker on the move, too honest to dissemble, who startles himself with his own discoveries. In this respect it is comparable to the internal books of Aristotle's *Metaphysics*.

Here James catches himself in the act, as it were, of procrastinating, of postponing urgent issues. In the opening pages of Chapter Nine he had written:

> No thought ever comes into direct *sight* of a thought in another personal consciousness than its own. Absolute insulation, irreducible pluralism, is the law. It seems as if the elementary psychic fact were not *thought* or *this thought* . . . but *my thought*, every thought being *owned*. Neither contemporaneity, nor proximity in space, nor similarity of quality and content are able to fuse thoughts together which are sundered by this barrier of belonging to different personal minds. The breaches between such thoughts are the most absolute breaches in nature.[1]

He went on to admit that he was using terms like "thought," "insulation," and "personal consciousness" that badly needed definition; but he would put that off to the next chapter, he said.² But in the "next chapter" (on the self) he has progressed so far in exposing the presuppositions which lie incongruously under his dualistic program that at the slightest touch of the attempt to define, the terms change their shape radically.

Clearly James is impressed by the fact that every thought is part of a personal, and apparently private, consciousness. If two minds think of the constellation of stars, Orion, there are *two* thoughts and *one* constellation. He wishes to do justice to what is evidently the particularity and plurality of thoughts. If as cognitive functions the two thoughts are just the known-ness of the known, and if the known is the same in both instances, it is hard for James to see in what the particularity and plurality of the thoughts consist. Thus he wishes to speak of the "being" of a thought as something distinct from its cognitive function.

But the upshot of Chapter Ten is that the self is not a sealed container full of intrinsically private thoughts. It is as if the self were blasted open and distributed across the face of the lived-world. The result: I can know that I think of Orion only after I know what Orion is, i.e., something anybody else with eyes can see too. There is total reversal: the problem is not how thoughts can be public but how they can be private.

In this chapter James loses interest in "imagery" as a candidate for private psychical entity (No. 2) and concentrates on "acts of thought" like affirming, dissenting, and remembering. But all he can make out of these is that they are movements of his own body of which he is aware. Awareness "itself," however, is empty. His body is "out there" with everything else, just not so far out, just always there at the center of the world as it is phenomenally presented. James is on his way to a reinterpretation of mind, subjectivity, and personality. We get the impression of a man who is thinking as if his life depended on it. The subject being the self, the analogy is not so farfetched.

James asserts that the self or thinker is nothing more than the passing thought itself. Thus category No. 1 in his abortive conceptual framework (the psychologist himself) becomes absorbed into category No. 2 (the thought). But category No. 2 is itself absorbed into the burgeoning Object (No. 3). Thus James admits in the closing chapter of the abridgment that a change in our concept of thought must involve a change in our concept of the thinker, and a radical change it turns out to be.[3]

Again we find that he takes as his point of departure thought's Object, that which is immediately presented to thought but is not thought itself. Accordingly, James begins his specification of the self from "the outside." Instead of beginning with a notion of thought as an internal psychic existent of some sort, and from this basis developing a view of the self as an internal psychic source or repository of such existents, James begins with thought's Object. As a result of his refusal to specify thought initially as that which is inside something, he does not initially specify the thinker (the self) as something which has an inside. The question is, will he *ever* so specify the thinker? But this question, according to James, involves the question of how he will specify thought itself (No. 2), which will be a matter of what reflection reveals. The paucity of reflection's report and the skepticism toward programmatic dualism which it inculcates are the startling things about James's analysis of the self.

My self, says James, my "me" in the widest sense, is whatever I can call mine.[4] What a person can call mine falls roughly into three categories, so James speaks of three selves. Now his talk of plural selves is disconcerting, for he is not talking about split personalities. Yet his locution, though possibly exaggerated, is not inconsistent with his view as a whole. The general point is that he does not consider the self to be a stable, isolable, and self-identical particular in the sense that a diamond is such a particular. James considers the self to be a chronically unstable item—"we are dealing with a fluctuating material." Indeed, he asserts, the self at times is at the point of vanishing altogether.[5]

Thus what James calls "my material self" does not reside somewhere within the envelope of my skin; it is comprised by my possessions and my family, etc. I know them to be mine and I am concerned with them and value them; they take on the warmth of things prized and cared for by me. My self is present to them cognitively—which is not to be inside the envelope of my skin. The point is that my physiological "here" is not my cognitive "here"; the suspicion being that physiology cannot specify the whole me. To attack my collection of paintings, say, is to attack me; this is the case even though my paintings be thousands of miles away, or even destroyed. It may even be the case, James suggests, that this attack on my paintings is more of an attack on me than a criticism of the shape of my face would be.

One hardly sets foot in James's chapter on the self before he is struck by the implications it contains. The thinker is specified in terms of the thought and the thought in terms of the Object. The thinker is tied into the Object: the thinker is all the things in the world which are judged by him to be his, just as they are judged. It becomes necessary to introduce into this Jamesian commentary the notion of the worldliness of thought.

It is not the case that all "things" in the world judged to be mine are things strictly speaking; some are persons, e.g., my family. So, along the same general lines, James launches an exposition of what he calls the "social self." The social self exhibits the most instability. The social self is the person's reputation. It is his "image" in other persons' eyes. It is what other persons "see in him." Better, it is what the self in question sees other persons seeing in him; it is what he takes the other to be taking him to be.

> The most peculiar social self which one is apt to have is in the mind of the person one is in love with . . . To his own consciousness he *is* not, so long as this particular social self fails to get recognition [from the loved one] . . .[6]

However, James notes a third self which is much more nearly stable and continuous, that of our "psychic dispositions"—"our ability to argue and discriminate . . . our moral sensibility and conscience . . . our indomitable will . . . Only when these are altered is a man said to be *alienatus a se*."[7] He remarks that this self seems to be central ("this self of all the other selves"), and adds that most men think of it as the seat both of freedom of action and continuity of action: it goes out to meet the objects of the world, while they seem to come in to be received by it. James adds the important observation that most men think of it as the "spiritual self" which is distinct from any of the objects which thought reveals.[8] This is important because if it is distinct, and if it is nothing but the passing, judging thought itself, then thought itself (No. 2) will be distinct and James will have a good chance finally to pin it down.

But his conception of thoughts and objects in the world does not turn out to be naïvely dualistic, or at least not consistently so; i.e., it is not consistently that which most men entertain, and the inconsistency is nowhere more evident than in James's analysis of the self. He is ever and again drawn into the Object as the common ground combining thought and things in the world. See how it happens in this pivotal case. James says that this self of selves with its psychic dispositions and its thoughts *is* felt.[9] But he speaks of it as "an abstraction." By this he means only that, as he explains:

> . . . in the stream of consciousness it never [is] found all alone . . . just as the body is felt, the feeling of which is also an abstraction, because never is the body felt all alone, but always together with other things.[10]

Note that the central self is like the body. Indeed, as we shall soon see, one's own *body*, phenomenally revealed, *is* the spiritual self!

James proceeds to speak of the body not as the physiological, causal source of our consciousness (not that he would deny this), but as a topic that can reveal itself phenomenally in our "field" of consciousness.[11] Notice again the metaphor for consciousness which suggests that he is attempting to supply the element of permanence and sameness in meanings. He treats the body as a topic known always as the same within an Object that has field-like as well as stream-like characteristics.

Starting from the field of consciousness—the Object in its prereflective totality—James attempts to "turn around quickly enough" in introspective reflection to capture his "spiritual self," this "self of selves," with its "thoughts themselves." This is a test case for the long-touted ability of introspection to grasp the data of compartment No. 2. He records the startling results as follows:

> But when I forsake . . . general descriptions and grapple with particulars, coming to the closest possible quarters with the facts, *it is difficult for me to detect in the activity any purely spiritual element at all. Whenever my introspective glance succeeds in turning round quickly enough to catch one of these manifestations of spontaneity in the act, all it can ever feel distinctly is some bodily process, for the most part taking place within the head* . . .
>
> In the first place, the acts of attending, assenting, negating, making an effort, are felt as movements of something in the head. In many cases it is possible to describe these movements quite exactly. In attending to either an idea or a sensation belonging to a particular

sense-sphere, the movement is in the adjustment of the sense-organ, felt as it occurs. I cannot think in visual terms, for example, without feeling a fluctuating play of pressures, convergences, divergences, and accommodations in my eyeballs. The direction in which the object is conceived to lie determines the character of these movements, the feeling of which becomes, for my consciousness, identified with the manner in which I make myself ready to receive the visible thing . . .

My glottis is like a sensitive valve, intercepting my breath instantaneously at every mental hesitation or felt aversion to the objects of my thought, and as quickly opening, to let the air pass through my throat and nose, the moment the repugnance is overcome. The feeling of the movement of this air is, in me, one strong ingredient of the feeling of assent.[12]

The startling upshot of this is that introspection, when finally employed in a full-fledged attempt, discovers no thoughts (No. 2) at all! All it can discover are just more topics within the Object which are curiously atomized portions of one's own body. The balloon-like Object has no inside. All topics are picked out of an original field which is objective. Portions of the body known in the field of consciousness are presented as responding to bodies other than one's own as these are known in the very same field. And whatever spontaneity these portions of one's body are felt as having is felt as responsive, not initiative, which is a curious sort of spontaneity.

The conclusion to be drawn from his own analysis shocks James. This conclusion is, in his own words:

. . . that *all* that is experienced is, strictly considered, *objective;* that this Objective falls asunder into two contrasted parts, one realized as 'Self,' the other as 'not-Self'; and that over and above these parts there is nothing save the fact that they are known . . .[13]

A dualism without an "inside"—without a clear-cut domain of psychical existents—is like a couple composed of one entity. It is incompatible with his dualistic natural scientific program. Understandably he recoils from his own conclusion. Every philosophy, he says, has recognized thought as the one sort of existent which skepticism cannot touch: "I will treat the last few pages as a parenthetical digression, and from now to the end of the volume revert to the path of common sense again."[14]

James employs various measures to set the inquiry back on the dualistic track, each of which can be damagingly criticized on his own terms. First, he points out that it is a fact that the Object is known. After all, it is thought's Object. What about this thought which has, supposedly, this Object? James remarks that only this Object is immediately given, and that therefore we should not really speak of a stream of consciousness, because the "con" in "consciousness" suggests that the stream thinks its own existence along with whatever else it thinks, which is not the case. In first-intention or in a prereflective knowing, the stream is just a stream of knowns, so it should be called a stream of "sciousness" or "sciousnesses," James maintains. And though he says the contention that there must be knowers for all these knowns is a mere hypothesis, he lets it pass as one. He again leaves us with the now-familiar supposition that an act of second intention, a reflective act of introspection, will reveal the thought itself if we just employ such an act. For the present moment of consciousness, he writes, is "the darkest in the whole series."[15]

But the point which the reader is unable to forget is that when James himself actually employed such an act of introspection, as immediately above, he failed to discover any such thought (No. 2). The reader is left with the suspicion that on James's own analysis the darkness of the present moment of consciousness, assuming it to be a fact, does not consist in a thought hidden behind an Object which can be discovered in a subsequent moment of introspection, since all that James actually discovered was a curiously atomized portion of the Object.

The second measure which he uses to set the inquiry back on the dualistic track is to employ the language of the common man, the putative language of common sense, and to speak of thought itself as if it were a thing which goes out to greet or reject things in the world. But on his own terms this is a misleading physicalistic analogy, and can be stigmatized as a commission of the psychologist's fallacy. The things in the world known by thought are not at first "out there" awaiting contact by it. Thought does not go out like an embracing net which is cast or a speeding arrow which is shot. In its cognitive aspect, as James makes clear in his example of thinking about Orion, thought is *already there* among the things known by it, if it is anywhere. How could thought contact these things in a way analogous to that in which a net enwraps or an arrow pierces? A thing known is a kernel or topic in thought's Object in quite a different sense, evidently, from that in which an apple is an arrow's object, since to begin to think is to be already there among the things thought about, while an arrow takes time to get to its object—if it ever does. Furthermore, it is not at all established yet, on James's own terms, that thought can be specified independently of its Object (which includes the topic) as an arrow can be; i.e., we know an arrow to be an arrow regardless of whether it strikes an apple, a head, or anything else—and regardless of whether it is shot at anything.

There is a third measure employed by James to restore dualism: Although he admits that all which is known in the Object is objective, still he says that one of the parts into which the Object falls is the self. And he leaves open the possibility that his analysis of his experience may be mistaken and that there may be a feeling of pure "subjectivity as such."[16] This possibility is heightened when he distinguishes within the self an objective person known, the me, and "a passing subjective Thought" which does the knowing, the I. It may be just the I which is masked off from awareness in the present, prereflective moment. But if the I is just the passing subjective thought itself, and if the moment of reflection or introspection does not discover it, then it is simply not to be discovered. Thus James's third and final measure to set the inquiry back on the dualistic track fails.

The reader cannot believe James when he says that he will treat the antidualistic tendency as a digression. There is too much of it, and it approaches too near coherence, to count as one.

II

James's further analysis of the self confirms the view that the Object has no inside. To be consistent with the analysis which he himself has initiated he must replace references to thoughts with references to one's body. It is the body—that of which there is some awareness in all cognitions, no matter how marginal—which swings into focal view in the moment of reflection. The body takes its place in the Object when the Object is no longer artificially limited to highly conceptual ones like Columbus-discovered-America-in-1492—i.e., the body swings into view when the full perceptual Object is adumbrated.

James had maintained that thought itself, though unaware of itself in the present moment, can become aware of itself in a later one through introspective reflection. In the reflective moment one thinks: I thought X then. James notes that in reflection what one thought about is "appropriated" by the thinker (the self) who thought it; i.e., "The thought was mine—it was thought by my 'I.' "[17] Now, since according to James's program the I is supposed to be nothing but the passing thought itself (No. 2), we would expect him to say that the reflective moment reveals that what one thought about is appropriated to that thought itself, and even though that thought itself is now past rather than present and passing, still that thought itself is now finally pinned down and ready for specification. The present passing thought which is doing the reflecting will be ready in a subsequent moment.

However, James's own analysis of the reflective moment does not succeed in pinning down and specifying any thoughts themselves. He notices that the present reflecting thought does not appropriate to itself a past Object; it cannot know anything about itself, a fortiori it cannot know that it appropriates anything to itself. This, however, is not surprising; on James's own grounds we should not have expected to learn anything about the present thought itself through introspection, only the past thought. What is surprising, at least to the reader who expects dualism, is that nothing is learned about the past thought either. For what is revealed to the present reflecting moment, says James, is not a past thought itself with its corresponding Object appropriated by it; rather, what is revealed is that past Object as appropriated by a topic which is part of the present Object—one's body cognized as the *same* body as before.[18]

> . . . *the body, and the central adjustments*, which accompany the act of thinking, in the head. *These are the real nucleus of our personal identity*, and it is their actual existence, realized as a solid present fact, which makes us say 'as sure *as I exist*, those past facts were part of myself.'[19]

That is, all that is revealed in reflection is more Object, not thought itself. The past Object is now presented as "knit-on" (appropriated by, owned by) a topic in the present Object—one's own body.[20] The nature of this new Object is just what we should expect in the light of James's initial and startling analysis of the "self of

James's conception of the self 133

selves." It really boils down to nothing more than "this same old body—the same today as it was yesterday." This is the basis for the judgment of personal identity—a judgment, James says, which is the same in principle as the judgment of the identity of anything else.[21]

To say, then, that I remember that I thought something is just to say that I remember that a past Object was mine, and this is just to say that within the present Object there is given the past Object as past and as belonging to the same tall, black-haired, irritable being that can even now be given as present in the present Object. The self is known as a living body. Indeed, the self is known as *this* living body. It is not sufficient to say that I become aware of myself as an instance of the genus animal, species *homo;* nor is it sufficient to say that I become aware of myself as a creature of flesh and bones. I become aware of *this* face, *these* lips, *this* nose, *these* legs. My particularity can appall me.

And at every moment this particular face and body *mean* something particular. Even a "blank stare" is not really such but characterizes me at that moment. If my face and body do not reveal myself to others, then this lack of revelation is itself a revelation. I reveal that I am hiding something. I am bound and tied to meaning.

And yet, as Merleau-Ponty has said, there is still something elusive about this self in its particularity: it is not all naked detail and bald finitude. To bring my own face to focal consciousness I must look into a mirror, and this act changes the meaning of my face. To be sure, I could have movies taken of me when I am unaware they are being taken, and to see them might very well be shocking, but the movie would not make focal for me my face and body as they are perpetually but incompletely given on the margins of my own field of consciousness. James initiates an intriguing and, until recently, vastly neglected topic for phenomenological study: what Merleau-Ponty calls "the phenomenology of the body-subject." Given our present inadequate conceptual tools, all that I can say of my own self as I actually experience it is laced with paradox: my self is a bald and naked yet elusive particular body. There is no "inside," there is all "outside"—yet all is not clear.

But the paradox is not insuperable. Take that elusiveness. Could *that* be, at long last, what we really mean by the *depth* and inwardness of the mind? Perhaps. My depth is on me, not in me.

Better, I am within the depth, not the depth within me. That helps to explain the difficulty of self-knowledge and the strange areas of darkness in life.

Still, it might be objected, James speaks of "the central adjustments in the head" as "accompanied by" the act of thinking.[22] So he must wish to assert that there is a distinct "internal" act of thinking. Of course he does; the whole point is that the result of his own inquiries show his assertion to be untenable.

But what can this present awareness be? What is the thing for which the present Object is an Object? James can really give it no other specification than Object-as-known, which is no more than the Object itself fully unpacked. The elements in the cognitive relationship, far from comprising an external relationship between "inner" and "outer" entities, are all laced onto the Object. Everything is *out there* in the elusive area of life itself. This is the actual upshot of what James has discovered. The cognitive relationship links the topic which is one's own body and the *rest* of the Object. The self thinking is just the known, elusive body.

As James says later in the *Principles*, to know something as real is to know it in a fringe of relationships, the central one being a practical relationship to one's bodily self. It is to say, "The thing stands in the same world in which I stand." The thing is known as fringed in this way. Not all things are known as real because not all things are known as so fringed. James's incipient philosophy of mind emerges directly in his metaphysics of radical empiricism: mind will simply be a particular network of relationships—it is *all* fringe.

His reinterpretation of the I-aspect of the Self is the crucial part of his reinterpretation of consciousness. He wants to say that the I is the thinker, and that that is the passing thought: specifically "a remembering and appropriating Thought incessantly renewed."[23] His analysis reveals that a thought (let us take, "I thought X then") can be specified without ever mentioning a subjective psychical existent, whether thought or thinker. It reveals a thinker solely specified by a present complex Object—almost literally a field: The-body-that-was-part-of-yesterday's-Object-is-the-same-body-that-is-part-of-today's-Object.

Though one, the Object must have two dimensions: things known as the same (the field) and the different times of their being

James's conception of the self

known (the stream-in-the-field). The analysis of the knowing apparently requires no mention of psychical existents which emerge and pass away; all that is required is an Object which changes in some respect, in some of its relationships. A past thought is recognized to be mine because an Object known as past can become incorporated in a more complex Object known as present.

The identification of one's own body as the same is the central core uniting the Objects. For example, I know now that I thought then that John is a kind person, because it is known that the bodily person who was responsive to John then is the very same bodily person who is responsive to that responsiveness now.

When the self is remembered, it is as a living body; it is remembered as the same self which now does the remembering, because the body involved so centrally is identified as the same body. The self so construed becomes a permanent part of James's philosophy. He writes in 1904:

> The world experienced (otherwise called the 'field of consciousness') comes at all times with our body as its centre, centre of vision, centre of action, centre of interest . . . The body is the storm centre, the origin of coordinates, the constant place of stress in all the experience-train. Everything circles around it, and is felt from its point of view. The word 'I,' then, is primarily a noun of position, just like 'this' and 'here.' Activities attached to 'this' position have prerogative emphasis, and, if activities have feelings, must be felt in a *peculiar* way.[24]

We spoke of "responsiveness": "the bodily person who is responsive to that responsiveness." James says that ". . . acts of attending, assenting . . . are felt as movements of something in the head . . . In attending to either an idea or sensation belonging to a particular sense sphere, the movement is the adjustment of the sense organ, felt as it occurs."[25] In the case of memory the felt movement is usually a rolling up of the eyeballs.

This marks the introduction of a third sense of the word "feeling" and another candidate for thought itself (No. 2). Known movements of the body are treated as if they were mental acts. When he equates "attending" with the movement which is the adjustment of the sense organ felt as it occurs, he is not equating the felt movement of the sense organ with the sensation which belongs to the sense organ in question, and which is felt by that sense organ. The feeling of a sense organ is not a feeling of what the sense organ feels.[26] The latter sense is, evidently, imagery: that which pertains in some way to what is sensed in the world, and this of course need not be one's body. We classified the latter sense as the second sense of the word "feeling"; it emerged as the first candidate for "thought itself" (No. 2). This sense occurs hardly at all in James's analysis of the self. What does occur is this new third sense. James talks about *acts* of attending and assenting, and it seems that he is endeavoring to reinterpret the traditional notion of mental acts. But again we find data, which at first seem to belong to the second compartment of his conceptual framework, falling out as tag ends in his analysis of the Object-directedness and worldliness of mind (No. 3). For example, James writes, "The direction in which the object [thing in the world] is conceived to lie determines the character of these movements," e.g., as in the visual sense sphere.[27]

What sense can be made of this third sense of "feeling" as a candidate for thought's themselves (No. 2)? Obviously, this responsiveness of sense organs in the body is felt to be *in the body*, and the body is felt to be in the world along with everything else. There is evidently no need to postulate psychical existents (No. 2). Furthermore, James declares that the body is felt along with everything else, and this suggests that it is only a topic within a total Object—a topic that emerges with some clarity only in reflection and directed attention. James is not saying that the Object is reducible exclusively to movements in the head.

It might be contended, however, that he is trying to introduce the germ of an odd and crude sort of physiologically oriented behaviorism—a behaviorism "from within," in which the person observes his own body without the benefit of objective measurements. Although there is a particle of credibility in such a contention, there are several reasons for thinking that it is disastrously misleading as it stands. For James is not liquidating all reference to consciousness and replacing it with reference to the physical organism qua physical. Rather, he has begun a reinterpretation of consciousness: we are not to speak of consciousness, but instead of "sciousness," because all that is given is Object, or things *just as they are known*, and not thought itself. The whole point is that introspection never does find thoughts which are psychical existents; it is not that the Object, things as known, is never found or that there is no knowing. Just the reverse, James is claiming that more of the Object is found; in this case it includes more of the physical organism than might have been expected, and these parts "do" the knowing. But it is not the physical organism qua physical, rather the physical organism as known. Some reference to some form of consciousness is being retained.

James's talk of movements in the head is an attempt to describe his own body as a phenomenal presentation; it is not an attempt to discover the causal bases of consciousness. This is true because, if for no other reason, he believes that the causal bases of consciousness lie exclusively in the brain, and he is not opening up his own skull and observing his brain. It is an attempt—drastic in its orientation and implications—to specify mental states. It may be a faulty attempt, but we cannot tell that it is unless we understand what is being attempted. It is true that there is a pervasive physiological aura about it all. But perhaps this is the way a physiologist and doctor of medicine sometimes experiences his own body.[28] Moreover, he is perfectly aware that identifying the movement of the glottis, say, is a new feeling *sui generis*, even though the glottis is the same glottis and the same "organic starting point" both before and after the identification.[29]

Ludwig Wittgenstein has written that James's introspection gave him

> . . . the idea that the 'self' consisted mainly of 'peculiar motions in the head and between the head and throat.' And James's introspection showed, not the meaning of the word 'self' (so far as it means something like 'person,' 'human being,' 'he himself,' 'I myself'), nor any analysis of such a thing, but the state of a philosopher's attention when he says the word 'self' to himself and tries to analyze its meaning. (And a good deal could be learned from this.)[30]

There are three distinct elements of truth in Wittgenstein's remark. First, it is true that James does not sufficiently heed his own observation that the body is always felt *with* other things—the rest of the world. He forgets his admission that his account tears the body from its natural context and reduces it to an atomized fragment; he goes on to speak of it as if it existed in splendid isolation as "the self of selves." He does not tell us nearly enough about its relationships in its role as the social self. Second, and related to this, James does not tell us enough about prereflective awareness of the body. If some awareness of the body accompanies all our awareness, and if awareness of body is awareness of self, then there must be some continuous awareness of self, even though marginal and prereflective. If James had elaborated this, it might have turned out that such an awareness of the body is quite a different matter from the focal awareness of movements in the head, for example. It might have turned out that we are aware of the posture and attitude of the body—how we confront the world, how we attack and retreat from it—the *meaning* of the body, if you will. The body may be more meaningful in being nonfocal. All that the body means when it is focally conscious in a social situation is "self-consciousness"; its meaning is limited and straitened.

This elaboration James does not give us, although his approach prompts it. Put in his own language, he offers an impoverished account of the fringes of the body.

Third (referring back to Wittgenstein's remark), James gives us no more than a hint of how differences in the feltness of the body could account for differences in modes of cognition, e.g., how we pass from perception of a thing to memory of the thing and all along know it to be the same thing. We will consider this incompleteness in his account later.

But Wittgenstein's remark would be misleading if it caused us to think that James is just giving us more physiology. What he is attempting to do, in no matter how faulty and incomplete a manner, is to give us a specification of thought and self which relies exclusively on descriptions of phenomenal presentations, and which eschews mentalistic talk (a project not uncongenial to Wittgenstein himself who studied James in depth[31]). In James's view it is not the case that the identity of my organism guarantees my identity as a person. The body must figure in the Object, as a *body known*, and it must be judged to be identical and judged to be mine. There is no guarantee that it will be so judged. It must be known with a modicum of concern, care, and interest; this is a function of the person's total orientation to the world, which includes, in James's treatment of Objects, the person's language. For example:

> Now I say that he identifies himself with his body because he loves *it*, and that he does not love it because he finds it to be identified with himself.[32]

My body is something known to be such within a field of consciousness (or sciousness) like everything else; and, as a rule, happily, it is (or can be) the most interesting and important thing there.[33] Consciousness must be more than a mirror-like cognition or intention; a partiality for certain things in the world must be exhibited as a feature of the field. In James's own terminology, some things are "warmer" (more prized and valued[34]) than others. That which exhibits a peculiarly constant warmness, and which for this reason can become the core of the personality if anything can, is the body which is judged to be one's own.

James makes much of this. For him there is no substantial self that the person can carry around with him like a diamond sewn into his pocket. The self is whatever is cared about, judged to be one's own—and the body here takes preeminence. The self is knit together only by virtue of this judgmental Object. If the judgment disintegrates so does the self.[35] The maintenance of self-identity is a continuous achievement, and one marked by peril. The danger for the person is either that all things will cease to be interesting or that things other than the body will usurp such a share of his interest that self-destruction, either psychological or organic, will ensue. Thus James is opposed to the associationist doctrine that altruistic interests are contradictory to the nature of things. This is so because he denies that thoughts are contents of one's subjectivity, which refer immediately only to one's self. Thoughts are "out there" with the things cognized, and the self is something "out there" along with all the rest of the things. As grave a danger as becoming too selfish is the opposite danger of becoming so dispersed and widely attached that the abiding center of one's personality is lost:

> I might conceivably be as much fascinated, and as primitively so, by the care of my neighbor's body as by the care of my own. The only check to such exuberant altruistic interests is natural selection, which would weed out such as were very harmful to the individual or to his tribe. Many such interests, however, remain unweeded out —the interest in the opposite sex, for example, which seems in mankind stronger than is called for by its utilitarian need; and alongside of them remain interests, like that in alcoholic intoxication,

or in musical sounds, which, for aught we can see, are without any utility whatever.[36]

This emphasis on the world known is an inevitable outgrowth of his thought about thought.

III

When James actually analyzes the field of consciousness and employs the method of introspection, rather than just talking about these things, then he sees that mental states cannot be construed as psychic existents which are the contents of a container we call self. We might try to replace the metaphor of the balloon by that of the stocking. It is as if James had begun by talking about thoughts as one would talk about the contents of a stocking, but when he comes to analyzing and itemizing these "contents" he can do so only by turning the stocking inside out to send them flying. They are no longer contents. James is embarked on a reinterpretation of consciousness.

Although his talk about the various selves does not pertain directly to split personality or schizophrenia, but is rather the broadest sort of theoretical exercise in normal psychology, still his analysis suggests interesting new approaches to such abnormalities. A self is not a self as a diamond is a diamond; the unity and continuity of the self depends on a continuous achievement: a thread of sameness, involving primarily but not solely one's body, must be picked out of a shifting welter of phenomena. Not to be up to the task—to be insane—is rendered more understandable. As James says in his monument to empathy and sympathy, *The Varieties of Religious Experience*, we are of one clay with lunatics; the difference is of degree rather than of kind; nearly all of us have our disturbed moments.

Walking the razor's edge of Chapter Ten is even more harrowing than it need be, however, because James's emerging reinterpretation of the self is incomplete and somewhat inconsistent. For example, in view of his own insights concerning the "peculiar" phenomenal presentation of the body identified by normal persons as their own (see above 135), it seems hard to believe that "I might conceivably be as much fascinated, and as primitively so, by the care of my neighbor's body as by the care of my own" (p.

139). I do not say this could not happen; I simply would have liked James to provide the conceptual structure which would enable us to conceive it. It seems to me that one could hate his body and still identify it as his own. How else would he know which body to loathe or to strike? Finally, it is difficult to see how a body other than the one identified by the normal person as his own could occupy that central place in the phenomenal field which the one so identified does occupy when in the focus of consciousness, or how another body could frequent the margins of this field in the way his own does when his own is not in the focus. The body which I as a normal person identify as my own floods a great deal of the margin when I am thinking focally of something else, and if I am in pain, say, colors deeply almost everything else. It is hard to see how another body could play exactly the same role. Thus knowledge of the self along the lines of James's reinterpretation of consciousness may not be quite as difficult as his somewhat inconsistent reinterpretation itself suggests.

But to detail all that James's account lacks would be to become involved in another study: one which explored the Jamesian repercussions for existential phenomenology and alluded to valuable work done by Maurice Merleau-Ponty and to some of Sartre's. Although I will have something to say about this later, here I am more concerned with clarifying fully what James's sketch for a phenomenology does contain. I wish to touch on every fundamental aspect of classical phenomenology. I wish to point out, for example, that James at least initiates a provocative new interpretation of mental acts in terms of felt movements of the body, and of the internal relationship of these acts to their objects in terms of what we shall call "interlocking spheres" in the total Object; this latter involves him in an incipient reinterpretation of Kant's distinction between synthetic and analytic apperception. Occasionally phenomenologists assert that James does not clearly distinguish act of thought (*Erlebnis*) from object of thought (*Erscheinung*); though there is some truth in this claim, as we shall see more fully below, those who make it have not fully appreciated all that the *Principles* does contain.[37] Indeed, Husserl himself suggests that James could not appreciate all the phenomenological implications of his concept of fringe because consciousness for James is ultimately "anonymous."[38] But James's reinterpretation merely rejects the transcendental Ego, not any self, and it can be wondered in any case how important is such an Ego for phenomenology.

For James, the knower is itself objective—a topic that can be isolated only because it is embedded in a total field or Object—and the latter is not within anything. One is reminded of G. E. Moore's response to the half question, half charge, "But you don't believe that the self is located at a definite place, do you?" "Why yes," he is reported to have replied, "it is right here"—pointing to the area around his eyes.[39] Or again there is the story of his students' asking him, "If we started chopping you up and throwing parts of your body out the window, when would *you* go out? With your arms? Legs? Trunk?" Moore is said to have replied, "With my nose."[40]

Of course, it is not easy to see how the hypothesis of a mental state could be replaced. It is not easy to see how James's talk of different known changes of the body could do all the work previously done, e.g., how we pass from perception of a thing to memory and all the while know it to be the same thing.

Yet he makes some strokes of a sketch for such a replacement. Take, for example, his contention that it is logically impossible for us to have the same thought twice. It cannot be the case, James reasoned, because if we had exactly the same thought twice we would fall into a state of timelessness; we would not know that the second instance of the thought *is* second. But we do know that the second instance of the thought is second; therefore we cannot have exactly the same thought twice.

Now the beginnings of an account of this can be found within the emerging framework of James's reinterpretation of consciousness. Each time that we think of something again we think of it in a fresh manner. That is, we do not think of something different, but we think of it in a different set of relations from the first (as James himself says[41]). In terms of the latent strand of the *Principles*, the change could occur within some "part," "dimension" or "sphere" of the fringe or Object: the "sphere" which pertains to our changing relations to the thing thought about. These certainly do change, and we can know them to change. In the account of our knowledge we need not allude at all to changing bits of psychic stuff; if the latter do somehow occur, the account we render of our knowledge would in no way count as evidence for their existence.

Considered from the point of view of James's reinterpretation of consciousness, what is constantly changing is our relation to things (even if it be only temporal), not the internal psychic components of a subject. And we *are* our bodies. But as outlined by James, the relationship should not be construed physicalistically, i.e., geometrically or optically. James indicates that the constantly changing relationship which we have to things known is a relationship of knowing. The tacit reference to consciousness is retained.

If James is to attack the problem of things known to be the same in different modes of cognition (e.g., perception and memory), his reinterpretation of consciousness requires as a next step an account of the fringe-and-Object which provides for the distinction between changes in our relationship to the thing as knower of that thing, and changes within the thing itself known. The latter may be known changes in the relationship which that thing has to things other than oneself, or those known changes in the thing's relationship to us other than changes in the knowing itself. In other words, what must be accounted for is the distinction between changes in our knowing a thing (with the account mentioning nothing but known changes in the body), and changes in the being of the known thing itself. In James's new terms, both kinds of relationships and the changes within both would be known by virtue of the complex Object-and-fringe within which the thing itself is known. But clearly they can be known as being what they distinctly are only if they occupy different parts or "spheres" of the fringe. For example, I perceive something now; I remember it later. I must distinguish the change in my knowing of the thing from any change in the known thing itself. If I knew all changes as being in the thing itself, I could not even say that my knowing of that thing had changed. We shall extrapolate on James's embryonic theory of mental acts.

Notice how we equate Object and fringe and speak of the *total* Object. We do this because James asserts that some awareness of the body, no matter how marginal, inattentive, and prereflective, accompanies everything else of which we are aware. The known body must, then, occupy some "place" within every Object. James does not adequately specify this "place," so we must supply it. We do not have to reflect in order to tell that we have passed from a seeing of a thing to a hearing of it, and from both of these to a remembering; therefore it must be apparent in some shift in the prereflectively given total Object. In James's new sort of terms, the shift must involve some change in the prereflectively given known body. He wants to "save the vague" and he speaks of cognitions

> whereof the objects are as yet unnamed, mere nascencies of cognition, premonitions, awarenesses of direction are thoughts *sui generis* as much as articulate imaginings and propositions.[42]

Their very vagueness would seem to be their virtue. For without it we would lose the sense of our body as the abiding *background* against which, and around which, our life in the world is oriented, related, and played out. The body-as-background would be sufficiently abiding if its changes as knower, prereflectively given, were distinguished from changes in the things known. To lose this distinction would be to lose our sense of our own selves as distinct from other things—a disaster.

This is why we were reluctant to equate outright James's "Object" and Frege's "sense." It is not that James means something less or something different from Frege; he seems to mean what Frege means, *and something more*. James wants and needs to include in the Object not only the meaning of what is thought about, but also the meaning of our thinking it. But in his explicit treatment of Object he never offers an exposition of an Object sufficiently complex for his own purposes. He speaks of the range of simple Objects up to complex ones, but the complex ones are not complex enough:

> What I . . . have called the 'object'[43] of thought may be comparatively simple, like 'Ha!-what-a-pain,' or 'It-thunders'; or it may be complex, like 'Columbus-discovered-America-in-1492,' or 'There-exists-an-all-wise-Creator-of-the-world.' In either case, however, the mere thought of the object may exist as something quite distinct from the belief in its reality.[44]

Little is mentioned about the body as knower, and this would have to be a distinct addition to the account; for when we say or think "It thunders," we mean something explicitly at least only about the thunder—not something about the knowing or our bodies. For James the Object of thought pertains to something judged (usually), and the structure of the judged has a marked affinity to language and statement in the form of propositions. Even the simplest Object he gives us, "Ha! what a pain," could be construed

James's conception of the self 145

as the judgment "This is a great pain." The Object is not a psychical sensation.[45] But just what the *judging* would be like in his own bodily terms he does not tell us.

Yet it is essential to grasp the import and the implications of what James has initiated. It is not merely that he engages in one act of introspection which dislodges his certainty that mental states are infallibly given psychical existents and that he then postulates them as hypothetical entities. It is that he has embarked on a reinterpretation of consciousness which seems to imply that the postulation is unnecessary, if not absolutely wrong. In fact, James does make a few further remarks about the Object which suggest that it can be regarded as all-encompassing, that the act of cognition itself and mental states can be construed in terms of the shifting topics of the cognized body, and that, in sum, he has embarked on a new program for psychology.

These remarks occur within his commentary on Kant. He maintains that his idea of Object is similar to Kant's: a systematic unity of things, qualities, or facts thought in relation. This agreement does not surprise us. James's notion of the fringe as that which contains a reference to expected satisfactions of standards is markedly similar to Kant's notion of a conception as a synthesis of actual and *possible* sensations and it is similar also to Kant's notion of the faculty of judgment as the faculty of rules. James quotes Kant with approval, "Object is that in the knowledge (*Begriff*) of which the Manifold of a given Perception is connected."[46] He qualifies his agreement in one respect, however. He disagrees emphatically[47] with what he takes to be Kant's tendency to regard the manifold as something *in* thought, something composed of discrete psychical existents called sensations which are then synthesized by an activity called the Understanding. James claims that separable parts are outside of thought not, as he says Kant implies, within it.[48] The Object comes already unified if it comes at all; it is just a matter of different degrees or kinds of unity. Thus, for James, nothing is needed to acount for the unity beyond the given Object itself: no principle of the unity of consciousness per se and certainly no principle of a unifying agency or agent, e.g., the Ego. James declares that our thought is not "an elaborate internal machine shop," for there are no parts to be assembled, and that "the Ego is simply *nothing:* as ineffectual and windy an abortion as Philosophy can show."[49] He rejects the idea that one must postulate a permanent agent or ego to account for the fact that "the 'I think' must be capable of accompanying all our representations." One *does* think "I think" along with certain Objects, but when this actually occurs it can be accounted for on the basis of the (total) Object itself without any reference to an Ego; and from the fact that one always *can* think the "I think," along with whatever else one thinks, nothing can be inferred concerning an allegedly permanent Ego. James says in effect that Kant is guilty of hypostatizing a possibility, and he adds, "a thought which is only potential is actually no thought at all."[50] He does not deny of course that the judgmental Object, "I am the same I that I was yesterday," *is* presented. Nor does he deny that it is important to the maintenance of self-identity (although we wish he would say more about its function on the prereflective level). But he does deny that anything like a permanently existing agent or Ego has to be thought before such an Object can be thought—i.e., before such an Object is conceptually possible. If we are to speak of its possibility at all, says James, it can only be in terms of states of the brain.

Yet the extent to which he does agree with Kant concerning the nature of the Object of thought is considerable and significant. He couples his agreement with still another which bears directly on his need to distinguish, in his own terms, between the being of the thing cognized and the mode of its cognition. James takes over Kant's distinction of synthetic and analytic apperception, and calls it "objective and subjective synthesis." He quotes Kant who writes:

> "Also nur dadurch, dass ich ein Mannigfaltiges gegebener Vorstellungen in *einem Bewusstsein* verbinden kann, ist es möglich dass ich die *Identität des Bewusstseins* in diesen *Vorstellungen* selbst vorstelle, d.h. die analytische Einheit der Apperception ist nur unter der Voraussetzung irgend einer synthetischen möglich." In this passage (Kritik der reinen Vernuft, 2te Aufl. p. 16) Kant calls by the names of analytic and synthetic apperception what we here mean by objective and subjective synthesis respectively.[51]

James elaborates:

> This sort of *bringing of things together into the object of a single judgment* is of course essential to all thinking. The things are conjoined *in* thought, whatever may be the relation in which they

James's conception of the self 147

appear to the thought. The thinking them is *thinking* them together, even if only with the result of judging that they do not *belong* together. This sort of *subjective synthesis*, essential to knowledge as such (whenever it has a complex object) must not be confounded with *objective synthesis* or union instead of difference or disconnection, known among the things.[52]

He is saying that a distinction must be made within the Object of thought which sets off things which are thought of together (subjective synthesis) from things which are thought of *as being* together (objective synthesis). Now this distinction *could* do what has to be done: to distinguish in the Object the thing qua thing from the mode in which it is known. And it would do it without any reference to psychical entities (No. 2): subjectivity would be construed solely in terms of one's phenomenal body.

The point is that one's body can be thought of together with, or along with, everything else, but it need not be thought of as *being* together with everything else. On this basis a distinction could be made between the cognitive activities which are mine and the things on which they are directed. Each could be presented as varying without the other being so presented. It would seem that nothing could be known about either "sphere" of the fringe unless each was first known to be distinct.

Let us see how a particular example of cognition could be accounted for in terms of this central distinction. My thought (memory) that I perceived Orion last night would be broken down as follows: Within the current Object this body is presented as *being* identical with the body which was presented in the past Object *along with* those celestial bodies which themselves were presented as *being* Orion. That is, my bodily self—and there is no other—is presented as having looked at Orion last night.

Thus the notion of the distinction of subjective and objective synthesis could make possible both the identification of the self and all that is not self.[53] In the same sweep, it could make comprehensible the distinction between things appearing *to be* such and such and things just appearing such and such. Recall James's analysis of the consciousness of the painter: Things would just appear such and such relative to an odd way of looking at them, and the odd way of looking would be reducible, presumably, to an odd positioning of the body as it is apprehended on the margin of the field of consciousness. Things would *be* such and such relative to a normal way of looking at them and a normal positioning of the body; the body would thus supply standards and rules of being. The distinction between the "mere looks" of a thing and the looks qua reality of a thing would reduce itself to a difference in the way one's body is *along with* the rest of the elements in the Object.

This extrapolation on James's hints fits into the general phenomenological formula: modes of being are correlated to modes of being presented. But it throws new light on the concept of "being presented" and it adds needed explication and elaboration to the suspiciously mentalistic scholastic phrase "act of thought" which appears so often and so centrally in Husserl. Certainly an act of thought is more than a string of thing-appearance or *hyletic* data flowing in the stream of consciousness; James gives us some idea of what more there may be. Therefore there is, I think, some definite value in working from within the framework of classical phenomenology and modifying it.

IV

As we shall note in our examination of James's analysis of the sense of reality, things are apprehended as being what they are because they are apprehended as standing in a definite relationship to our bodily selves—one that arouses our belief and "stings" our interest. What he tells us is not conclusive, but some pattern does emerge when we take the initiative and tie together various loose ends of inquiry which protrude from *The Principles of Psychology* at various points. For now we hold this "lead" in abeyance and pass on. Awaiting us is the crucial Chapter Twelve on conception, the "keel of the mind," "the sense of the same," so long required but so long delayed. That it is presupposed by his analysis of the Self seems too obvious to require comment: there is no self and no self-identity without a body identified as the same old one—one's own. And if our extrapolation is correct, there is without this no sense of the same old world.

In Chapter Twelve James deals with our basic ability to pick things out from the field of consciousness, to identify them as the same, and to apprehend the single, stable world which is the encompassing reality of our existence. He comes very close to an explicit doctrine of intentionality in which "thought itself" is linked internally and necessarily to a topic in the Object of thought. Unfortunately, however, the distinction between imagery and known movements of the body is not kept clear in his analysis of "thought itself"—that which "passes in the stream." Accordingly, his insights concerning the role played by one's body in the performance of "mental acts" do not come to full fruition but remain tantalizing possibilities.

SEVEN

Phenomenology: intentionality and worldliness of thought

I

James uses "conception" for the sense of the same, and says, "This *sense of sameness* is the very keel and backbone of our thinking."[1] As simple a thought as "I thought that then" requires two conceptions of sameness—the "I" and the "that"—which act as polarities and which impart direction in the stream-like turbulence of changing circumstances and myriad images. Indeed, even the "that" which "we mean to point at may change from top to bottom and we be ignorant of the fact. But in our meaning itself we are not deceived; our intention is to think of the same."[2] "We are masters of our meanings."[3]

The associationist's account of the ordering of the flux of experience, his postulation of two successive copies of the same thought, is repudiated by James:

> Thus, my arm-chair is one of the things of which I have a conception; I knew it yesterday and recognized it when I looked at it. But if I think of it to-day as the same arm-chair which I looked at yesterday, it is obvious that the very conception of it as the same is an additional complication to the thought, whose inward constitution

must alter as a consequence. In short, it is logically impossible that the same thing should be *known as the same* by two successive copies of the same thought.[4]

What does James mean by "logically impossible"? The latent tendency in his work is toward a confrontation with the question of logic. We examine this below.

James defines conception as the "function" of a mental state's signifying "a permanent subject of discourse." He says that it is not the mental state, and it is not what is signified; rather it is the "relation" between them. In giving us an account of conception, then, he is giving us an acount of the cognitive relationship. But if conception is the "keel of the mind," then the cognitive relationship must be also. We witness a radical departure from the manifest thesis of the *Principles:* Instead of the cognitive relationship's being an ultimate matter which is not to be discussed or being a simple external relation, it assumes a pivotal role in a pivotal discussion. Note carefully James's definition of conception:

> *The function by which we thus identify a numerically distinct and permanent subject of discourse is called CONCEPTION;* and the thoughts which are its vehicles are called *concepts.* But the word 'concept' is often used as if it stood for the object of discourse itself; and this looseness feeds such evasiveness in discussion that I shall avoid the use of the expression altogether, and speak of 'conceiving state of mind,' or something similar, instead. The word 'conception' is unambiguous. It properly denotes neither the mental state nor what the mental state signifies, but the relation between the two, namely, the *function* of the mental state in signifying just that particular thing.[5]

What James is saying, then, is that conception is not the mental state nor is it the particular thing signified by the mental state; rather, it is the relation or function of the mental state in signifying that particular thing. He says that the word "conception" is unambiguous: it stands in contrast to the ambiguous word "concept" which can mean either the mental state or what is signified by it ("the object of discourse").

But the univocality of the word "conception" is already suspect because of the unmentioned ambiguity of the phrase "object of discourse"; similarly ambiguous is "the signified." For James has already told us that there are two senses of the word "about," just as there are of "meaning": A thought can be about a particular thing (topic or referent), but also it can be about an Object (sense). Thus "conception" could be unlike the ambiguous "concept" by not being *merely* about a particular thing (topic), but it could be equally ambiguous by virtue of connoting both the mental state in its functioning and what the mental state is about *in the sense of Object*. This possibility is further strengthened by James's practice of regarding the topic in its incessant, minute changeableness as "the mere topic" and by his suggestion that it becomes known only because it falls under a concept (or essence)—that which is applicable to an indefinite number of particular things. And it should be noted that James is a conceptualist, not a nominalist:

> We saw . . . that the image *per se*, the nucleus, is functionally the least important part of the thought. *Our doctrine, therefore, of the 'fringe' leads to a perfectly satisfactory decision of the nominalistic and conceptualistic controversy*, so far as it touches psychology. *We must decide in favor of the conceptualists* . . .[6]

As sure as fate, on the very next page of the *Principles*, James does exactly what he said he would not do: he discusses conceptions in terms of what they are *about*. Not only that, they are about concepts (in the sense that "concept" may mean that about which we think), or about particulars as instances of concepts. So we can only conclude that the sense of sameness is embedded in the Object, and no mental state can be specified in isolation from its Object.

> Thus, amid the flux of opinions and of physical things, the world of conceptions, or things *intended to be thought about*, stands stiff and immutable, like Plato's Realm of Ideas.[7]

The ambiguity of "conception" is precisely what we would expect on the basis of our reading of the *Principles*. James cannot speak specifically of a mental state's function in signifying a permanent subject of discourse unless he specifies the latter (Object). He must speak both of the mental state and its Object in order to speak of its signifying function or cognitive relation. Accordingly, we soon find him asserting that each thought must be understood to have *two aspects:* its structural, psychical, or subjective aspect as a numerically distinct passing feeling (No. 2, construed apparently as *either* imagery pertaining to the topic of thought *or* cognized movements of one's body) in the "stream," and, on the other

Phenomenology

hand, its cognitive aspect as a cognition *of* something known—the rest of the Object:

> The contrast is really between two *aspects* in which all mental facts without exception may be taken; their structural aspect, as being subjective, and their functional aspect as being cognitions. In the former aspect, the highest as well as the lowest is a feeling, a peculiarly tinged segment of the stream. This tingeing is its sensitive body, the *wie ihm zu Muthe ist*, the way it feels whilst passing. In the latter aspect the lowest mental fact as well as the highest may grasp some bit of truth as its content, even though that truth were as relationless a matter as a bare unlocalized and undated quality of pain. From the cognitive point of view, all mental facts are intellections. From the subjective point of view all are feelings.[8]

The *Principles* has come full circle: so intimately are data No. 2 and No. 3 related that they are aspects of the same thing.

Next James comes as close as he ever does to an explicit admission that mental states can be discriminated and specified only in terms of their cognitive Objects, and that their specification as psychical, as numerically discrete and temporal, is parasitical on an initial specification of identical things known:

> If every feeling is at the same time a bit of knowledge, we ought no longer to talk of mental states' differing by having more or less of the cognitive quality; they only differ in knowing more or less, in having much fact or little fact for their object . . . Concept and image, thus discriminated through their objects, are consubstantial in their inward nature, as modes of feeling . . . Both concept and image, *qua* subjective, are singular and particular. Both are moments of the stream which come and in an instant are no more. The word universality has no meaning as applied to their psychic body or structure, which is always finite. It only has a meaning when applied to their use, import, or reference to the kind of object they may reveal. The representation, as such, of the universal object is as particular as that of an object about which we know so little that the interjection 'Ha!' is all it can evoke from us . . .[9]

Notice the phrase, "concept and image, thus discriminated through their objects." The inference would be that the "representation as such," the real being or "psychic body" of the thought, can be specified only because the initial presentation, which is the cognitive aspect or object, is specified.

The sense of the same emerges as pivotal: Even in the peculiar way of looking in which the very being of sensations is supposedly revealed, the mental state cannot be specified independently of the cognitive aspect—the what that is cognized—and in the case of the green grass seen in the shadow it is the *same* dark brown—either the same as what has been seen before vis à vis the grass or the same as some other dark brown thing. Therefore if the psychical aspect must be specified in conjunction with the cognitive aspect, and if the cognitive aspect involves the sense of the same, then the psychical aspect must be specified in conjunction with the sense of the same. That is, the comings and goings in the stream cannot be specified in isolation from a stable world cognized—a world intended to be thought about.

The phenomenological breakthrough is unmistakable. With it goes the confession of the poverty of introspective psychology. In sum, to know the mind is only (but this is not easy) to know the world-known:

> We never can break the thought asunder and tell which one of its bits is the part that lets us know which subject is referred to; but nevertheless we always *do* know which of all possible subjects we have in mind. Introspective psychology must here throw up the sponge; the fluctuations of subjective life are too exquisite to be arrested by its coarse means. It must confine itself to bearing witness to the fact that all sorts of different subjective states do form the vehicle by which the same is known; and it must contradict the opposite view.[10]

As we shall see, to name a sensation is to name a place!

Even some of James's language was taken over by Husserl in his classical statement of phenomenology, the *Ideen* of 1913. For Husserl, each *Erlebnisse* or lived-through mental act passes in the "stream of consciousness," and it is linked intentionally and internally (qua *noeses*) to its intended object (*noema*). Moreover, each *noemata* is linked to others in a nexus of noematic phases; that is, the intended object is embedded in a context, and the primacy of the whole lived-world (*Lebenswelt*) becomes increasingly clear in the course of Husserl's long career of writing.

What we find in James is a tacit admission that in *ordo cognoscendi* the Object holds primacy, and that regardless of what is meant by the psychical, whether it be imagery or cognized movements of the organism, the psychical can be specified only in dependence on the cognitive. Thus if the causal analysis cannot get

Phenomenology

started unless the psychical is specified, and if the psychical cannot be specified in isolation from the cognitive, then the analysis of the cognitive holds primacy over the analysis of the causal. James's programmatic philosophy of mind undergoes a wrenching on its foundations.

With all this in mind, we can understand why James's notion of conception has been linked by some interpreters to the phenomenological notion of intentionality. Johannes Linschoten, in his helpful book, *Auf dem Wege zu einer phänomenologischen Psychologie: die Psychologie von William James*, writes of James's definition of conception:

> Konzeption ist also die Funktion, durch die wir einen numerisch unterschiedenen und permanent möglichen Gegenstand (subject of discourse) identifizieren. Dieser Ausdruck bezieht sich, streng genommen, weder auf den Bewusstseinszustand, noch auf dasjenige, worauf dieser verweist, sondern auf die Relation dieser beiden. Konzeption is die Funktion eines Bewusstseinszustandes, der genau das besondere Ding meint [I, 461]. Konzeption, so könnten wir sagen, ist die Bezogenheit des Erlebnisses auf *etwas: 'Konzeption*' ist hier James' Ausdruck für *Intentionalität!*[11]

Because for James conception is not the mental state "itself," and because it is the cognitive reference of the state to something (a permanent *possible* subject of discourse, Linschoten says), this scholar is willing to say that "conception" is James's expression for intentionality.

Now the question of intentionality is central to our inquiry. Are the logical conditions Linschoten cites sufficient conditions for applying the concept of intentionality to James's notion of the cognitive relation? I think so—with qualification. Moreover, I agree with Herbert Spiegelberg who says that James's notion of the active nature of the cognitive function could very well have influenced Edmund Husserl in his refinement of the concept of intentionality.[12]

II

What is intentionality? It is easiest and best to answer this historically. The most influential formulation is found in the writings of the central thinker in the phenomenological movement, Husserl. But he refined the idea as it was presented to him by his teacher, Franz Brentano. Brentano in turn derived it from the scholastics, who in turn derived it from Aristotle. Can any doctrine so old possibly have relevance to the question of a scientific psychology? Let us see.

Aristotle writes in his psychology, *De Anima*, that the mind is in some sense all things.[13] It is identical in the sense that when it knows something, *what* it knows is identical to what the thing itself is; i.e., the thing's essence or intelligible form. He did not mean the thing's physical form necessarily; for, in brief, he thought that what a thing is, is what it does (its function), and many things have the same function without having the same physical shape; e.g., all surgical instruments have the same intelligible form because they all have the same general function, i.e., the repair of the body; but they do not necessarily have the same physical shape. Aristotle's doctrine has a platonic element: when something is known, it is known as an instance of a form, a kind, a universal.[14] Needless to say, a form is what more than one particular could share; in a sense it is the very principle of sameness, so that in linking mind to the apprehension of form Aristotle also links it to the sense of sameness. When something is known, the mind cognizes the intelligible form of the thing, i.e., the thing itself minus its matter.[15] Mind, then, is intrinsically referential, intrinsically significatory for Aristotle.

What is meant by the word "intrinsic"? This question was treated fully by the scholastics, but the roots of their discussion can be found in Aristotle. Consonant with his view that what a thing is is what it does, and what it does depends on the end of the doing, Aristotle writes, "For Nature, like mind, always does whatever it does for the sake of something, which something is its end,"[16] and he goes on to assert, ". . . it is right to call things after the ends they realize . . ."[17] It is the latter we wish to stress: things and processes are rightly *called* in terms of the end they realize.

But this is very broad: It applies both to nature and to mind, and mental acts, according to Aristotle, exhibit traits which are not shared by processes of nature which are divisible and which move from incompletion to completion in time. In the *Nicomachean Ethics* he writes:

> Seeing seems to be at any moment complete, for it does not lack anything which coming into being later will complete its form; and pleasure also seems to be of this nature. For it is a whole, and at no

time can one find a pleasure whose form will be completed if the pleasure lasts longer. For this reason, too, it is not a movement.[18]

Like all activities, mental acts are named after their ends, but since it is the case that if the mental act *is* at all it is complete, then it follows that if it is at all it has already attained its end; and it follows that it already is *what* it is if it is at all. Mental acts are specified and determined by their ends—what they are of or what they are directed on—and these ends must always be present, in some sense of the word present. Thus Aristotle declares that seeing is specified by what is seen, and our pleasure is of a kind which is determined by what we take pleasure in. We have the roots of the scholastic adage: *Objectum specificat actum.*

The scholastics, particularly St. Thomas, expanded and attempted to clarify the idea that mental acts[19] are specified by their objects. The object of a mental act is the *id quod* ("that to which"), the act itself is the *id quo* ("that by which")[20]; the object is the *ens intentionale*, and the act the *intentio*—thus the source of "intention."

Now most acts of any sort have objects; e.g., there is no pounding unless something is pounded, and what is pounded specifies the kind of pounding taking place; e.g., pounding a man is a specifically different kind of pounding from pounding a piece of dough, and killing an innocent man is a killing of a kind which is specifically different from killing a guilty man—one is murder while the other is manslaughter or execution. But one can know that he is pounding without knowing exactly what he is pounding—one may be doing more than he knows. However, how can one be thinking more than one thinks, knowing more than one knows, at any one moment? It is not immediately clear that he can.

In specifying *mental* acts the scholastics went beyond the distinction of act and object and introduced that between material object and formal object. Anthony Kenny writes:

> Anything which can be ϕd is a material object of ϕing. Beer, for example, can be seen, and so beer is a material object of seeing; when the executioners burnt Joan of Arc, Joan was the material object of their burning. The formal object of ϕing is the object under that description which *must* apply to it if it is possible to ϕ it.[21]

Is it possible to sense something? Only if the object of the sensing —the something sensed—is sensible. To describe the mental act of sensing we *must* describe it as a sensing of something sensible. Its description presupposes a description of its object.

But even this is not sufficient to specify mental acts. For demonstrably nonmental ones are also specified by their formal objects: e.g., only what is edible can be eaten, only what is dirty can be cleaned, and only because a person is inflammable can he or she be burnt; eating, cleaning, and burning are not specifically mental acts.

Although not sufficient to specify mental acts, it is true, the identification of their formal objects is a necessary condition. Certain definite logical restrictions are placed on the type of object which a mental act can have. And from this it follows that a mental act cannot be specified as an internal event nor even as a set of molar movements of the body (nowadays called "behavior patterns"); for there is no logical restriction placed on the kinds of objects such events or such movements can have. The relation between a mental act and its formal object is a logical one, not a contingent one—a fortiori not a causal one. It has been argued by phenomenologists, among others, that many philosophers, from Descartes until Brentano, mistakenly construed the relation as causal.[22]

What then, according to the scholastics, will be sufficient to specify mental acts qua mental? Again the roots are found in Aristotle. In defining anger, for example, he declares that it is a desire for *what appears to be* revenge for *what appears to be* an insult.[23] The description of the formal object of a mental act such as an emotion, unlike the description of the formal object of a nonmental act, must contain reference to what-appears-to-be, and probably to what-one-believes-to-be as well. Only what is dirty can in fact be cleaned, but something which merely appears to be dirty may be the object of anger—indeed, the appearance provokes the anger in some sense of "provoke."

The scholastics attempted to amplify and clarify this idea with still another distinction. A *mental* act is a strictly intentional one, and it need not necessarily produce any actual change in its object; e.g., the appearance of dirt may provoke us to passionate anger, but nothing gets cleaned. St. Thomas writes:

> There are actions of two kinds: some actions, such as heating and cutting, pass over into external matter; others such as understand-

Phenomenology 159

ing, perceiving and wanting, remain in the agent. The difference between them is this: actions of the first kind bring about a state not of the agent which initiates the change, but of what is changed; whereas actions of the second kind bring about a state of the agent.[24]

Most of these scholastic distinctions were revived by Brentano in the 1870's. Searching for a characteristic which would identify psychical phenomena and set them off from physical ones, Brentano first considered and then rejected the suggestion that the uniqueness of psychical phenomena was that they lacked extension (cf. Descartes). He then advanced a different criterion of distinction in his *Psychologie von empirischen Standpunkt:*

> Every psychical phenomenon is characterized by what the medieval scholastics called the intensional (or mental) existence of an object, and what we, not quite unambiguously, would call 'relation to a content,' 'object-directedness' or 'immanent objectivity.' ('Object' here does not mean reality.) Each such phenomenon contains in itself something as an object, though not each in the same manner. In imagination something is imagined, in judgment something is accepted or rejected, in love something is loved . . .
>
> This intensional existence is a property only of psychical phenomena; no physical phenomenon displays anything similar. And so we can define psychical phenomena by saying that they are those phenomena which contain an object intensionally.[25]

In his statement, "Every psychical phenomenon is characterized by what the medieval scholastics called the intensional (or mental) existence of an object," Brentano seems to have intended that the word "characterized" carry the same force as it carried for the scholastics: the mental act is literally characterized or specified by its formal object as this object is presented phenomenally to consciousness, and the act is only specified this way. It is a matter of what we *mean* by mental act.

But Husserl, his pupil, came to criticize Brentano on this score: Brentano, he charged, was excessively empirical in his method and mode of formulation, and thus only imperfectly captured the logical force of the concept of intentionality (or what Husserl calls the "eidetic" nature of it, together with the statements that can be made about it with "essential necessity," i.e., necessary truths). In particular, Husserl charged that Brentano is seriously ambiguous when he talks of the "content" to which consciousness is directed, as to an "immanent objectivity"; we are never sure if Brentano means some "material phase" of consciousness itself (what Husserl not unequivocally called "the hyletic data") or to the object in the world insofar as it can be intended.[26] However, this charge of Husserl's takes place within a wider context of criticism: intentionality cannot properly be conceived as just a criterion for distinguishing one empirical science (psychology) from another, or one factual domain from another; nor can it properly be studied by empirical methods of observation. Rather, intentionality is a matter of meaning, of *eidos*—a matter which is logically prior to the pursuit of any empirical inquiry—and one which can properly be treated only by an eidetic method. Matters of meaning must be distinguished from matters of fact.[27] *Was meinen wir?*—this is the rallying cry for Husserl's inquiry, as Pierre Thévenaz points out.[28]

Phenomenology has been described as a descriptive science and as an exercise in seeing. But what is described and what is seen? Phenomena—it will be said—the things of the world just as they appear to us: their appearance freed from the overlay of scientific and philosophical theorizing. Back to the things themselves and the bedrock of our experience!

This is true as far as it goes, but it is misleading because it does not go far enough. The phenomenon *is* seen, but it is seen in the sense that what is seen discloses the very possibility of the phenomenon. The possibility of the phenomenon is disclosed when seeing it discloses how we can *mean* the phenomenon. A thing can appear in our experience only because we can mean that thing, and we can do so only because we know *how* it appears. Phenomenologists attempt to correlate what a thing means to us (its essence) with how it appears to us. If physical things appear to us perspectively then that at least in part is what we mean by them—they are that *kind* of thing. Thus the statement, "Physical things appear perspectively," is necessarily true, because what we mean by the predicate is involved with what we mean by the subject; it is known with "eidetic insight" which no conceivable future observation of experience could prove false—for if something did not appear perspectively it would not count as a physical object. Thus the truth is a priori and knowable a priori insofar as it is true independently of any future experience. We say future experience, since its truth is not independent of all experience: after all, its

Phenomenology

truth is a matter of what it means (essence), and essence a matter of how things appear in experience. Thus Husserl searches for that which makes experience possible, as does Kant, but he differs from Kant in thinking that essence is directly intuited (or seen, *Wesenschau*) in experience.

For Husserl there are mental acts. What kind of things are they? They are the kind of things which appear, but do not appear perspectively.[29] Also they are *of* something else. They are intrinsically referential; they could not be anything else, because that is what, in part, we *mean* by them. Indeed, intentionality is the main phenomenological theme,[30] and the truth about intentionality is a truth of essential necessity. It cannot be discovered by empirical (in this case empirical-psychological) methods of observing and testing facts, for it is a matter of meaning, discoverable only through eidetic intuition or insight; and just as certain basic meanings must be presupposed by all empirical inquiry, so must be also the method of eidetic intuition.

Since for Husserl the cognitive relation of mental act to object is not conceivably false, the relationship is not contingent or empirical in any way. He writes emphatically:

> We must, however, be quite clear on this point that *there is no question here of a relation between a psychological event—called experience (Erlebnis)—and some other real existent (Dasein)—called Object—*or of a *psychological connexion* obtaining between one and the other *in objective reality.* On the contrary, we are concerned with experiences in their essential purity, with *pure essences*, and with that which is *involved in* the essence "*a priori,*" in *unconditioned necessity.*[31]

There are no rays connecting thought and what it is of, no wires or rods, nothing that could be verified or disverified empirically. Husserl's point is one of meaning: we cannot even mean the mental act without at the same time meaning the thing cognized or intended by it. That thing might not even exist—but it would still be intended. For *if* it does exist, then *what* it is (its form or essence, cf. Aristotle) is just what one intends it to be. Indeed, Husserl would add, one cannot even begin to search to see if it does exist until one knows *what* he is looking for. Husserl maintains that all "metaphysical enigmas and riddles of the theoretical reason" lead us eventually back to the doctrine of intentionality.[32]

We reach the apotheosis of the Aristotelian and scholastic tendency to identify mind in conjunction with an identification of its formal objects.[33] It is a reaffirmation of *objectum specificat actum* when Husserl writes of mental acts or experiences:

> In the very essence of an experience lies determined not only *that*, but also *whereof* it is a consciousness . . .[34]

The *whereof* is part of what we mean by it—we cannot identify the mental act without identifying the *whereof*. A thought is identified as, say, "Thought A," only because we have already identified it as "Thought of A'." Thus the statement, "Thought A is thought of A'" is a necessary truth.

III

In the light of this exposition can we say that James's doctrine of conception is a doctrine of intentionality? Prima facie there are similarities. James affirms the omnipresence of cognition. Both James and Husserl repudiate the notion that what we immediately cognize is something mental, a notion that gained widespread currency after Descartes.[35] We do not, say, immediately perceive a sensation which we then take to be a sensation of a horse because we reason causally (i.e., there must be something in the physical world which produces this sensation in my mind), but rather we immediately perceive a horse.[36] Husserl maintained that Descartes' analysis of mind (and ego) was faulty and had to be corrected by a transcendental analysis of meaning and its constitution: Descartes mixes in factual and causal considerations and leaves the mind as a "tag-end of the world"—a point of departure for causal investigations.[37] Husserl regarded James as "a bold and original man—unbound by tradition—whose influence upon me was not without significance."[38] Husserl also thought that James's analysis of presentational experience was brilliant.[39] It could very well be that James's idea of the cognitive relation and conception influenced Husserl.

James's exposition of sensation immediately emphasizes its referentialness and worldliness. As we have seen, he compares it closely to perception:

> They are . . . different cognitive *functions*, not . . . different sorts of mental fact. The nearer the object cognized comes to being a

Phenomenology 163

> simple quality like 'hot,' 'cold,' 'red,' 'noise,' 'pain,' apprehended irrelatively to other things, the more the state of mind approaches pure sensation . . . But in both sensation and perception we perceive the fact as an *immediately present outward reality*, and this makes them differ from 'thought' and 'conception' whose objects do not appear present in this immediate physical way.[40]

This comes close to saying that part of what we mean by "sensation" and "perception" is that their objects appear as present in an immediate physical way.[41] Furthermore, he seems to say that we can never perceive a thing without perceiving a world. He writes:

> *The first sensation which an infant gets is for him the Universe.* And the universe which he later comes to know is nothing but an amplification and an implication of that first simple germ . . . In his dumb awakening to the consciousness of *something there*, a mere *this* . . . the infant encounters an object in which (though it be given in a pure sensation) all the 'categories of the understanding' are contained. It has objectivity, unity, substantiality, causality, in the full sense in which any later object or system of objects has these things. Here the young knower meets and greets his world.[42]

Passages such as this have led some phenomenologists to assert that James hit on the companion notion to intentionality: *Lebenswelt*; i.e., the lived-world as the ground of meaning from which all other meanings, however refined, technical, or scientific they finally become, are initially derived—a ground which is then usually forgotten. Linschoten observes:

> Das Empfinden ist bereits Welterleben, es ist die Wirklichkeit selbst, so wie anfängt zu erscheinen.[43]

John Wild asserts that James grasped the importance of "primary reflection"—the world as it is lived before it is overlaid with scientific interpretation. He goes on to say that the basic distinction between the *Lebenswelt* and the science-world is "already implied in James's own thinking," and that "this central core of James's teaching has been ignored in his own university and in the Anglo-Saxon world until recently."[44] James Edie makes a similar point.[45]

It is understandable that such assertions have been made. Even though James does not explicitly affirm that mental states are specified by their intentional objects, there are many passages in which he implicitly treats them as if they were; there are particularly vivid ones in the second volume of the *Principles*. Furthermore, these passages give the unmistakable impression that the intentional objects themselves are not to be regarded as discrete, but as part and parcel of the whole lived-world. Take James's treatment of sensations in his chapter on space, for example. Sensations, he says, are immediately given as "voluminous," or intrinsically spatial.[46] Loud sounds, for instance, "have a certain enormousness of feeling": they occupy a whole *volume* and present themselves from a definite *direction*. Odors have a spatial quality: they envelop us. Even tactile sensations have an acute voluminousness; they are not mere impressions of resistance; sticking one's tongue into a hollow tooth which has lost its filling affords a vivid sensation of the three dimensions of space.

James is undercutting the traditional distinction between primary and secondary qualities. For him it is not the case, as it was for Locke, for example, that the secondary qualities are nothing in the spatial things themselves except the power to produce ideas in the mind, while the primary qualities can really be in the things themselves in such a form that they accurately match (in some way) their mental correlates in the mind. For James it is not the case that what we immediately know are nonspatial ideas in the mind, nor that we then infer that in the case of some of these there are point-for-point physical correlates in space. It is not necessarily the case that what we immediately know is mental: even sounds, which in the Lockian tradition have been construed as secondary qualities, are presented *in space*, and in this they differ not at all from lengths, widths, and motions, say—those qualities which have been traditionally construed as primary.

As a consequence, James undercuts the traditional dualistic distinction which sorts the world into two different kinds of stuff, the mental and the physical. It is a burgeoning of the latent strand that was so apparent in his analysis of the self: Following through with "the original cognitive function of our sensibility," he finds no fixed point like a substantive self—in which he can stand, as it were, and pocket all the presentations of experience into one of two mutually exclusive and exhaustive categories, the mental and the physical. Thus he cannot preserve his own fundamental dualistic distinction. Instead he is led into a single field of experience in which the cognitive relationship is basic and in which many distinctions proliferate as a result. He wants to leave room for the

Phenomenology

psychical, it seems, but he cannot characterize it simply as that which is nonphysical. He can characterize it in terms of an aspect of the thing known which is immediately relative to us as its cognizer (the image) and he can characterize it also in terms of our own cognized body, but he cannot characterize it through simple contrast as nonphysical because the thing known is not always cognized as physical: There are things cognized as "mental realities" (like fictions) and as formal entities (like numbers) and these too, presumably, have a psychical aspect. In his chapter on the perception of reality he speaks of such "mental realities."

No matter what mode of cognition or what kind of "mental states" James chooses to examine, he finds himself thrown into the cognized and examining that instead. Moreover, he has great difficulty in isolating a discrete thing known, because he finds that it is interwoven with the whole lived world; and this whole lived world is really a whole, it is not something on which one can get an initial purchase through an initial characterization of it as nonmental or nonself. No indeed, for the self and the mind are out there with everything else—out in the single vast and variegated field of experience. The lack of a conventional fixed point, a center for all coordinate systems, is vividly apparent. All that is available is the phenomenal body judged to be the same in a world which is the same.

This development is particularly obvious in the case of sensations: they are no longer the *ne plus ultra* of reality, bits of mental stuff in the absolute here and now which analysis can initially lay hold on and feel confident in, though all else should fail. When James lays hold on sensations, he lays hold on space. He cannot begin with sensations as mental and plot their cognitive and causal connections with the physical world, since he tells us that when he begins with sensations he begins with the physical world as cognized by sensation. How can he begin with sensation and then plot its relationship to the world, when what he begins with is this very relationship? This has profound repercussions. It means that any attempt to break up the world into an extended and a nonextended realm and then to connect thoughts to things through causal reasoning must fail. Descartes, after proving to his own satisfaction that a good God existed who would not deceive us, asserted that a geometrically specifiable physical world existed. He then asserted that our sensations, which are specifiable in their own nongeometrical and mentalistic terms, are given a reference to the world through causal reasoning: e.g., a red sensation is the red of an apple, an apple's red, because an apple is that kind of thing which can cause the sensation of red in the mind under such and such conditions of observation.[47]

James's break with Descartes on this matter marks him as a precursor of phenomenology. As Husserl did after him, he maintains that all scientific (e.g., geometrical) knowledge of space is possible only because there is already a direct experiential notion of space from which the scientist can start: by progressive refinements and modifications of this he eventually achieves a mathematized system. For Husserl and for James the notion of sensation as a mental state, insofar as it is an element in the stream of consciousness, is specifiable only internally, or in conjunction with that which it is of, i.e., things in space. Thus the attempt to relate them through contingent and causal reasoning is an absurdity.[48]

Since for James sensation is not known as a mental particle, it cannot be as a mental particle that it supplies a fixed point, a founding level if you will, for philosophical reflection. However, sensation serves as a founding level in terms of what it *is* known as. We remember that James said that sensation is either our reality or "our test of reality"; conceived physical realities must show "sensible effects" or else be disbelieved.[49] In what sense does he use the words "test" and "sensible effects"? His use of these words is tied to his use of "originals of experience." It is here that his relationship to phenomenology and the phenomenological notion of the *Lebenswelt* as the founding level of meaning is closest. Notice his use of the word "original" in this key passage on the voluminousness of sensations:

> In the sensations of hearing, touch, sight, and pain we are accustomed to distinguish from among the other elements the element of voluminousness . . . Now my first thesis is that this element, though more developed in some than in others, is the original sensation of space, out of which all the exact knowledge about space that we afterwards come to have is woven by processes of discrimination, association, and selection.[50]

Even pain is an original sensation of space: a pain is felt in the foot or in the head, and the foot and the head are in definite *places*. Pain is an original sensation of space, thus it cannot be the case that pain is first cognized as mental and then by an inference of some sort projected into what we take to be space; it is already spatial: it is part of what we *mean* by space, James says.[51]

He also declares that the original of time is immediately sensed, not inferred; it is the specious present. It is the "prototype of all conceived times." Again we encounter the idea of originals, archetypes or founding levels of meaning in James.

> But the original paragon and prototype of all conceived times is the specious present, the short duration of which we are immediately and incessantly sensible.[52]

An event in the distant past is cognized as past because it is cognized "in the direction of the objects which at the present moment appear affected by this quality."

> What is the *original* of our experience of pastness, from whence we get the meaning of the term? . . . To think a thing as past is to think it amongst the objects or in the direction of the objects which at the present moment appear affected by this quality.[53]

Note that the world in which we find ourselves at any given moment, the immediately presented world, is not just a fact among other facts—a peculiarly "psychical" fact, say, the truth of which could conceivably be deduced from some supremely general theory of psychophysical reality—rather it is the *foundation* of *all* our meanings, the most sophisticated and technical as well as the most naïve.

I think that James's notion of the "originals of experience," which he develops in the *Principles*, is the root-notion of his later metaphysics of pure experience. The key idea of that metaphysics is that experience is pure in the sense that "it leans on nothing"—it is the self-contained foundation.[54] A pure experience is a "specific nature"—a "fact" in the sense that it has an irreducible meaning, *not* in the sense that it is necessarily a truth about the actual physical world. In 1905 James wrote:

> It boots not to say that our sensations are fallible. They are indeed; but to see the thermometer contradict us when we say 'it is cold' does not abolish cold as a specific nature from the universe.[55]

Specifically in regard to the experience of activity, but having a general significance, James writes:

> . . . for the word 'activity' has no imaginable content whatever save these experiences of process, obstruction, striving, strain, or release, ultimate *qualia* as they are of the life given us to be known . . . The *percipi* in these originals of experience is the *esse;* the curtain is the picture. If there is anything hiding in the background, it ought not to be called activity, but should get itself another name.[56]

And again:

> . . . a philosophy of pure experience can consider the real causation as no other *nature* of thing than that which even in our most erroneous experiences appears to be at work. Exactly what appears there is what we *mean* by working, though we may later come to learn that working was not exactly there . . . To treat this offhand as the bare illusory surface of the world whose real causality is an unimaginable ontological principle hidden in the cubic deeps, is, for the more empirical way of thinking, only animism in another shape. You explain your given fact by your 'principle,' but the principle itself, when you look clearly at it, turns out to be nothing but a previous little spiritual copy of the fact. Away from that one and only kind of fact your mind, considering causality, can never get.[57]

This trenchant argument is fundamental to James's philosophical outlook. He turns the tables on those who accused him of subjectivism, anthropomorphism, and animism, views which amount to an erroneous assignment of a causal role to (mainly) human traits: it is the seeing of human activity where no such activity exists—e.g., "the geyser acts because there is an actor in it." But to treat an original of experience as if it were nothing but an epiphenomenal effect of the "real" world is itself nothing but a subtle form of animism, James claims. What we mean by causality, say, must be given within our human experience. To say that the experience is illusion, and that what is real is that hidden process which causes us to have the experience, is to engage in animism: because all that we can *mean* by causality is the very thing we experience; because human experience is "explained" by what in actuality is just more human experience—but experience displaced from its proper role and misidentified. In effect, James is accusing his critics of saying that we mean X because X causes us to mean X. But how can we mean or intend X in the first place? What his critics say is no better than "a geyser acts because there is an actor in it"; indeed, it is worse, since to undercut the foundation of meaning is to live more insecurely in the world than if we

Phenomenology

believed that things are animated by spirits. At least the savage knows what he means! A counterfeit causal explanation of meaning conceals the real foundation, for "causality" itself is a matter of meaning; to place it beyond our knowledge ("in the cubic deeps") is worse than hiding something with the left hand and pretending to hunt for it (and placate it) with the right. It is to forget where one has hidden it, and to be haunted by a peculiar sense of loss—a loss of something we know not what.

It is no accident that James used the word "humanism" synonymously with "radical empiricism," i.e., the metaphysics of pure experience.[58] The usage reflects his attempt to heal the rift between modern science and the immediately experienced significance of life and his attempt to overcome "alienation," that unusual kind of nightmare (which he thought was growing typical of modern life) in which we have power and no motives (in an ordinary nightmare one has motives but no power); i.e., the world is strange and alien; it contains nothing which answers to our intentions and emotions; the real conditions of consciousness lie beyond the scope of consciousness.[59] As John Dewey put it, James's metaphysics is an attempt to overcome the rift between nature-lore (science) and individual-fate-lore.[60]

It is true, I think, that James's "originals of experience" in the *Principles* is the root-idea of his later "pure experience." It is the direct consequence of the dominating position which the Object of thought comes to assume in the *Principles*. Mental states are *of* something, and this something is ineluctable. The Object must be discussed on its own terms—terms which are entirely independent of those which refer to the causal ground of thought in the brain. For example, James makes hypotheses about a feature of the brain process which could causally account for the original of time, i.e., immediately experienced duration, or the specious present. He writes:

> we must suppose that this amount of duration is pictured fairly steadily in each passing instant of consciousness by virtue of some fairly constant feature in the brain-process to which the consciousness is tied. This feature of the brain-process, whatever it be, must be the cause of our perceiving the fact of time at all.[61]

He immediately appends a footnote to this: "The cause of the perceiving, not the object perceived!"—and the emphasis given by the exclamation mark is appropriate. It must be remembered when one reads the later essays, such as "Does Consciousness Exist?" For their whole intent seems to be to apply the lesson that was so painfully taught by the *Principles:* the causal analysis of mind must give up priority of inquiry to the descriptive and cognitive. It seems to me misleading for Professor Perry to have asserted that "James is the brother of Mach," for James only inadvertently tries to specify a visual sensation in terms of the retina, whereas Mach makes a systematic attempt.[62]

This represents a pivotal difference in philosophical point of view. It represents the distinctness of James's *comminuted Identätsphilosophie* and his admitted "squinting towards idealism," an idealism which has points in common with the objective idealism of the Continent, more so than with the subjective variety of the empiricist Berkeley.[63] It is the latter idealism, one featuring punctiform particulars, which Mach echoes to some extent. For the same reason I think Professor Lovejoy's complaint over the lack of physiological psychology in James's "Does Consciousness Exist"? and his bafflement in the face of the fact that James knew more about such psychology than any other philosopher of the time, reveals a fundamental misunderstanding of James's philosophical intentions.[64]

While it is true that James develops the idea of the originals of experience in the later *Essays*, it is also true that the whole account is "thinner" than in the *Principles*. This is due not only to the fact that they are merely a sequence of articles and not a systematic treatise, for the *Principles* itself is not a *systematic* treatise. James (perhaps unjustifiably) applies Occam's razor to the philosophical content of the *Essays* in a way that sets them off substantively from the *Principles*. For example, he asserts that a pure experience like that of coldness, say, figures in two contexts of experience at once: as a part of the context we call the physical world and as a part of the one we call the mental, the context making all the difference.

In the *Essays* James conceives of a single pure experience as being both the knower and the known. This is exceedingly spare substantively, and it puts a great theoretical load on the concept of pure experience: a single pure experience must be perceiver, perception, and perceived. Of course, as a perception, say, the total content of the mental context would be different, presumably, from

Phenomenology 171

the total content of the physical context—the perceived. Presumably one's own body would figure differently in each (James emphasizes breathing in the *Essays*), but he does not work this out. The relationship (the mode of cognition or the act of the cognizer, e.g., perception) is not spelled out, and he reiterates that pure experience is itself the knower. It is only in his very last works that he begins to sketch-in what has been well described by Millic Capek in his article, "The Reappearance of the Self in the Last Philosophy of William James."[65]

When taken altogether, the latent strand of thought which we have been tracing in the *Principles* results in a richer and more nearly complete texture than is found in the *Essays*. It more nearly approaches James's ideal of concreteness and adequacy. Not only do we find the notion of the originals of experience, but the notion of experience itself is more fully adumbrated: To be sure, James had not yet explicitly affirmed that the same pure experience supplies the "stuff" of both mind and matter, but his *reasons* for believing this are clearer.[66] He does not confront us *ab ovo* with a set of discrete pure experiences, but rather with a whole livedworld of experience which is experienced by a person *as* lived by himself. He takes the first steps toward a direct linking of modes of experiencing and modes of the experienced, and so conceives experience that it never takes place outside a context. Indeed, the founding level of meaning is a context. As in phenomenology, then, modes of being are linked to modes of experiencing—modes of world-appearing.

IV

Nowhere in the *Principles* is the force of the phenomenological strand more evident, and its flowering more nearly complete, than in the second volume of the *Principles*, in the chapter "The Perception of Reality." Here is his version of the *Lebenswelt*. James the psychologist has merged with the thinker and the thought being studied: he does not stand outside of anything. The thought being studied is specified in conjunction with the thought's Object in all its fullness; and the psychologist's reality (No. 4) is in effect indistinguishable from delineations drawn within thought's Object. The conceptual structure of his dualistic and natural scientific program, with its four ostensibly irreducible compartments, is in conspicuous disuse. To be sure, he occasionally reverts to his program and insists that a natural scientific psychology must not attempt to determine the structure of ultimate reality; but he proceeds as if such a special determination were unnecessary and irrelevant—and the scope and success of his procedure is a lesson in itself. It is thought's object as a phenomenon presented within a lived phenomenal world which suffices in his account of reality. A single compartment denominated "thought's object" is no longer sufficient to contain his data. This compartment overflows, as it were, and covers the others.

What first greets the reader's eye in James's chapter on the perception of reality is the profusion of entities discussed. Gone is the attempt to say that there are only two basic kinds, mental and physical, and that the observing psychologist assigns the relations of veridicality or nonveridicality between them. For there are hallucinatory objects, fictional objects, formal objects (like numbers), objects conceived as not existing (like perpetual motion machines or round squares), objects conceived as existing but not as present to sense, objects perceived as existing and present to sense, objects sensed as aspects or qualities of immediately perceived things, etc. But this is not all. For what also greets the eye is his description of these objects as objects cognized within a *system* of objects. What is immediately presented is phenomena-within-a-system; thus James speaks of "the various orders of reality" and "the many worlds."[67]

Now some of these objects he calls "mental objects" (like unicorns), but the point is that they are not mental merely because they are thought about, for physical objects are also thought about and they certainly are not *mental* because of this. This simple dualism between the mental and the physical collapses and is replaced by something more subtle. In the first place, objects are the kind of objects they are because of the relations to other objects which they can be thought to have; they are not the kind they are because of the mere fact that they are thought about. James alludes to the thought about them as a "psychic attitude" which may be an attitude of "mere thought" or one of "belief"—the difference being an essential element in the determination of whether the object of thought (topic) is thought to be *real* in the primary sense of the term.[68] But the point for us to grasp immediately is that this thought qua psychic attitude is displaced from its comfortable position as a mental entity: James prepares the ground for an assignment of it to the total Object of thought. It is something I do and I am out there with everything else; it is a relating of me to the rest of the world, only it is more intimately presented and "warmer"; but it is basically worldly. The point is that thought qua psychic attitude is only one element in the specification of mind. The other elements can be discovered only when characteristics of the objects *thought about* are discovered, and since these can be discovered only when the various "worlds" are connected, the other elements of mind can likewise be discovered only then—so thoroughly worldly is mind.

How do the "worlds" become connected? As James conceives it, it is the most natural thing in the world. Objects thought about must find a place within a system or "world" if they are to be thought about in a determinate fashion at all, and an object thought about finds a place within that particular system of objects which will "tolerate its presence" and which will stand in a relation to it "which nothing contradicts."[69] For example, I can very well think of a horse with wings like Pegasus. I know exactly what I mean when I do so: wings are predicated of a horse, and this is part of the "inner constitution of the thought's object"; it is presented as just what it is.[70] The question of the reality of that which is thought about (topic) need not come up; it is a completely independent question. Of course, as James says, Pegasus is real in the sense that it is really a "phenomenon, or object of our passing thought, if nothing more."[71] Moreover, it is thought within a whole system of centaurs and satyrs, say, which adds content to what we are thinking about, because Pegasus is coherent with the system; and this system is real in the very same sense of "phenomena."

But for James there is a *fundamental* sense of the word "real." Things are thought to be real in this fundamental sense when they are thought to be in connection with "reality *par excellence*"—"existence for itself, namely, or *extra mentem meam*."[72] But what is the latter? For James it is that with which the person enters into practical relations; it is that which is *believed* to be sensibly at hand and to which the person turns with a *will;* it is all that, too, which is contained in the fringe of such believed things—all those things believed to be related in space and time.[73]

The sense of "belief," then, is linked to the most fundamental sense of "real." Belief is the sense of reality, James says.⁷⁴ But belief is something distinct from mere thought, mere entertainment of ideas. He quotes Brentano with approval: "belief presupposes mere thought," but not the reverse.⁷⁵ He also follows Hume and Kant: the judgment of existence or fundamental reality adds nothing to the concept, i.e., the inner constitution of thought's Object which delineates the single *what* judged about. In an existential judgment we "step outside of the concept." For James we step into a practical relationship between ourselves and the thing judged about, which relationship is belief. James says that belief is a "state of consciousness *sui generis*," but he adds significantly that it is a state of consciousness

> . . . about which nothing more can be said in the way of internal analysis, [so] let us proceed to the second way of studying the subject of belief: *Under what circumstances do we think things real?* We shall soon see how much matter this gives us to discuss.⁷⁶

What are the *circumstances* in which we think things real? James writes, concerning the unusual predicate "exists":

> The syllable *ex* in the word Existence, *da* in the word *Dasein*, express it. 'The candle exists' is equivalent to 'The candle is *over there*.' And the 'over there' means real space, space related to other reals. The proposition amounts to saying: 'The candle is in the same space with other reals.' It affirms of the candle a very concrete predicate—namely, this relation to other particular concrete things. *Their* real existence . . . resolves itself into their peculiar relation to *ourselves*. Existence is thus no substantive quality when we predicate it of any object; it is a relation, ultimately terminating in ourselves, and at the moment when it terminates, becoming a *practical* relation.⁷⁷

To say that an object is real in the fundamental sense, that it exists, is to say that it is over there *from us*—or that it is continuous in space and time with those things which are now over there from us. The sense of "exists" is grounded in this reciprocal practical relation. James is here anticipating Sidney Shumaker's idea of "token reflexives"—words that make an oblique and covert reference to the self, like "this" and "that" and "there."⁷⁸ If, following James, we insist on calling "exists" a predicate (and I think there are excellent reasons for doing so), we must nevertheless

Phenomenology 175

qualify our assertion with the rider that it is a most unusual one. For most predicates refer to qualities which are expressed by the sheer concept of the object, e.g., "four-legged," "rational," "solid," and so on. But James agrees with Hume and Kant that "exists" forces us "to step outside" the mere concept; adding his own insight, he asserts that "exists" forces us to step into a notion of the *practical relationship* of the object to ourselves.[79] A real horse is one I can ride, and it stings my interest in quite a different way from Pegasus. Indeed, the concept of existence is inseparable from the concept of the whole lived-world.

We can now make better sense of James's assertion that in naming a sensation we name a place. As the sensation directly and primitively refers to its object, so the object holds, in some way, a reference back to the knower who has the sensation. He writes:

> For the places thus first sensibly known are elements of the child's space-world which remain with him all his life; and by memory and later experience he learns a vast number of things *about* those places which at first he did not know. But to the end of time certain places of the world remain defined for him as the places *where those sensations were;* and his only possible answer to the question *where anything is* will be to say 'there,' and to name some sensation or other like those first ones, which shall identify the spot. Space *means* but the aggregate of all our possible sensations.[80]

But what *is* the sensation, then, "in itself," in its "psychical being"? By now we realize that such talk makes sense only within the context of the lived-body, and talk of the lived-body makes sense only within the context of the whole lived-world. James writes:

> Reality, starting from our Ego, thus sheds itself from point to point —first upon all objects which have an immediate sting of interest for our Ego in them, and next, upon the objects most continuously related with these. It only fails when the connecting thread is lost. A whole system may be real, if it only hangs to our Ego by one immediately *stinging* term.[81]

But he does not really mean the Ego—we already know this.[82] For him, the concept is the windiest abortion ever perpetrated. He means the self, and by the self he means the lived, phenomenal body—the cognized body. And by the cognized body he means something cognized within a totality of fringe or relationships: the web which is the cognized world. The cash value[83] of what he is saying is that the fundamental sense of position or place in the world is given to cognition as something in relationship to our bodies. When we believe that there is something real *over there*, we mean that it is over there *from our body*. When we believe that the thing over there is real, we believe that *the thing over against our body*—which can affect us, which interests us, which "stings" our interest and care—is real; and so are all other things which are related to it. Sensible things sting us the most, and thereby supply the basis of our sense of reality.

What has happened to the reciprocal reference to *sensation?* It quite drops out as an isolated matter. It is absorbed into the enveloping Object and the lived-world of space surrounding and containing the body.

For James we can believe that Pegasus exists only if we believe that Pegasus can enter into spatial relationships with those objects which comprise "the world of practical realities."[84] We cannot do this. Concomitantly, we can believe or assert the attributive proposition "Pegasus has wings" only if we do not assert the existential proposition "Pegasus exists"—that is, only if we do not believe that Pegasus belongs in the world of Maggie and Dobbin, the world of real horses, the world of practical realities. Either way, this world is the court of final appeals, the founding level of meaning.

> Each thinker . . . has dominant habits of attention; and these *practically elect from among the various worlds some one to be for him the world of ultimate realities.* From this world's objects he does not appeal. Whatever positively contradicts them must get into another world or die. The horse, e.g., may have wings to its heart's content, so long as it does not pretend to be the real world's horse—*that* horse is absolutely wingless.[85]

As we might expect, James speaks of the "paramount reality of sensations."[86] We can now see why he thinks that they are either our realities or our tests of reality: If something is conceived as existing it must be conceived as sensible. Its sensibility is part of what we mean by its existence.

We reach here the apogee of the development of the latent strand in the *Principles*. There is no suggestion that the physical existence of a thing is simply and passively registered in a mental

Phenomenology

substance called mind—no suggestion that the cognitive relation can be ignored or, at best, filled in later through an assignment of truth values. James is analyzing mind from within the cognitive relation, and cognition itself is a worldly activity of a worldly self. Mind and world are ineluctably connected: thought is specified only in conjunction with that which is thought about, and that which is thought about is specified only in conjunction with the principles of its system, i.e., principles of thinkability (e.g., a mythological system is what it is because it is thinkable in a precisely different way from that in which the physical world is thinkable). The "originals of experience" are the common ground for the specification of both mind and world; James has launched himself on a course which must lead to something like his radically monistic radical empiricism. In any case, the four conceptual compartments of his programmatic dualism are broken beyond repair.

John Dewey has already advanced an interpretation of the *Principles* which is similar to ours in some salient respects. He writes:

> There is a double strain in the *Principles of Psychology* of William James. One strain is official acceptance of epistemological dualism. According to this view, the science of psychology centers about a *subject* which is 'mental' just as physics centers about an *object* which is material. But James' analysis of special topics tends, on the contrary, to reduction of the subject to a vanishing point, save as 'subject' is identified with the organism, the latter, moreover, having no existence save in interaction with environing conditions. According to the latter strain, subject and object do not stand for separate orders or kinds of existence but at most for certain distinctions made for a definite purpose within experience.[87]

Of course, in identifying the subject or the agent with the organism Dewey is pursuing his own inquiry, which I will not consider here. The point is that Dewey recognizes two strands in the *Principles*, and that he sees that subject and object is only a distinction made for a definite purpose *within* experience. I observe, in passing, that it is not evident to me that a biological analysis employs categories which are adequate for cognition; it does not seem that fringes hover about things in the world as membranes or tentacles hover about certain organisms. But I do concede that James's account of the phenomenology of the body is laced with physiological terms, and that we look in vain for a completed phenomenological account of the way in which the act of cognition construed as a phenomenal presentation of the body is presented in necessary connection with the object cognized.

V

Not only does this apogee in the development of the latent strand point forward to James's later work, it also points backward to earlier sections of the *Principles* and gives them sense and coherence. Particularly is this the case with his notion of the will. As early as the chapter on the stream of thought he had made it clear that will, partiality, and selectivity are a constant feature of thought—cognition is not passive mirroring. But he could not do justice to the subject at that point in the book. For as it transpires, James construes will as a function of attention, and attention is obviously a function of cognition—or in phenomenological terms—intention. We can attend only to what we can intend. Thus it is only in the later portions of the book wherein he drops the dualistic conception of cognition as mirroring and begins to clarify an implicit (if incomplete) conception of cognition as intention that he can profitably deal with the conception of will (and also of belief, which James thinks of as a kind of volition). As John Wild aptly points out, James is a *noetic* voluntarist—not a voluntarist pure and simple.[88]

James writes of belief: "It resembles more than anything what in the psychology of volition we know as consent."[89] It is a matter of affirming what is thought about—saying yes to it. For him, some selecting, some choosing, some incipient affirmation is always at work in cognition, and the *inhibition* of that final affirmation of bona fide belief stands more in need of explanation than its occurrence. Affirmation is naturally attractive; it is the normal thing. In a synoptic and crucial passage, James writes:

> *The primitive impulse is to affirm immediately the reality of all that is conceived.* When we do doubt, however, in what does the subsequent resolution of the doubt consist? It either consists in a purely verbal performance, the coupling of the adjectives 'real' or 'outwardly existing' (as predicates) to the thing originally conceived (as subject); or it consists in the perception in the given case of *that for which these adjectives*, abstracted from other similar concrete cases, *stand*. But what these adjectives stand for, we now know well. They stand for certain relations (immediate, or through intermediaries) to ourselves. Whatever concrete objects have hitherto stood in

Phenomenology 179

those relations have been for us 'real,' 'outwardly existing.' So that when we now abstractly admit a thing to be 'real' (without perhaps going through any definite perception of its relations), it is as if we said "it belongs in the same world with those other objects.". . . All remote objects in space or time are believed in this way. When I believe that some prehistoric savage chipped this flint, for example, the reality of the savage and of his act makes no direct appeal either to my sensation, emotion or volition. What I mean by my belief in it is simply my dim sense of a *continuity* between the long dead savage and his doings and the present world of which the flint forms part. It is pre-eminently a case for applying our doctrine of the 'fringe.' When I think the savage with one fringe of relationship, I believe in him; when I think him without that fringe, or with another one (as, e.g., if I should class him with 'scientific vagaries' in general), I disbelieve him. The word 'real' itself is, in short, a fringe.[90]

We think of the savage as the being who used this flint which we now can feel and hold in our hands. We think of him as real (and believe him to be so), because we think him in the fringe of the flint. We affirm him to have been real because we think of him as a being who existed in the very same world which "stings" us with interest and affirmation now.[91]

James gives us here his consummate expression of the doctrine of fringe, and it supplies evidence for phenomenologists' assertion that he hit on the idea of the *Lebenswelt*. The point is that James is not giving us a causal analysis of cognition. He does not attempt to predict our belief in the savage's reality by deducing the occurrence of a psychical event from premises relating to stimulating objects in the environment and causal connections in the brain. No doubt he believed that such causal chains do occur. But he sensed that before we can talk, say, of an object in space that emits energy which impinges on our organism, we must first know what we *mean* by space and reality; indeed, these needs dovetail with one another: not only must we know what we mean by space and reality before we can talk technically about them, but we must know what we mean by them before we can talk about *the psychic event* we hope to predict; i.e., the psychical event (in whatever sense it is an event) is specifiable only in terms of that which is known by it, or at the most basic level imaginable, of the whole lived-world. The meaning of "real" is founded in the most encompassing of all fringes, i.e., the sense of the world as a spatial and temporal whole which includes me as being among other beings. To lose the sense of the *Lebenswelt* as the founding level of meaning would be disastrous for psychology, for James surely implies that psychology without the *Lebenswelt* has no valid basic conceptions with which to begin.

In comparing James to the heterodox phenomenologist Martin Heidegger, Walter Cerf has written:

> The rumor is that Heidegger is one of "those deep and obscure German metaphysicians." His books belong indeed to the hardest reading in philosophy. None the less, it is William James, the lucid, Anglo-Saxon William James who, among all modern philosophers, seems to me to be one of the closest spiritual associates of Heidegger. Not William James the pragmatist, rather the William James of the *Principles of Psychology*. Not William James in any definite position on which you may pin him down; rather William James in his most fervent inner tendency which was, I believe, directed towards a new concept of man, a new and fresh insight into what man is, a tendency led forward by the dissatisfaction with the traditional horizons in which the self-understanding of man is moving, those traditional horizons being the concept of substance, force, act, consciousness, and so on. It is this tendency towards a new insight into the essence of man which William James and Heidegger have in common, and which ranges them, I am convinced, among the thinkers most pregnant with the life of a new era.[92]

For Heidegger, as for most phenomenologists, a man is understandable only as a being-in-the-world, and the world itself is understandable only if we begin at least with the conception of it as it is ordinarily lived by a man, the *Lebenswelt*. The "fervent inner tendency" in James's *Principles* is a tendency in just this direction, and so it is not quite the case that one can find "no definite position on which you can pin him down." True, James's position is not as clear as a commentator would like, but precisely because James is not "lucid." In spite of the racy surface of his style, he is often an obscure and head-cracking writer. It is not hard to understand why he had such strong appeal for major thinkers like Husserl, Dewey, Bergson, and the later Wittgenstein, and why he is so often cavalierly dismissed by thinkers of lesser rank.

VI

Let us try to get a clearer view of James's relationship to phenomenology, and let us focus in a summary way on the central thinker in the phenomenological movement, Edmund Husserl. If one can be sure of anything about Husserl, it is that he did not intend to do empirical psychology. He intended to discover a "new *a priori* science."[93] He intended to discover what is logically prior to any empirical assertion about matters of fact, i.e., what must be understood before any empirical assertion is completely understandable. By "completely" is meant a total rational reconstruction of our ordinary empirical knowledge of the world (he would never deny that we have such knowledge).[94] Certainly we know such and such, Husserl would say. Now the question arises, how is it *possible* to know that? First and foremost, it is possible to know that only if we can mean that. The question then arises, how is it possible to mean that or—in Husserl's language—intend that? It is as if the ordinary direction of the mind were reversed; Husserl emphasizes that his philosophical investigation goes against the natural grain of the mind. Instead of saying we know such and such—now what else can we go on to know? Husserl says we know such and such—now how was that possible? And he is not asking for an evaluation of the empirical evidence on which the knowledge claim is made, for then he would ask how it is possible to intend anything as empirical evidence.

For Husserl, it is possible to have knowledge only because there are basic presuppositions involved in knowledge. These presuppositions are exposed and grasped only through an extraordinary or "reversed" method of investigation; it is, he says, a transcendental method.[95] A similarity to Kant's procedure is unmistakable, and he admits that there is an "inner affinity" to the *Critique of Pure Reason*.[96]

The presuppositions which Husserl claims to discover consist of meanings (*Sinne*) or essences (*Wesen*) and also of connections between meanings (which he calls connections of essential necessity). In either case they can be asserted in the form of a priori necessary truths—truths independent of future experience. Indeed, experience can be seen to be possible only when such truths are presupposed, thus no experience could happen which conflicts with them. What is the evidence of such truths? Simply an intellectual "seeing" which is an exhibition of thinkability. An essence or a connection of essences is intuited to be what it is, and intuition is capable of discerning necessary truths on the basis of self-evidence alone, because intuition is simply that which gives its own object (*Selbstgebung*); i.e., intuition is specified in only one way, thus that way must be the correct one.[97]

Let us cite one of Husserl's examples of a transcendental exposition of a priori presuppositions of knowledge. We are interested in only the broad outlines of his method, for Husserl's relationship to James is illuminating only when we adhere to broad outlines and ignore details (no matter how significant such details are in their own right). Take Husserl's example of looking with pleasure at a blossoming apple tree. Only a philosopher of some sort would doubt that any such tree is there, but Husserl is not of this sort. As Quentin Lauer has put it, Husserl identifies the true critique of cognition with the intentional (meaning) constitution (or reconstruction) of naïve objectivity.[98] He takes the point of departure for all transcendental exposition to be the "natural point of view," i.e., that there are numerically identical things existing in a common world which various knowers can know.[99] But though the natural point of view, as so defined, is the starting point for the transcendental exposition, it is necessary to nip in the bud the further elaborations of it that have become so "natural" to us twentieth-century thinkers dominated by natural science. Because of our sophistication (or quasi-sophistication) in physics and physiology it is "natural" for us to go ahead and think that the perceived, the tree, is one real thing, while our perception is another (a psychical "state"), and that between them real causal relations exist. But such causal relations are not phenomenally given; what we do, usually before we know it, is to contaminate what is thus given, the "pure dator intuition."

To avoid this, Husserl proposes that we "bracket" all affirmations of, or beliefs in, the empirical world. We do not cease to believe that the apple tree is really there, we merely become aware of our belief as a belief. The bracket does not cut out the belief and send it falling into discard, nor does it constrict it in any way; it merely delineates it; it helps to remind us that we *are* believing. This reminder is necessary, Husserl thinks, because of our "natural" tendency to overlook the act of knowing in the glare of the fact known—our tendency to be so close to the act of knowing (to "live in it") that we forget it and become absorbed in what is known by it. After all, it is only natural to do so, only natural to be practical and to find our way in the world—only natural to be absorbed in a world which clamps contingencies on us.

Husserl proposes that we look *at* what we ordinarily look *through*. He does not intend that reality be truncated or obscured. On the contrary, he intends that it be exposed and clarified. We do not cease to believe that the tree is real. Just the reverse, our belief in its reality is exposed, clarified, and saved from a contaminating admixture of theoretical speculation. The tree remains just as it presents itself: as a tree really believed to be really there—it remains as "reality phenomenon."[100] That the particular tree may not be real is true but irrelevant; that it appears to be real and is believed to be real is true, certain, and relevant. Because we do not make the *simple* affirmation of the tree's existence, Husserl wants to say that we do not affirm its existence. What the philosopher does is to become aware of his affirmation; the affirmation itself is the focus; only in this sense he does not *make* the affirmation. He no longer "lives in" the belief—so it is a bracketed or modified belief, not a simple one. Belief is not discarded.

According to Husserl, this bracketing is necessary to expedite the transcendental exposition of that which makes cognition possible. It enables us to become aware of exactly what we mean in an act of cognition. In stepping outside the belief (or positing) aspect of an act of cognition we modify it and are enabled to see the meaning (intending or constituting) aspect in its fullness. Husserl relies on the very distinction in Brentano which James acknowledges: that between mere thought and belief; also the doctrine that belief presupposes thought. Husserl claims that bracketing the belief exposes the presuppositions embedded in the thought qua sheer meaning-aspect; and as they are exposed within the bracket they reveal themselves as necessary truths. Within the bracket there can be no doubt about what we intend and how we intend it, because we are concerned with the intended object *only insofar as it is intended*, not with whether it actually exists in the world. Of course, *if* the object does exist—if we discard the bracket and *simply* affirm the object's existence—then *what* it is can be no other than what we intend it to be. This is nothing but an elaboration of Aristotle's doctrine of the formal identity of thought and thing known. As Pierre Thévenaz put it,

. . . the world, in this new perspective, "is not an existence but a simple phenomenon," it is a signification. Let us not imagine then two spheres which divide the whole of reality: the natural world and the transcendental field, which would be like a metaphysical ulterior world [*arrière-monde*] susceptible in turn of being described, grasped, known as a second nature. There is only one world . . .[101]

When we see in its fullness the meaning-aspect of the perception of the apple tree, what exactly, according to Husserl, is revealed? Though we see nothing of an empirical or causal relation between perception and perceived, within the bracket we do see a definite relation between them. We have not lost any meaning-content qua meaning-content; on the contrary, the meaning-content is now revealed.[102] The perception is still a perception *of* "this apple tree in this garden," and so on. What is perceived is the "perceived as such" (*noema*), and we see with "essential necessity" that part of what we *mean* by the perception (*noesis*) is that it is a perception *of* this very "perceived as such." We are concerned only with essence, not existence. The "perceived as such" belongs to the perception inseparably—it belongs to its meaning. The tree plain and simple can burn away, but the meaning of this perception (object, *noema*) belongs necessarily to its essence; it cannot burn away. It might be said that in one sense of "meaning" our meaning is just that physical tree itself, and it can burn away. But Husserl would reply: you forget the bracket. Within the bracket we intend the tree as something that can burn away, and *that* intention cannot burn away. Husserl would also say, I think, that we intend the tree as something that we might be mistaken about, but *that* intention we cannot be mistaken about. The object of the intention cannot be thought away from the experience without the experience itself being discarded: it makes the experience what it is.

Whatever cannot be thought away from the experience passes into the essence and is separated from all physics and physiology by "an unbridgeable gulf." It follows that psychology cannot rely on these sciences to supply the meaning of its mentalistic terms; nor can it rely on traditional introspection which is really nothing more than an odd and mistaken sort of empirical investigation; psychology can rely only on a transcendental exposition of the act of cognition. Thus Husserl conceives of transcendental phenomenology as a necessary propaedeutic to empirical psychology.[103]

Phenomenology

Husserl employs the method of "free variation" to determine what cannot be thought away from an act of cognition and thus to determine what belongs to its essence. He also calls this "fictive variation," for it is a matter of thinkability, and this is closely akin to supposability or imaginability. He concludes that there are limits to variability in the case of perception, say. Employing the intentional object (in this case the "perceived as such") as a "transcendental clue" (*Leitfaden*), he concludes that the intentional object must always be presented perspectively if it is to be the intentional object of perception. That is part of what we *mean* by perception, then. That *too* is part of what we mean by "thing."[104] He attempts to link *noema* to *noesis* in connections of essential necessity; this, in general, is an attempt to link modes of being to modes of being presented, and conversely. Moreover, a perceived as such (the apple tree, say) does not exhaust the *full* noema. It is only a nucleus which can be connected with essential necessity to a nexus or context of noematic phases; for example, since the tree presents itself perspectively it *must* present itself in space—that is its essence, it is that *kind* of thing. This holds though there should be no longer any trees to stimulate our sense organs.

In sum: Husserl does not bracket the world because he is uninterested in it. Precisely the reverse. He brackets it in the attempt to become fully aware of what he means by it.[105] He maintains that scientists and ordinary men actually do employ meanings (or essences) and connections between them, but working *with them* they are so close to them that they take them for granted and grow oblivious to them; needless to say they do not work *on them*, as he proposes to do.[106] Begin, Husserl recommends, with the ordinary experience of an apple tree, say, and then ask how this experience is possible. It is possible only because we employ meanings or essences like "physical object," "object," and "existence." But what exactly is it that we are employing? What is the essential structure of the essences as well as the structure of their essential connections, and what is their essential connection to the evidence appropriate to objects which instance these essences—in this case perception? Modes of being are linked essentially to modes of being given, and modes of being given are linked essentially to modes of consciousness. The generic mode of consciousness is intentionality itself; specific modes, like mathematical reasoning for example, are determined by the essential nature of the particular intentional objects of that mode—in this case numbers. Empirical psychology is quite unable to rule on these matters. It is the bipolar relationship of subject and object which is transcendentally fundamental, not object or subject by itself.

What else does Husserl tell us about the method of inquiry peculiar to transcendental investigations? First and foremost, these essences and essential connections are real or "experimental"—and, as he writes, they are "previous to all deduction."[107] They can be discovered only by a bracketing of ordinary experience, and ordinary experience is logically prior to any formal or deductive system—prior to the mathematization of space, time, and meaning itself. For how do we know what to begin with—how do we know what to mathematize? Essential connections, then, on the phenomenological plane, are necessarily the case—but they are *not deductively* so. For example, since the apple tree presents itself perspectively it *must* present itself in space; this is an inference, but not a deductive one. Consonant with this, William Kneale, the British philosopher and historian of logic, characterizes phenomenology as "The non-formal study of necessary truths."[108]

Now what on earth does this have to do with William James? It is just James's intent in the *Principles of Psychology* to do empirical psychology and nothing else, a fortiori not logic of any transcendental sort. Yet in regard to James's view of the fundamental or "native" character of our experience of space, James Edie has recently written:

> James's "nativism" seems to have been an original attempt to elucidate the "transcendental" pre-conscious structures of lived perception with which phenomenology has made us familiar. It is not a question here of "innate" forms or ideas, structures of the perceiving *subject*, but rather a question of certain "open" structures which arise *in* experience . . . While he was . . . wary of "transcendentalism," it is because he knew only Kant and Hegel.[109]

Though Edie does not document this remark, I think it is very perceptive, and that it can receive salient documentation from the *Principles*.[110]

Indeed, it could be said that our whole study up to this point supplies documentation. We have seen repeatedly how James's intent to write an empirical psychology replete with contingent

Phenomenology

statements of fact and contingent causal laws is repulsed, and how in spite of his intentions his inquiry takes a strange backward turn suspiciously like the transcendental turn. As things actually transpire, he cannot specify mental states unless he specifies what the mental state is *of*, and he cannot specify what it is *of* unless he specifies the whole lived-world in which the intended topic finds its place. He is drawn backward into an excavation of presuppositions. Moreover—though we have had to make the explicit inferences and extrapolations ourselves—his actual findings indicate that these presuppositions are connections of meanings which permit an expression in the form of necessary truths: e.g., "Thought A is thought *of* A'," and "A' is something in space."

Note the following fundamental passage in which James asserts that when we name a sensation, we identify a place in space:

> But to the end of time certain places of the world remain defined for him as the *places where those sensations were;* and his only possible answer to the question where *anything is* will be to say 'there,' and to name some sensation or other like those first ones, which shall identify the spot. Space *means* but the aggregate of all our possible sensations. There is no duplicate space known *aliunde* or created by an 'epoch-making achievement' into which our sensations, originally spaceless, are dropped. They *bring* space and all its places to our intellect, and do not derive it thence.
>
> By his body, then, the child later means simply *that* place *where* the pain from the pin, and a lot of other sensations like it, were or are felt. It is no more true to say that he locates that pain in his body, than to say that he locates his body in that pain. Both are true: that pain is part of what he *means by the word body*. Just so by the outer world the child means nothing more than that place where the candle-flame and a lot of other sensations like it are felt. He no more locates the candle in the outer world than he locates the outer world in the candle. Once again, he does both; for the candle is part of what he *means* by the 'outer world.'[111]

James is giving us connections of meanings, or connections of concepts qua concepts! He is asserting in effect that we cannot identify a sensation of pain, say, without identifying where it is felt (what it is *of*) in the body. And this is only to assert (and he does assert it): "that pain is part of what he *means by the word body*." Likewise he is asserting in effect that we cannot identify the object which the sensation is *of* without identifying it as having a location in, and being a part of, the outer world. And this is only to assert (and he does assert it): "the candle is part of what he *means* by the 'outer world.'"

But we must note carefully that James does not draw from this state of affairs—these connections of meanings—the conclusion concerning necessary truths which would seem to follow. If pain is part of what one means by the word "body," then it would follow that the statement "pain is felt in the body" is a necessary truth, since one could never speak of pain without implying that the pain is felt in the body. Likewise, if the candle is part of what one means by "outer world," then it would follow that the statement "the candle is in the outer world" is a necessary truth, since again one could never speak meaningfully of (real) candles without implying that the candle is in the outer or spatial world; the linkage of subject and predicate must always be assertable; thus the assertion must be necessarily true.

It is because James fails to draw this conclusion concerning necessary truths—a conclusion that is implicit within his own discoveries—that he fails to make the decisive shift which would once and for all lift his inquiry from the empirical to the transcendental level, and which would clear the way for a new area of investigations. He points the way, I contend, but he does not follow through. Put another way, I think that James never fully accepts the *necessities* which his own discoveries place on him. He never faces squarely the *presuppositions* in which he involves himself; e.g., in order to assert something about a sensation one *must* be able to assert something definite about what the sensation is *of*.

We can speak of presuppositions in terms of logical conditions for the application of concepts. On the basis of James's own findings, he can speak meaningfully of "thought A" only when he has already spoken of its object as "A'." But he does not infer from this that some of the necessary conditions for applying the concept "thought A" (which we shall call "A") are the very necessary conditions for applying the concept "A'" (which we shall call "A'"). Because he does not infer this he also does not infer that A presupposes A'. And because in turn he does not infer the latter, he does not infer that the statement (S_1) "Thought A is thought of A'" must be a necessary truth.

The same sort of reasoning would hold in regard to James's

Phenomenology 189

assertion that "the candle is part of what he means by the 'outer world.'" It would follow from this that if one asserts something about a real object (in the fundamental sense of the word "real"), then one *must* be able to assert something definite about the world in which it finds its place. But, as before, James does not make the inferences that stand open to him. Therefore I see no reason to revise my conclusion that the latent strand in James's *Principles* is incomplete; that he indicates a region of transcendental investigations which he himself does not explore. Thus I accept Professor Edie's remark that James's "nativism" is "an original attempt to elucidate the 'transcendental' . . . structures of lived perception with which phenomenology has made us familiar" only after I have hedged it about with qualifications. Of course, I think that the remark is penetrating and worthy of the study which goes into its qualification.

It is as if James felt the backward pull of the transcendental investigation, but that he would not, or could not, admit it. So instead of concluding that one can profitably retrace one's steps (viz., expose one's presuppositions) only by first turning around, he walks backward into the "backwards investigation." Inevitably, he cannot see where he is going. He insists that he is simply reading off more facts—more contingencies.

There is a rich supply of examples. At that crucial point at which he invokes "the world of practical realities"—that which *in effect* supplies the founding level of meaning for his investigations —he speaks of it as if it just happened to be that way, as if it were just another matter of fact that might have been different. Recall that he writes:

> Each thinker, however, has dominant habits of attention; and these *practically elect from among the various worlds some one to be for him the world of practical realities.* From this world's objects he does not appeal.[112]

From this we could conclude that it is a mere matter of fact that most thinkers' habits of attention happen to be such that they do not in fact appeal to a level more basic than what we, the majority, call the world of practical realities. James writes simply that most people *do not* so appeal, not that they *cannot*. He might very well have added: This is a fact—insane people do appeal to a different world. But I would rejoin: Of course that is a fact about insane people, and that is precisely why we call them insane: we believe them to be out of touch with reality. I would go on to ask: Is this belief of *ours* a mere matter of fact that might itself have been different? I would reply in the negative, because we cannot even imagine what belief in another sort of reality would be like, unless we imagine that belief as different in a definite way from our belief in the world of practical realities; the latter belief is ever our base line for comparison; it is presupposed. We cannot really understand the question, might our belief have been different? unless we understand what it is different *from*. This seems to be the case because what we *mean* by reality is the world of practical realities which James tells us about. It seems to me that the real force of his own argument in the *Principles* tends to push us to an admission of necessities of thought; but it is an admission which he himself does not explicitly make.

James's attitude toward Kant is telltale in this respect. Recall the cavalier way he dismisses Kant's contention, "The *I think* must be capable of accompanying all our representations." James asserts that a possible thought is not a real thought at all, and that Kant is not talking about anything substantive. He seems completely oblivious to the transcendental point which Kant is here making. Kant is saying that if one asserts something about thoughts (or representations) then one *must* be able to assert something about a thinker of these thoughts. He is not saying that there are potential thoughts existing in a state of potency—whatever that might mean. He is not making a statement about existence at all, but one about transcendental logic.

It is not our intention to demonstrate that the particular statements Kant makes in the course of his transcendental investigation are all correct, but only to point out that James does not seem to grasp clearly and fully what Kant had in mind when he spoke of a transcendental inquiry. His criticism of Kant's notion of space is a case in point. He maintains that Kant's description of space as a form of intuition which intuits space as one infinite continuous unit is mistaken.[113] This is not verified by intuition, James alleges, for the appearance which we really intuit is not this way at all. What Kant calls an intuition is really a complex intellectual notion which flies in the face of the phenomena; it cannot therefore legislate for the phenomena.

Phenomenology

Now, in its way, I think this is a shrewd observation on James's part. It may be necessary for us to intuit things as being in space, as Kant maintains, but why should we agree with Kant that the space we must intuit things as being in is necessarily infinite, for example? Is it not possible that Kant's belief reveals a contaminating element of contingency in his transcendental investigation, i.e., the state of natural science (e.g., Newtonian mechanics) and geometry during Kant's time? I believe that the question must at least be considered.

James's observation may even cause us to reevaluate the form of Kant's transcendental inquiry. This inquiry takes as one of its transcendental clues the synthetic a priori propositions which Kant believed to hold in mathematics and pure natural science. These propositions are possible because they are actual, Kant thought; he went on to ask, following the transcendental clue, *How are they possible?*

> By a transcendental exposition I understand the explanation of a conception as a principle from which the possibility of other synthetic *a priori* cognitions can be discerned. For this purpose it is required, first that such cognitions do really flow from the given conception, and secondly that these cognitions are possible only on the presupposition of a given way of explaining this conception.[114]

Thus, for example, beginning with certain synthetic a priori truths of mathematics, Kant shows that they are possible only because they are "constructable" and presuppose an intuition of space. In showing this he thinks he gives a transcendental exposition and explanation, indeed a proof, *of that which is presupposed*. What we begin with is actual, therefore that which makes it possible *must* be the case.

James's observation may provoke us to reevaluate a point of departure of Kant's transcendental inquiries, which is the synthetic a priori truths of mathematics and pure natural science, as well as unacknowledged suppositions like "sensations" taken over from the science of the time. We may be further provoked by James's observation that the distinction between synthetic and analytic cannot be made clear, and that "*all* our great truisms are ampliative," not just those which Kant denominated as "synthetic *a priori*."[115] It is up to experience—not to formal studies and the like—to decide which necessary truths hold, James asserted.[116] In fact, this is probably one of those points at which he influenced Husserl (though Husserl is not specific); for Husserl criticizes Kant on exactly these grounds. He charges that his point of departure for his transcendental inquiry (and his transcendental clue—*Leitfaden*) is incorrect, and that it leads him to a conception of the a priori which is "merely formal."[117] Husserl wishes to be true to ordinary experience, and thus his battle cry "back to the things themselves."[118]

Despite all this, it does not seem to me that James ever fully grasped what is generic to any transcendental investigation; i.e., the radical turnabout and exploration of necessity which are characteristic of the rational reconstruction of knowledge. As another example, take his analysis of time:

> *The knowledge of some other part of the stream, past or future, near or remote, is always mixed in with our knowledge of the present thing.*[119]

He does not say *must* be mixed. He does not say that we *must* perceive the thing in a fringe of temporal relations—that being part of what we *mean* by a thing perceived to be real. He goes to great lengths to preserve the appearance of talking merely about contingencies: He mythologizes to the effect that God might have implanted a memory of the past in the consciousness of the first man at the first moment of his existence.[120]

What we find in James is a tacit and incomplete transcendental investigation, and I doubt that he would have identified it as transcendental at all because of the connotation of Kantianism. (He once asserted that the true line of philosophical progress lies not so much through Kant as around him.[121]) He does begin with the actuality of knowledge, not the dualistic "problem of knowledge" vis à vis the external world, and he is drawn, in spite of himself, into an investigation of what this knowledge involves in the way of basic meanings and their interconnections. But we are never sure of the force of the word "involves," nor *why* one meaning is connected with another. We are not given a method for finding out, and this method would have to be some sort of transcendental one. There is no decisive awareness of the transcendental question, knowledge is actual; granted—not how is it possible?—and thus there is no attempt to construct a method of inquiry

Phenomenology   193

which is appropriate to answering the question. As P. F. Strawson has written in regard to the specific transcendental question, how is knowledge of particulars possible?:

> It is not that on the one hand we have a conceptual scheme which presents us with a certain problem of particular-identification; while on the other hand there exist material objects in sufficient richness and strength to make possible the solution of such problems. It is only because the solution is possible that the problem exists. So with all transcendental arguments.[122]

The message here expressed is corroborated by James's intellectual toil, as we have amply seen: There is no use beginning with thought (or conceptual schemes), on the one hand, and a physical world full of particulars, on the other, and then asking how they can ever meet in a relationship of cognition. We must begin within that relationship itself and then see what it involves. James lives out the truth of the message but does not express it clearly, and because of this it is almost inevitable that he should fail to express it completely. We agree with Thévenaz that

> it is a fact of history that the great initiators seldom know very well themselves what they are doing when they launch their new method . . . we think of Galileo and his fumbling attempts to state his "scientific method."[123]

As it happens, the quotation from Strawson is particularly appropriate because it focuses on an important omission in James's account. The transcendental problem of particular-identification is exceedingly acute in James. For example, do we know thoughts to be particulars? If so, how? What do we mean by a particular? What are the logical conditions for the application of the concept "particular"—thus what must we presuppose about them? Are pains particulars? If they are, is it then the case that they differ essentially from physical-object particulars? Could it be that one of the criteria for the identification of any sort of experience is that it be numerically distinct from its intentional object? Or could it be that experiences of any sort are distinct from physical objects of any sort because we do not identify the former as numerically identical with what someone else can talk about, while we do identify the latter as such? All these questions turn out to be central in James, and he does not give them adequate attention. As is typical in his case, he simply writes:

The judgment that *my* thought has the same object as *his* thought is what makes the psychologist call my thought cognitive of an outer reality.[124]

We never learn the force of the term "makes." For all we can tell, things just happen that way.

The central piece missing in the Jamesian puzzle is what phenomenologists and linguistic analysts have come to call, in our century, informal logic. James is a "great initiator," to use Thévenaz's phrase: There is enough of the puzzle present to enable us to see what is missing. Despite his notable disagreements with Kant, he is pursuing the same essential theme: Those fundamental aspects of the world which we call philosophical are philosophically treatable only insofar as they are experienceable in determinate ways. What *must* experience be like if it is to be experience at all? Take, for example, Kant's demonstration that experience must be structured by the categories. This demonstration shows how each category must apply, given the essential temporality of experience. Kant calls it a "deduction," but as Father Copleston has pointed out, it is not really a deduction at all.[125] It is akin to that phenomenological reasoning which Husserl says to be "previous to all deduction," and he goes on to say that in the first edition of the first *Critique* Kant "already moves strictly on phenomenological ground; but . . . misinterprets the same as psychological, and therefore eventually abandons it of his own accord."[126] James is also concerned with the structure of experience, but instead of misidentifying the method of its discovery as "deduction," he fails to specify the method at all. He *does* something, however: he begins to touch the rock bottom of specification, and in so doing he feels his way toward fundamental connections of concepts—or what Husserl would call essences. It is understandable that Husserl should acknowledge James's influence on his thought and should in particular credit him with helping him to throw off psychologism.

Although Husserl is not more specific in his allusions to James, it seems likely that he is referring more to his anticipations of necessary truths within the latent strand of the *Principles* than he is to his explicit treatment of them in the last chapter of the *Principles*. It is true, of course, that we find an attack on psychologism in this lengthy last chapter. James denies that necessary

Phenomenology 195

truths are generalizations from experience which can be explained by the empirical order of that experience in conjunction with an empirical account of the psychological processes of abstracting, generalizing, and habituation.

> *There are then ideal and inward relations amongst the objects of our thought which can in no intelligible sense whatever be interpreted as reproductions of the order of outer experience.*[127]

The structure of necessary truth pertains to the *objects* of thought. This is only what should be expected in the light of the whole development of the *Principles:* the locus of importance shifts from the psychical to the cognitive aspect of thought, and the latter cannot be divorced from the object of thought (No. 3). When we intend something in the world we intend it in terms of "permanent and fixed meanings, ideal objects or conceptions"; just how we come into possession of such a stock of meanings (James is inclined to attribute it to the congenital structure of the brain), though an interesting question, is irrelevant to the structure of that which is *meant*.[128] He writes:

> In chapter XII we saw that the mind can at successive moments *mean the same*, and that it gradually comes into possession of a stock of permanent and fixed meanings, ideal objects, or conceptions, some of which are universal qualities, like the black and white of our example, and some, individual things. We now see that not only are the objects permanent mental possessions, but the results of their comparison are permanent too. The objects and their differences together form an immutable system. *The same objects, compared in the same way, always give the same results;* if the result be not the same, then the objects are not those originally meant.[129]

It is not conceivable that a future experience would invalidate the necessary truth (the "principle"). "Instead . . . of correcting the principle by these cases, we correct the cases by the principle."[130] He proceeds to talk of the system of ideal objects which is mathematics:

> That confident tone is due to the fact that they deal with abstract and ideal numbers exclusively. *What we mean* by one plus one *is* two; we *make* two out of it; and it would mean two still even in a world where *physically* (according to a conceit of Mill's) a third thing was engendered every time one thing came together with another. We are masters of our meanings . . .[131]

Necessary truths pertain to relationships between ideal objects, and they arise because the "presented order of experience is broken" and comparisons between ideal objects are made.[132] Ideal objects are linked in series which transcend the spatiotemporal order of experience. James asserts that the "axiom of skipped intermediaries" seems "to be on the whole the broadest and deepest law of man's thought";[133] it is the basis of rationality.[134] For example, as in logic, if a thing belongs to a kind (an ideal object[135]), then of necessity it belongs to the kind's kind; the intermediary kind is skipped, and of necessity the connection holds.

But James's account of logic in the last chapter of the *Principles* is quite definitely formal and deductive. As sketched by him, logic involves an act of abstraction from the stream of experience and an explicit comparison within a structure which features the traditional logical constants in pivotal roles. First and foremost, it is the structure of the categorical judgment with its copula "is" which supplies a paradigm of logic. A logical argument is a sequence of such judgments.

> But we never say that it is an M without M's properties; for by conceiving a thing as of the kind M I mean that *it shall* have M's properties, be of M's kind, even though I should never be able to find in the real world anything which is an M. The principle emanates from my perception of what a lot of successive is's *mean*.[136]

It is not at all clear how this conception of logic throws light on the validity of statements based on observations (like James's own) to the effect that, "Space *means* but the aggregate of all our possible sensations," and "The candle is part of what he *means* by 'outer world' "; if this is the case then certain concepts are linked with necessity, and necessary truths appear. But the linkage of these concepts has nothing to do with an explicit act of comparison nor with the meaning of the word "is." It has to do with the meaning of "sensation," "object," "outer world," and so forth. It would seem that although James involves us in a kind of informal logic, when it comes to an explicit discussion of logic, he has nothing to tell us about it. For this reason we think that Husserl may have been more interested in James's chapter on reality than he was in the one on necessary truths.

It is interesting to note in this connection what Gilbert Ryle has said about the differences between formal and informal logic.

Phenomenology

Whether meaning to or not, Ryle throws light on the distinction Husserl made between formal studies and studies of the connections of "experimental essences" (or senses).[137] Ryle maintains that the formal logician is mainly interested in the logical powers of "topic neutral expressions" like "not," "some," "all," "a," "is."[138] By "topic neutral" he means that if all except such expressions were deleted from a manuscript the reader could not tell what is being talked about. On the other hand, the informal logician is concerned with the logical powers of expressions which are not topic neutral—like the concept of *seeing*, say. (Why not the concept *perspiring* as well? Because "the former is charged with paradoxes and the latter is not."[139]) Noting that philosophically relevant, nontopic-neutral expressions cannot be dealt with in a formal system, Ryle writes:

> They can, for the most part, be the hinges of legitimate and illegitimate inferences; there are parities of reasoning between inferences pivoting on one of them and inferences pivoting on some others of them; but there is, ordinarily, no way of extracting from them some implicit logical constant or web of logical constants to be credited with the carriage of those inferences.[140]

It is instructive to observe that, in Ryle's terms, it is precisely the logical power of a topic-neutral expression—"is"—which concerns James in his explicit discussion of necessary truths; thus James is there concerned with formal logic only.

One reason why James does not discuss the logic of his basic terms like "sensation" and "space"—though there are doubtless other reasons as well—is that he reverts to the manifest program of his work in key passages of his last chapter. Logic arises, he thinks, only when the spatiotemporal order of experience is broken. This order simply "stamps copies" of itself on the mind. Here, he declares, the associationists are right: the internal relations of the mind follow passively the external relations of the environment. "Here the mind is passive and tributary, a servile copy, fatally and unresistingly fashioned from without."[141] In other words, James has here lost his grip on his own insight, expressed in his critique of Helmholtz, that the cognitive relationship is no less fundamental and difficult to understand in the cognition of spatiotemporal sequences than it is in any other kind of cognition. He forgets that conception and intention must always be at work. It is a lapse which conflicts with his own tendency, elsewhere expressed, to accept and develop Kant's notion that a conception is a synthesis of actual and *possible* sensations. We can only agree with him that we learn from sequences of experience that heat melts snow and fishes die on land; still, how could we know snow at all, say, if we did not know it as the *kind* of thing which appears perspectively?[142] This would hold even though it should happen that snow did not melt, or that it melted today in the heat of the sun and did not melt tomorrow in the same heat. Instead of breaking the order of presented experiences, why do we not look for necessary truths *in* the order? We could assent to such truths without denying any empirical fact—e.g., snow might not melt tomorrow, but it would still present itself perspectively in space. But James is so interested in showing the independence of necessary truths from the contingent order of presented experience that he does not look for necessary truths within the order itself, e.g., truths which pertain to kinds of presentations (perhaps distinguished according to sequence) of definite kinds of objects. For example, we would particularly like to know how pain presents itself in contrast to the way a billiard ball or a snowflake presents itself. One cannot get all the way around a pain as one can a billiard ball; the pain is stuck, as it were, in the corner of one's being; that may be a part of its oppressiveness.

In sum, James simply asserts that the world of practical realities is the base line of all our thinking, the irreducible context of meaning. He does not assert that it *must* be so, and because he does not he cannot be termed a transcendental phenomenologist—at least not without qualification.

But there may be advantages to James's approach as well as disadvantages. Perhaps something is missed when the bracket is always focal. Interestingly enough, the bracket is not found in *existential phenomenologists*, and some good reasons for its absence may be suggested by reading James.

Martin Heidegger maintained in his earlier writings that the Being of human existence is care, and that this gives us some clue to Being qua Being. Husserl sometimes examined interest and care phenomenologically, but (with the possible exception of his very last work) only within the field of disinterestedness—the bracket. It is at least a provocative question whether the Husserlian account

Phenomenology

of Being ("a sense for consciousness") is entirely adequate. We should even ask whether Husserl's notion of essence is adequate. James states unequivocally that the essence of a thing—*what* it is—is just a matter of its most important characteristics;[143] and importance would seem to be inconceivable apart from the concerned and active being: man—the only being that can find things important and know that he does so. As James put it, interest is the a priori element in cognition.

It is just here that Husserl may be lacking. Of course, he would say that the bracket can be expanded to include the whole existential relationship of man and world. But he can say that the bracket can include everything only because he assumes that all acts of mind are in principle reflectable. James, I think, would differ here, since he states that most of the stream of consciousness is gone forever once it passes, and that the reflecting observer picks up "only the crumbs which fall from the feast." Moreover, he liked to quote an aphorism of Kierkegaard's: "We live forward but understand backwards." This is telltale. The central fact of our existence for Kierkegaard is a geyser-like immediacy of consciousness which is intrinsically elusive because most of it slips through the meshes of inevitably subsequent reflection.

Now James agrees here, I think, and his agreement has provocative ramifications on which I speculate: If consciousness is not completely reflectable, then the active interest and concern which is in functional relationship to what things are would not be completely reflectable either. But then *what* things *are* would not be completely reflectable either. This would not mean that things are unknowable, but only that they are not completely knowable at any point in time (and I mean more here than that one cannot, say, look at all sides of a thing at once). Such speculation grates harshly against the whole rationalist tradition from Plato down through Husserl.

Because James construes essence somewhat differently from Husserl, he is a forerunner of existential as well as transcendental phenomenology. Recall his contention—amazing for a philosopher of the West—that our lives are in some respects really vague; we must not distort this vagueness through secondary reflections which "clarify" it all. At every waking moment of our lives there is a margin of things known vaguely. James wants to grasp the environment in which we actually live—that which shades off on all sides into the dense, opaque, and vague; that which lies in the corner of the eye. What presses on us all around is "the immediate push and pull of the cosmos"; either we apprehend it in primary, prereflective awareness or we do not apprehend it as it really is.[144] James has a knack for grasping it: for example, a negative moment of our experience when we feel that "just around the corner something is wrong." And we know there are other corners around which lie things which elude our awareness altogether. We intend the world as that which contains more than can be intended at any one time.

It is this sense of an overabounding world, too rich and fluid to be contained by any set of concepts—as truthful as that set might be—which sets James off from Husserl and which places him nearer to Heidegger and Merleau-Ponty. The idea that experience is overflowing one's concepts and pouring in all around them—that our concepts as we actually employ them in everyday life are insufficient to sop it all up—is one that is hard to imagine Husserl emphasizing. He is too fastidious and his notion of rationality too exalted.

For James the essence of a thing is its most important characteristics, and what is important about a thing cannot be understood in isolation from its relation to a finite human being's interests, needs, and purposes. He puts it tersely: *"This whole function of conceiving, of fixing and holding fast to meanings, has no significance apart from the fact that the conceiver is a creature with partial purposes and private ends.*[145] Essence—the *what* of a thing—must be understood teleologically; the interest and purpose of the knower is no mere psychological impertinence, no mere detail of a detached and worldless mind.[146] After the essence is gotten something is still left over.

> What is a *conception?* It is a *teleological instrument.* It is a partial aspect of a thing which *for our purpose* we regard as its essential aspect, as the representative of the entire thing . . . the essence, the ground of conception, varies with the end we have in view . . . Ueberweg's doctrine that the essential quality of a thing is the quality of most *worth* is strictly true; but Ueberweg has failed to note that the worth is wholly relative to the temporary interests of the conceiver. . . . If, without believing in a God, I still continue to talk of what the world "essentially is," I am just as much entitled to

define it as a place in which my nose itches, or as a place where at a certain corner I can get a mess of oysters for twenty cents, as to call it an evolving nebula differentiating and integrating itself. It is hard to say which of the three abstractions is the more rotten or miserable substitute for the world's concrete fullness. To conceive it merely as "God's work" would be a similar mutilation of it, so long as we said not what God, or what kind of work.[147]

All this can be put another way. James says that the present moment is the darkest in the whole series; darkest in regard to itself *and* to the world presented within it. And every moment of our lives is a present moment.

In sum, the idea of essence involves the idea of value. A thing *is* those characteristics that are most important to us as revealed under conditions of observability which are normal or optimum, *relative to us*. These conditions comprise a standard or ideal which cannot be understood apart from the cognitive relation of finite mind to world. But for James, despite his existential awareness of the overabounding richness of the ground of meaning, there can be no "thing in itself," if by that phrase is meant essentially unreachable and unknowable things in the world. His dualism still undergoes internal attack from both sides: the intrinsic referentialness of thought to world, and the intrinsic intendability of the world. We can say that a thing's essence is given in its fringe: what we *would* perceive under standard conditions of observability and manipulability.

Now, as Chauncey Downes has pointed out, the essence of a thing for Husserl is not something laid up in heaven, but is merely the thing's essential characteristics.[148] But we dare say that James makes this clearer. He is more existential in this respect than is Husserl. James makes us aware of the knower as a being-in-the-world who is forever concerned, choosing, valuing, and who is forever limited by his partial purposes and private ends. For Husserl the essence is just given to pure dator intuition; he gives us only a thin idea of how the essence is constituted, which is rather odd in a philosophy of constitution, as Harmon Chapman has pointed out.[149] In this respect I think that James's conception of essence is more adequate than is Husserl's.*

---

* But I would demand the privilege of explaining just what is meant by the "private ends" of the perceiver.

But what we find lacking in James is a full-scale connection of essences—essential necessities and necessary truths. The reason for this is that there is also lacking a clear-cut method for the discovery of such. His desire to be empirical precludes the admission of necessary truths on any level except that of the formal one of abstract reasoning. We need not think that Husserl's method of bracketing is the only applicable method, but we do need some tool for the exposure of basic connections of meaning, e.g., "sensation," "body," and "space." Above all, James needs to provide us with some method of exposing the connection between the act of thought and that which is thought about, the object. He attempts to construe the former (at least in part) in the phenomenal terms of one's own body, e.g., the "rolling up of the eyes" as in memory. There may be difficulties in this attempt; be that as it may, given the attempt, he must provide some method of discerning the connection between such phenomena of the body and that which is thought about. He admits that his account leaves such phenomena in an "atomized" and thus artificial form, but he provides no remedy. Part of the reason, of course, is that he never makes perfectly explicit the essential connection between act of thought and object of thought which is intentionality itself.

Since this general matter of the connection of act of thought and object of thought is never cleared up, it is unreasonable to expect that the more specific matter of the connection *within the act of thought* of the feeling of the body and imagery (e.g., the brownness of the green grass in the shadow) will ever be cleared up either. In fact it is not. We are left with two disconnected senses of "feeling" to cover the act of thought: as feeling of the body, and as feeling of the thing cognized in the world insofar as this feeling is relative to the bodily and sensory situation of the cognizer (imagery).

All in all, the concept of the act of thought is left in an egregiously unsatisfactory state in the *Principles*. We note in passing that this is not rectified in his later *Essays in Radical Empiricism;* if anything, it becomes worse. In the context of experiences which is mind we are never sure if James is talking about the act of thought (and bodily presentations such as breathing construed as part of the act) or about that which is thought about. For example, he says that breathing accompanies all our presentations. But

Phenomenology

surely we do not always think *about* our breathing. If we do, we are in trouble.

James's deficiencies in this area must be noted in order to forestall an error into which existential interpretations of him may fall. In becoming existential, phenomenology need not become non-transcendental, and this is particularly true of the most important existentialist of all, Martin Heidegger. True, the intentionality of *consciousness* is no longer referred to, but that of existence itself, and the internality of the relationship of existence to world, is the abiding assumption of the whole discourse. Moreover, no sense at all can be made of Heidegger's constant allusion to the ontological as opposed to the ontic nor to his employment of the existentialia of mood, understanding, and speech as the categories of existence unless the reader understands how Heidegger is rooted in Kant and the transcendental method.[150] Heidegger wishes to display the necessities which make experience possible.[151] The elements in James's account which prevent a transcendental phenomenology from coming to full bloom are among those which prevent an existential phenomenology from doing likewise.

The fact of the matter is that the phenomenological latent strand of the *Principles* never does completely supplant the manifest program of the work. James's failure to make internal relationships perfectly explicit introduces a vacillation and cluttering into his account which impedes the development of phenomenology.[152] Throughout the *Principles* one can find passages which suggest that mind is built up by a fabulous quasi-empirical process which then mirrors the "outer" world. James deserves an existential interpretation and an honest one.[153]

Notice the one passage in which James uses the word "intend" just as phenomenologists do, i.e., not in the popular, volitional sense of "intend to do something," but just "the mind intends something":

> All that a state of mind need do, in order to take cognizance of a reality, intend it, or be 'about' it, is to lead to a remoter state of mind which either acts upon the reality or resembles it. The only class of thoughts which can with any show of plausibility be said to resemble their objects are sensations. The stuff of which all our other thoughts is composed is symbolic, and a thought attests its pertinency to a topic by simply *terminating*, sooner or later, in a sensation which resembles the latter.[154]

First focus attention on his contention that mental states intend some reality by *leading* to a remoter state of mind which either acts on the reality or resembles it. It is not clear whether he means an *actual* leading which would occur if the cognizer acted on his thoughts and followed them out, or an expected or anticipated leading. In the work which follows the *Principles* he seems to suggest the former,[155] although the ambiguity is present even in the *Principles* itself in some passages.

Key difficulties in James's later work are traceable to this key vacillation and ambiguity in the *Principles*. In his later work he spoke of experiences as "flat," with one leading to the other very much like a contingent sequence of events.[156] Mind is simply one context of these experiences, but it is not clear how the relationships in this context (and thus the context itself) differ from the context which is the physical world. According to James, if we think about Memorial Hall, all that is happening is that a sequence of experiences is being initiated which, if followed out, would lead directly to Memorial Hall itself; our meaning is just that very building, i.e., what the sequence terminates in. This doctrine led to the charge that James was solipsistic, and it is not difficult to see why.[157] In the case of actually being led to the building, the difficulties inherent in the doctrine may be obscured; for in *one* sense of meaning, i.e., the topic or reference, the building itself truly is the meaning. But what if our thoughts of Memorial Hall lead us to a smoking pile of debris? Our experiences do not terminate in the building, yet we *do* know we were thinking about *it* and nothing else: if we cannot know that we were meaning it, then we cannot know that Memorial Hall has been destroyed, nor that we are now standing where it once was. James's occasional doctrine, it could be charged, not only cuts us off from physical reality but cuts us as well from our own future and past experience. It provides no basis for knowing what one has just meant or will mean; thus it could lead to a double-edged solipsism. And, incidentally, not only does being led to Memorial Hall fail to be a necessary condition for meaning it, but it fails as a sufficient condition as well. For if I fell into Memorial Hall from an airplane, we would not say that for *that* reason I was thinking about it. James was thus forced to admit in 1905 that in some sense thoughts are self-transcendent—that they are not "flat" but have a "point"—that they are like the "com-

Phenomenology

pass needle which points to the pole without stirring from its box."[158] This of course is *also* a position which is found in the *Principles:* the omnipresence of cognition—the view that thought is already about an Object, whether a real referent in the world is to be found or not for the topic which the Object may contain. The reason this view did not hold constant can only be that James did not bring the internality of the cognitive relation to a decisive and clear awareness.

In his later work James conceded that he sometimes had a "wavering opinion" on this matter of intention and meaning.[159] It seems to me that in his later work he sometimes confused meaning and truth.[160]

Let us also mention what seems to be another confusion in his later work, traceable to the same ambiguity and indecisiveness in the *Principles*. In his reply to the charge of solipsism in 1905, he makes clear that what he most objects to in "intellectualistic" theories is their practice of concluding that the meaning and value of a thought resides exclusively in what one can presently pin down about it and express. James declares that this self-conscious fixing blocks the flow of creative thought: let the thought be, he exhorts us, let it lead where it will, for it—and only it, perhaps—may lead to a brilliant thought.

Here again, as was the case with his assertion that the psychic aspect of a thought cannot be adequately introspected, I think that this is true—but irrelevant to the question of the meaning of the thought. Thus his assertion is more misleading than if it had been false. I do not deny that a vague thought (one whose Object is incompletely characterized) may be the only entrance to another thought which is clear and brilliant. But the first thought is distinct from the second, and its meaning must be just what it is. This is Aristotle again: thought, like seeing, is at any moment complete, and it is not a movement.

This need not involve us in a denial that all experience is temporal and that one experience does lead to another; indeed, how could we deny that experiences occur which are shocking and unexpected? James's own assertion is plausible:

> The knowledge of some other part of the stream, past or future, near or remote is always mixed in with our knowledge of the present thing.[161]

It may well be both that meaning arises only in a temporal flow and that it is sustained only in a network of relationships in which the temporal strand is ineluctable. But if this strand is present in the fringe, and if the fringe is present, then it is *anticipated* or *prospective* time. Moreover, it should be pointed out that James himself was one of the first to make theoretical room for anticipated time in his notion of the specious present. "The unit of composition of our perception of time is a *duration*,"[162] he writes, not a punctiform "now." Consequently, the future is already present in this small duration as the anticipated "not yet."

Probably Husserl was influenced by James on this point also. When he writes in *Ideen* of "retention" and "protention" as the primary dimensions of the time-sense,[163] he is echoing the following words of James's:

> These lingerings of old objects, these incomings of new, are the germs of memory and expectation, the retrospective and the prospective sense of time.[164]

And Husserl's idea of "meaning intentions" and "meaning fulfillments" may well reflect a Jamesian influence. Husserl points out that a meaning intention is conceptually tied to its fulfillment: we know what a sign marked "dip" means because we know what a dip in the road will be like if and when we come to it—time is of the essence, in a way. But what that way is is just the point: Husserl is quick to point out that not all meaning intentions actually have (or get) meaning fulfillments; some meaning intentions are never actually fulfilled—though they may be variously fulfillable.

Focus next on James's contention that a state of mind can intend a reality when it leads to a later state of mind which acts on the reality. Even in his later writing all that he may mean is that this may happen: in the case of speaking about thinking of the tigers in India he asserts that if we followed out the thought we would be led "into some ideal or real context, or even into the immediate presence, of the tigers."[165] What, pray, does he mean by an "ideal context"? If he only means that we *may* be led into the "real context" and *may* "act upon the real tigers," then he is in line with the scholastic dictum that a mental act produces a change in its object only *per accidens*. The point is simply that James is not

Phenomenology

perfectly clear on this all-important matter of the internality and necessity of the cognitive relation.

Consider finally his contention that a state of mind can intend a reality when it leads to a remoter state of mind which resembles the reality. This is the only case in which our thinking is not "symbolical," James says. First, we note that this conflicts with the implication contained in his attack on Helmholtz that *all* thought is symbolical.[166] Second, we note that he admitted that he had exaggerated the importance of resemblance in his earlier work.[167] It is particularly sensation which resembles the reality, according to James. Sensation involves no leading, for we are already there, so to speak; we do not "operate" on the topic using a conception as our "teleological instrument," for we "have" it—just as our "hands may hold a bit of wood and a knife, and yet do naught with either."[168] Recall that he also said that in the case of viewing under normal conditions the sensation "coalesces" with the reality. The word "coalesce" is a gross physicalistic metaphor redolent of the psychologist's fallacy.

All this adds up to the suggestion that in this passage at least sensation is construed nonintentionally by James. Sensation involves no leading, either actual or anticipated. Thus it is fringeless —outside an Object. Indeed, there is the added suggestion that sensation involves no sense of sameness and therefore it cannot involve conception, and thus even if conception is regarded as intention (as Linschoten wishes us to do) and intention as leading, sensation is again nonintentional. James writes in a closely related passage:

> . . . our mind may simply be aware of a thing's existence, and yet neither attend to it nor discriminate it, neither locate nor count nor compare nor like nor dislike nor deduce it, nor recognize it articulately as having been met with before. At the same time we know that, instead of staring at it in this entranced and senseless way, we may rally our activity in a moment, and locate, class, compare, count and judge it. There is nothing involved in all this which we did not postulate at the very outset of our introspective work: realities, namely *extra mentem*, thoughts, and possible relations of cognition between the two. The result of the thought's operating on the data given to sense is to transform the order in which experience *comes* into an entirely different order, that of the *conceived* world. There is no spot of light, for example, which I pick out and proceed to define

> as a pebble, which is not thereby torn from its mere time-and-space-neighbors, and thought in conjunction with things physically parted from it by the width of nature. Compare the form in which facts appear in a textbook of physics, as logically subordinated laws with that in which we naturally make their acquaintance. The conceptual scheme is a sort of sieve in which we try to gather up the world's contents. Most facts and relations fall through its meshes, being either too subtle or insignificant to be fixed in any conception. But whenever a physical reality is caught, and identified as the same with something already conceived, it remains on the sieve, and all the predicates and relations of the conception with which it is identified become its predicates and relations too; it is subjected to the sieve's network, in other words.[169]

Here he does not pause for a moment to consider the possibility that a "spot of light" can be "stared at" in even an "entranced and senseless way," only because it is recognized as the "same with something already conceived" in some respect. It need not be recognized as numerically the same as a previously seen spot, but it is formally the same as some other spot of light—or at least some other possible spot or some other possible light—or at the very least some other entity or quality. There may be some sense in saying that we can be aware of something without recognizing it articulately as the same as some other possible thing, but then we have to explain how inarticulate recognition is possible without the sense of sameness, and this he does not do. Here we find a gap dividing James from the tradition of intentionality and the key place which the sense of sameness, form, and essence occupies in that tradition.

We also note the pinching off of James's notion of conception in this passage. It becomes curiously abstract—as if he were talking about concepts as opposed to percepts.[170] But his thought will not allow any prolonged treatment of perceptions in terms of nonintentional sensational bits.[171] Accordingly, in his last book, he speaks of percepts as "the much at once"—the "field" at any moment, the whole world.

We find in these passages in the chapter on conception a tendency, previously noted, to think of sensations as if they were independent of the Object and fringe; a tendency to think of them independently of the cognitive relation—as if they were psychical existents which could be correlated straightaway (through resemblance) with physical existents. As such this is a relapse into the

Phenomenology

manifest program of the *Principles*. It bespeaks an attempt by James to detour around the Object and to forget his own observation that sensations are the results of a highly discriminating attention applied to the topic of an Object—a cognized thing in the world. (Either this or sensations are cognized as qualities that such things *could* have.) This tendency is an attempt to detour around the only bridge across the chasm of the subject-object relation; that it is the only bridge and that there is a chasm are facts which James's own text attests to. We have found no evidence to dissuade us from our position that the latent strand does not completely supplant the manifest thesis of the *Principles*.

Throughout the book the reader can find passages in which James attempts to specify mental states in isolation from the Object. He attempts to detour around the Object. He speaks of sensations as punctiform existents around which fringes are later embroidered.[172] As there are punctiform things in *rerum natura*, so there must be punctiform mental bits which know these things through a point-for-point, one-for-one sort of mirroring. Here remain remnants of dualism: There are two kinds of existents in the world, standing face to face, with one "known unto the other." It is an example of the psychologist's fallacy: confusing what the natural scientist knows about the being of particular things in nature (e.g., that they are atomic) with what the thought being studied knows; in effect, it amounts to the confusion of the being of particular things in nature with the being of the thought that knows nature, for what the thought knows, its Object, is decisive, as we have seen, in the specification of the being of thought—so far as it can be specified. It amounts to a forgetting of the initial grasp on nature through the Object which makes even the fallacy itself possible. In other words, it amounts to treating elements known only through knowledge as if they antedated knowledge and were the elements out of which knowledge had been constructed in some fabulous, quasi-empirical process.[173] In the most obvious way this is an example of James's forgetting his own observation that sensations are the *results* of a highly discriminating—or even idealizing[174]—attention.

There are other passages which exemplify the same sort of fallacy but which concern relations and processes of change known to take place in nature:

Some parts—the transitive parts—of our stream of thought cognize the relations rather than the things; but both the transitive and the substantive parts form one continuous stream, with no discrete 'sensations' in it . . .[175]

His assertion cannot even have surface credibility unless we limit the kinds of relations considered to temporal ones. (And perhaps this is just what he has done: his example of thunder's following silence is one of the few examples of relations he cites.) If we consider spatial relations, his assertion has no credibility whatsoever: my index finger is known as being smaller than my middle finger without my cognition of this state of affairs being any more "transitive" than my cognition of my index finger alone. His assertion has no credibility either when we consider, say, the relationship of an individual to the species it instances—and in talking about fringe as the characteristics of things known he invites us to consider all kinds of relationships. His assertion loses even its surface credibility when we recall his own dictum: the feeling of succession is not a succession of feelings.

He does consider another example: the relationship intended as Columbus-discovered-America-in-1492. He maintains that this cognition takes time and involves a transition. It is not a transition cognized as being in the thing itself cognized, but rather as being in the cognition of it. It takes time to think it. Now we might grant this, at least in regard to the psychical *aspect* of thought, to use James's own distinction. But if we do, we would also have to maintain that it takes time to look at my index finger, too. This, according to James, would be the cognition of a *thing*, and takes place in a substantive state. But if the cognition of Columbus' discovering America is a transitive state because it takes time to think it, so must the cognition of my finger be a transitive state because it takes time to look at it.

Yet James in some passages does not draw the inference. The only reason we can discover for this failure is that in these passages he attends exclusively to the changing imagery involved in thinking about (or saying) the business about Columbus, while the imagery involved when I look at my finger does not change, he wants to say. Surely this is an instance of attempting to specify thought independently of thought's Object—an attempt to specify

Phenomenology

it just on the basis of the thought "itself," the imagery. And, as surely, it is an instance of confusion. It would not have happened if he had concluded finally and decisively that the specification of thought is logically dependent on the specification of the Object. There is nothing in the intended Object of Columbus' discovering America in 1492 which determines that its cognition be transitive and changing while the intended Object of my finger determines its cognition to be a substantive state.

> Sensorial images are stable psychic facts; we can hold them still and look at them as long as we like.[176]

But if anything is stable it is the cognitive aspect of thought; the psychical or image-aspect comes closest to being constantly changing.

In view of his own latent strand of thought, James should just have said that meanings (fringes) are stable, and so are things meant as stable. He says the above because, in this passage, he has forgotten the Object; he attempts to detour around it in his account of cognition and to treat what is only an aspect, the psychical, as if it were the whole of mind.

VII

The Principles of Psychology is an important work at odds with itself. As we look back over it we discern the lines of internal struggle. On the one hand, we see the manifest thesis which attempts to treat thought as a psychical existent specifiable in its own terms, that is, independently of its Object, and which attempts to correlate this straightaway with a physical state of the brain. On the other hand, we see the latent strand: James's growing realization that he cannot correlate until he has specified, and his efforts at specification which land him in an involved and incompletely carried out analysis of thought's Object; the upshot of this is to throw him out into the lived-world and to cast doubt on the very notion of thought as a psychical existent. The traditional psychophysical dualism, whether it take the interactionist or parallelistic form, is imperiled; no correlation of existents seems to be possible. We face the prospect of a wholly different dualism—of analyses not of existents—a conceptual dualism. What must be correlated—in whatever sense of the word "correlation" is applicable—are two different analyses: the cognitive analysis of being-in-the-world and the causal analysis of the organism.

We have concluded that the tension between the two strands of the *Principles* is unresolved: the latent strand does not supplant the manifest thesis and then unroll in full development. It would not be true to say, however, that there is total confusion in the *Principles*. The latent strand is a tendency of thought which exhibits promising horizons for further development. What is more, a study of it throws light on some of the problematical passages of the *Principles* itself. Take the first chapter, which we regarded as problematical. We can see now why James dwells so little on mental states as psychical existents, and stresses the teleological nature of mind as that which seeks out goals within an environment. This is actually a portent of the latent strand which is to follow: mind can be discussed only in terms of worldliness, purposiveness, and intentionality. We encounter ourselves as beings-in-the-world.

Other passages, however, reveal a deadlock between the two strands. The most notable of these is James's famous theory of the emotions, too famous to my mind—Sartre and Merleau-Ponty give him credit for little else. I do not propose to examine this theory in detail, but only to the extent that it bears on my thesis that there are two opposing strands at work in the *Principles*. James's theory of the emotions has internal complexities all its own, and contains both virtues and vices which fall beyond the scope of our discussion. Besides, it is one of the topics in the *Principles* which has already received something approaching adequate attention from commentators.

The gist of James's theory is that the feeling of bodily disturbances *is* the emotion.[177] For example, a person does not run from a wild beast because he is afraid, but he is afraid because he runs (or flexes to run—incipient running). Immediately, with our study behind us, this strikes a chord of recognition: a "mental state" like an emotion is not a psychical existent; therefore it cannot cause a person to do anything. In the light of the latent strand we might expect something like this: We are beings-in-the-world engaged in projects; awareness of the body as phenomenon is central to our sense of self; the body is disturbed in definite ways when our projects are aided and abetted or when, on the contrary, they are blocked. Why may not joy, for example, be the full experience of success in our projects (which would include experiences of our body), and grief, say, the full experience of blockage and defeat?

But as we might expect in view of the fact that the two strands conflict and preclude a consummating development in either of them, James again regards the body in an "atomized" way. He had admitted that the body is felt *together with* the environing world, not alone; but he does not remain true to his own insight. He maintains that an emotion is only the feeling of a localized part of the body—like the stomach:

> We have, as Professor Lange says, absolutely no immediate criterion by which to distinguish between spiritual and corporeal feelings; and, I may add, the more we sharpen our introspection the more *localized* all our qualities of feeling become (see above, Vol. I, p. 300) and the more difficult the discrimination consequently grows.[178]

The reason why he maintains this is that he thinks he is here advancing a *causal theory* of emotions; after all, only one's own organism is the proximate cause of emotions, not the things in the environment.[179]

This is a clear example of the two strands blocking and entangling one another. James is sufficiently acute in the meaning analysis to see that an emotion, like any "mental state," cannot be specified in the traditional introspectionist terms of psychical existents: it must be specified as worldly. But this strand is blocked before it can attain completeness. It is blocked by his attempt to advance a causal theory. James maintains that problems of classification and description are the lowest stage of any science: "They sink into the background the moment questions of genesis are formulated."[180] But the obvious retort is that he has hurried away from "the lowest stage" before he has completed his necessary business there. He writes:

> . . . *any classification of the emotions is seen to be as true and 'natural' as any other*, if it only serves some purpose; and such a question as 'What is the 'real' or 'typical' expression of anger or fear?' is seen to have no objective meaning at all.[181]

This is cavalier because it does not consider an obvious rejoinder: The variousness of human emotions and the looseness of our classification of them make the problem of describing them not less important, but more so. Granted the conditions for the application of a term in psychology ("afraid," say) may not be as rigidly specifiable as they are in physics or physiology, this would only mean that concepts in psychology are open-textured and demand more, not less, care in their application.

It seems to me that James has mistaken what may be one necessary condition for the application of terms of emotion (i.e., bodily disturbance) for a complete set of necessary and sufficient conditions. Let us use James against James. How can we be emotional unless there is something we are emotional *about?* And how can we be emotional about something unless we *believe* something about the world? James leaves these considerations out of his account of emotions.

We see here the incompleteness of his account of intentionality and the worldliness of mind. To be more specific, we see the consequence of lumping both sensations and emotions under the exceedingly ambiguous phrase "feeling of the body." An emotion is a feeling of the body in quite a different sense from a pain or a pleasure. An emotion like fear refers beyond the body to what we are emotional about. We are not thinking about the palpitations of our heart or the sickening lump in our stomach when we face a wild beast; we are thinking about the *wild beast*—we believe it to be *there*. These are crude considerations, but basic; this is no time to think about the odd and subtle way in which lumps or pains may be intentional (e.g., when we are cold, the pain is not only there, in the body, but we huddle *against* a cold world). James's description of emotions seems quite inadequate, particularly in view of his own admission that when we perceive an emotion in isolation from its object it evaporates.[182]

We see here another intrusion into the meaning analysis by the causal. In order to do justice to the varieties of human emotion he is forced to postulate that the difference in emotion, however slight, correlates one to one with differences in bodily disturbances, however slight. He goes on to assert that all differences in bodily states are felt.[183] Again we note what we have before: the circularity in his criteria and the resulting deficiency in the meaning analysis. The question arises, What is the criterion for the occurrence of such a feeling of minute bodily change? If it

Phenomenology

is the nonverbal behavior of the subject, the criterion must be his display of emotion, which by hypothesis is his only behavior at the time. (Differences in bodily changes detected by an outside observer are not tantamount to the agent's feeling of them.) If this is so, then James is merely renaming the emotions "perceptions of bodily changes," and his theory, allegedly causal, loses its explanatory force. There must be ways of identifying a cause independently of its effect if our assertion about the cause is to be anything but a useless truism. On the other hand, if James's criterion is the verbal behavior of the agent—what he can say about himself—then his theory is patently false.[184] One of the bodily changes in fear is the increased secretion of the adrenal glands. According to James's theory, fear consists in part in the feeling of this secretion. But people felt fear, and knew it was fear, long before they knew about adrenal glands. Nowadays some of us can infer the state of our adrenals from the state of our feelings; but we infer the secretion from the fear, not the fear from the secretion. Of course, one can feel the adrenals without being able to speak of them, but the *equating* of this feeling with the emotions is not warranted.

James's theory of the emotions reveals as nothing else can the incompleteness and internal conflict of the *Principles*. It is evidence for Santayana's cruel but perceptive remark that James was "self-interrupted"—like a bird attached by a wire to a peg in the ground: the bird takes wing only to be jerked to a stop in mid-air.[185] But this is only evidence for James's own insight that he had a genius for allowing himself to be interrupted.[186] In this instance it is tragic, for his theory of the emotions undercuts his own intention to preserve the integrity of experience. He writes:

> But our emotions must always be *inwardly* what they are, whatever be the physiological ground of their apparition. If they are deep, pure, worthy, spiritual facts on any conceivable theory of their physiological source, they remain no less deep, pure, spiritual, and worthy of regard on this present sensational theory.[187]

But if an emotion is *nothing but* a feeling of bodily disturbances, if it tells us nothing about the quality of our world, how can we preserve and appreciate its "deep, pure, spiritual" nature? There is not a chance. It might be noted that he attempted to remedy this in his later work. In 1905 in "The Place of Affectional Facts in a World of Pure Experience," he writes that a feeling must be treated as an original or pure experience, and that it is sorted out into mental or physical only later, and only by virtue of particular purposes. Of affections:

> their ambiguity illustrates beautifully my central thesis that subjectivity and objectivity are affairs not of what an experience is aboriginally made of, but of its classification. Classifications depend on our temporary purposes.[188]

And again,

> The various pleasures we receive from an object may count as 'feelings' when we take them singly, but when they combine in a total richness, we call the result 'beauty' of the object, and treat it as an outer attribute which our mind perceives . . . Single sensations also may be ambiguous. Shall we say an 'agreeable degree of heat,' or an 'agreeable feeling' occasioned by the degree of heat?[189]

The whole point of this essay of 1905 is that affections, feelings, and emotions cannot be simply localized as can events occurring within the envelope of the skin. Our affections disclose the world to us. If I am full of joy then the world is joyous.

We all know the difference between tears of sorrow and tears of joy—a gulf as wide as nature divides them. But how similar the bodily disturbances! Indeed, this similarity may help to explain the strange similarities on the psychological level which have intrigued writers since the dawn of history. However, these similarities are strange precisely because of the gulf between the two kinds of tears which remains; there is still a *world* of difference.

This is a point which James the humanist would never miss. But James, the self-appointed natural scientist—tantalized by causal theory—certainly does miss it. And what are we to do with the *rationality* of emotions? The world supplies good reasons for many of our emotions; e.g., we feel disgust because things really are disgusting, but we do not learn about this quality in things by examining our own bodies—a bodily disturbance is immediately felt or learned about (at least usually)—while learning about things in the world may take time. What prolonged probing of the world and ourselves is often required to learn how we really feel about something or somebody. It is hard to imagine how the writer of "The Perception of Reality" could have neglected to see this.

EIGHT

Conclusion: toward philosophy of mind
and reconciliation of natural science
and phenomenology

W illiam James's *Principles of Psychology* raises more problems than it solves. But to raise a problem can be a contribution, and in this sense, as well as in others, I believe that James's work makes a major contribution to philosophy of mind and to the culture generally. Even his errors are important because they arise in connection with important problems and provoke new thought about them. As James Joyce once put it, the mistakes of genius are the portals of discovery. One commentator has said that James was a noteworthy psychologist but "was [as a philosopher] at best little more than a brilliant and slightly irresponsible amateur."[1] While I recognize that James was loose in his use of certain philosophical terms, I could not disagree more with the main point of the allegation. I believe that it is only because he is an important philosopher that his work in psychology is still noteworthy and timely today. For the philosophical problems that his work raises pertain to the philosophical foundations of psychology, and, as Wittgenstein and others have indicated, it is here, in its philosophical foundations, that psychology requires the most urgent attention.[2]

Not only does James raise significant problems, he also offers certain suggestions for their solution. The suggestions are in some cases only that: It is as if we were left the fragment of a building and asked to reconstruct in imagination the whole edifice. Yet it is an important fragment: like the groin of a vaulted ceiling—we have a basis for projection in several dimensions.

A central problem raised by James's work is that of how mental states can be correlated to brain states.[3] It is made abundantly clear that mental states cannot be correlated until they are specified, and that they cannot be specified in isolation from their cognitive objects. If what they are *of* is something in the world—which need not be one's brain at all—then how can this be correlated with a state of one's brain? We cannot simply say that that which the mental state is *of* is in causal relation to the brain, for what it is *of* need not even exist. The relation of mental state to cognitive object is entirely "in" the mind, James says, yet he cannot specify the force of "in." An object is not in the mind as a piece of brain tissue is in the skull.

In modern parlance we would say that we use an entirely different set of predicates to describe thoughts from what we use to describe brain states. Thus there is an odd incommensurability between the two. We use predicates like "clear" and "unclear" to describe thoughts, and we ascribe such predicates on the basis of how clearly the things thought *about* are delineated and set off from one another. Or we use predicates like "true" or "untrue" to describe thoughts, and we ascribe such predicates on the basis of how accurately the things intended to be talked about *are* talked about. Or, again, we use predicates like "valid" or "invalid," and we ascribe such predicates on the basis of how consistent thoughts or utterances are among themselves, etc.

We use an entirely different set of predicates to describe brains: e.g., valent or nonvalent, contiguous in space and noncontiguous, conductive of electricity and nonconductive. It does not make sense to cross these predicates, and if we do, we are guilty of "falling into the other kind." What sense does it make to say that a thought is either conductive of electricity or nonconductive? It can be neither; it is not that kind of thing. What sense does it make to say

Conclusion

that a thought is either contiguous in space with another thought or thing or noncontiguous? Thoughts can be neither; they are not that kind of thing. To cross the sets of predicates is to make jokes. It is the kind of incongruity which leaves us stunned, speechless, or laughing: A man falls to the earth and says, "I've just been struck by a thought."

It is just such difficulties that assail us when we attempt to discover the being of a thought. We say that a thing like a brain is a substance because, for one reason, it can be specified independently of whatever altering attributes it has: though it turn yellow and shrink in size, still it occupies a definite position in space—a position which no other substance can occupy at the same time. But prima facie a thought is not given such localization and continuity in its specification. How then can we call it a substance? This problem cannot be solved by calling it a "mental substance"—since we do not know how it is a substance in any sense.

It is very difficult to know what is meant by the "being" of a thought. What *is* it? The only specification we can give it is in terms of what it is *of*—which is not itself. But the word "itself" plays tricks on us. Our language is so "thingy" that we think there must be some substance (presumably "mental") lurking behind the cognized attributes,[4] but there seems to be no good reason to think that there is. And even if the possibility can be conceived, what good would it do? why is it needed? We can speak of our thoughts perfectly well without speaking of some putative "mental substance."

The "being" of a thought—in the only sense of the term that concerns us as ordinary persons—is all in its meaning. Must there *be* something *to do* the meaning? If this question makes any sense on the practical level the only answer would be that we, as selves, do the meaning. Mental substances need not be mentioned.

But is there any nonpractical or theoretical sense in which the term "being" can be applied to thoughts? Perhaps there is. U. T. Place has suggested another sense of the verb "is" which may be appropriate here.[5] It is what he calls "the compositional sense." For example, even though the operations for determining the occurrence of lightning are different from those involved in determining the occurrence of a motion of electric charges, still it is true to say that the lightning *is* the motion of electric charges (in the compositional sense of "is"); furthermore, it is true to say that the motion of electric charges provides, in part, a causal explanation of the experience of lightning.[6] Likewise, Place maintains that the thought *is* the brain state in the specified sense.[7]

Place's theory is plausible and provocative. However, it houses the very same danger, in a subtle form, which lies in every causal theory, no matter how grossly reductionistic and simplistic. It is that of hurrying on to the specification of the nervous system before an adequate specification of consciousness has been achieved. For example, what if one says that the spot of light he sees is just a bit of electrified brain tissue? This is misleading because one does not see just a spot of light (except perhaps in primitive states of consciousness like incipient sleep), but rather a spot of light against a ground of darkness, and one also sees or knows, no matter how marginally, that it is *he* who knows it. Consciousness is always consciousness *of* (or at least we must say that human existence is always existence *of* or *toward*), and this relation of of-ness can only be grasped by a necessary truth.

But once we recognize this danger, Place's theory is helpful. We can go on to say that this surprisingly large "bare minimum" of consciousness is—in the compositional sense—a complex brain state. We will bear in mind that the complexity of consciousness which features internal relations is only an indirect and partial indication of what the complexity of the neurological structure must be; for no matter how complex the latter, its complexity cannot be a matter of internal relations; it must be a matter of empirical complexity featuring external relations which are the subject matter of biochemistry and cybernetics.

Whether true or not, however, Place's theory is in the spirit of James. The overriding point is that we must already know what a thought *is* in the sense of *means* before we can go on to determine what it *is* in the sense of composition, just as we must already know that lightning is the kind of thing that lights up the sky and burns things before we can determine that it is composed of electric charges (and before we can start to control it). Moreover, what a thought is in the compositional sense is almost ridiculously irrelevant to what the thought means. It is like a mosaic in this respect: it makes no difference if a particular mosaic is composed of gems, clay, dung, or bits of electrified brain tissue—the same thing can be depicted in all instances, say a portrait of St. Bartholomew. Of course, a rearrangement of the material may produce a change in the meaning; well and good, natural science has an important role to play, e.g., drug therapy. But for a therapist to know what he is doing when he injects chemicals for the purpose of altering a patient's thought patterns, he must already know what the thoughts to be produced *mean*. Natural science does not tell us this.

Place's theory is in the spirit of James, I feel, even though James himself asserted that something *happens* when a brain state corresponds to a mental state.[8] But something happens (sometimes) only when two substances correspond or impinge, like paper and shears. If a mental state is not a substance, then *nothing* happens. "Brain state" and "mental state" may just be different ways of conceptualizing the same "thing."

The primacy of the cognitive, conceptual, or philosophical analysis asserts itself over the causal. But just the reverse of curtailing or limiting the causal-physiological analysis, it rather frees it from muddles and distractions. In this sense James's work prefigures a reconciliation of natural science and phenomenology. There is no more temptation to look for thoughts inside skulls and—not finding them there—to dismiss consciousness as scientifically irrelevant. Once the physiological psychologist has recognized the primacy of the conceptual analysis, and with this has realized that he, say as a monolingual New Yorker, will have exceeding difficulty in mapping[9] the cerebral cortex of a monolingual Eskimo because he cannot understand fully the meaning of the Eskimo's mental life, then he can attempt with some confidence to map the cortex of those persons with whom he does intimately participate in the world. To comprehend the primacy of the conceptual analysis is to comprehend the worldliness of thought; but to grasp this is to grasp the primacy of civilization, for what things in the world can be taken to *be* is a function of what we can *mean* about them (essence), and this in turn is a function of our command of language and of our mastery of the institutions of civilization which language involves. There is no virtue in a simpleminded understanding of the world.

The significance of the worldliness of thought extends beyond physiological psychology and reaches into psychology as a whole and into the culture generally. The problems and suggestions which James's work generate point to the possibility that psychology imposes a gratuitous limitation on its own development when it proceeds as if human behavior can be understood as contingent responses to contingent stimuli. For example, the influential B. F. Skinner extrapolates his conception of animal behavior to include human beings (he usually conceives of responses operationally in terms of bar-pushing data). A human response of talking about a physical object is conceived by Skinner as "under the control of extremely subtle [physical] properties" of the object.[10]

Now let us take as an example some tower about which we talk. First, there is no operational connection here between the response and the actual tower. I need never have been in the physical presence of the tower—need never have received stimuli from it—in order to talk and think meaningfully about it.[11] Second, Skinner gives us an egregiously undefined term, "control," which houses a metaphysical ghost. What on earth does "under the control of an extremely subtle [physical] property" of the tower mean? The phrase gives the appearance of expressing a contingent and causal relationship, but it is not actually doing that. Because it gives this appearance it cloaks the fact that we can identify the talk as being what it is (talk about the tower) only because we identify the tower talked about; it cloaks the internality and noncontingency of the response. And we can identify the tower talked about without ever alluding to its existence. Indeed, the tower need not even exist for us to talk about it!

As Plato knew long ago, the life of mind or spirit (we need one word like *Geist*) is conditioned by realities which do not exist at all —the Forms, what we call concepts. This means both the glory of truth and the danger of error. To apprehend the present and the actual we must constantly range beyond it in the possible. The thrill of the spirit is inseparable from its precariousness. There is something abysmal about Skinner's thought and so much else of "behavioral science"—pre-Socratic, but with the wonder gone, untimely.

A linguistic response is *non*contingently tied to what is talked about. This is not an empirical condition or limitation. It is a logical limitation pertaining to what we can mean by human responses; it is not learned in the laboratory. To think that it can be so learned is to set ourselves on the trail of occult powers and

Conclusion 223

"controls." It is ironic to think that Professor Skinner, the devotee of science, has unwittingly championed a new spiritualism.

Regardless of how inadequate is James's notion of mental state or act construed as imagery or felt movements of the organism, still his work suggests the necessity of conceptualizing that part of human behavior which can properly be called mental in terms of its intended or cognized object, i.e., the cognitive relation must be construed as internal. There is for example a difference between bar-pushing and pushing the bar. In the first kind of behavior a muscle spasm can do it; in the second *you* do it. In the first kind I can raise your hand for you; in the second you must raise your own hand, otherwise it cannot satisfy the concept "raising your hand." It is an intentional act: you do it because you intend to accomplish something by it, which others understand (e.g., gaining the floor to speak). That is what your behavior *is*, because that is what your behavior *means*.

There is always the danger that when a psychologist specifies a bit of behavior as a directed response, he does so only because he unwittingly presupposes an internal cognitive relationship which he will not or cannot acknowledge. For instance, the psychologist must assume that when he shows a subject a blanket and the subject says "elephant," the subject is behaving in response to the blanket, but just talking about it nonveridically. For how does the psychologist know that the subject is talking about the blanket, and not instead about Africa and elephants? Perhaps because of the total linguistic situation in which the psychologist and subject both participate. But language is not related contingently and externally to the world: To know what the talking means we have to know what is being talked about.

What if the psychologist says that he looks into the subject's eyes and sees him focusing on the blanket? "Sees him focusing on the blanket"? Is the psychologist seeing an empirically specifiable fact—a movement or angular fixation of the eyeballs that can be adequately specified in terms like centimeters, centimeters per second, or geometrical degrees? Rather, is not the psychologist seeing an intentional or cognitive action which can only be construed as intrinsically referential, i.e., which *means* that something in the line of sight is being looked at?

All of this suggests that we must know something about the subject's world in order to know about his mind. That is, it suggests that at some point we must make reference to what has always seemed to be the core of our existence anyway: *what the world means to us*. We must make reference to the subject's consciousness, and by this we would not be referring to a substance but to an internal relation: one which is variously open both to the subject and the psychologist.

But if it must be open to both the psychologist and the subject, then there is something which forever envelops the psychologist—something he cannot stand outside of. It is that which renders questionable every attempt to begin a thoroughgoing psychology with the assumptions of physics, however fine they may be for physics. For it does not seem that the psychologist can begin with the physical world alone, but only with what this world means to us. It is meaning which envelops the psychologist and which structures his point of departure. Call it the linguocentric predicament if you wish. Only this is rather thin, since it does not call attention to the nonverbal meaning in our ordinary existence—our gestures, facial expressions, silences—nor to the background of civilization against which the project of our existence takes shape and finds its meaning. It is civilization which envelops us and from which we cannot escape; for even the attempt to escape it, in whatever cunning and thoughtful way, must be structured by it. In this sense the *plenum* of meaning exhibits a similarity to what St. Paul asserted of God: It is that in which we live and move and have our being.

No distinction of reason, it seems to me, has been more unreasonable and damaging to us than that which divides matter and spirit. James's greatest contribution is that he helps to overcome this distinction by the only means which is not worse than the disease meant to be cured: by working from within the evolving tissue of civilization, not by a futile and damaging attempt from without. What I am suggesting, with James's help, is that spirit *is* the *meaning* of matter at the level of human existence. To think that matter per se is nonspiritual is to distort the spirit in an agony of overbearing manipulation and control of the body. It is to treat ourselves and others like things. It is, ironically, to become materialistic.

Conclusion

But the irony which arises from the distinction of matter and spirit is very cruel and cuts both ways: To be a materialist who thinks of matter under the rubric of the distinction is to think of matter without its full complement of meaning. This thinking, too thin to cover the full range of human behavior, splits apart. The result is the materialist's bastard spiritualism (his talk of pseudophysical "controls") which is as damaging to human life as is the bastard materialism of the spiritualist who thinks under the aegis of the same distinction.

The distinction of matter and spirit—meant to liberate from rampant sensuality and having perhaps this value at one time—has finally bound and confused us. Materialists and spiritualists, helpless in their mutual dependency, have been like blind combatants hacking away at one another on an empty field. The prize lies in a different arena governed by wholly different rules. James helps to free us because he prompts us to see that an adequate materialism is at the same time an adequate philosophy of the spirit, and conversely.

BIBLIOGRAPHY

Aiken, Henry David, "American Pragmatism Reconsidered: II; William James," *Commentary*, September, 1962.
Barrett, William C., *Irrational Man: A Study in Existential Philosophy*, New York: Doubleday & Company, Inc., 1958.
———, *What Is Existentialism?* New York: Grove Press, Inc., 1964.
Biemel, Walter, "Persönliche Aufzeichnungen herausgegeben von W. Biemel," *Philosophy and Phenomenological Research*, 1955–6, p. 295.
Bosanquet, Bernard, "Review of Bertrand Russell's *Problems of Philosophy*," *Mind*, Vol. 21, 1912.
Bradley, F. H., *The Principles of Logic*, 2d ed., Oxford University Press, 1922.
Brentano, Franz, *Psychologie von empirischen Standpunkt*, Leipzig: Felix Meiner, 1924–5.
Capek, Millic, "The Reappearance of the Self in the Last Philosophy of William James," *Philosophical Review*, October, 1953.
Cerf, Walter, "An Approach to Heidegger's Ontology," *Philosophy and Phenomenological Research*, December, 1940.
Chapman, Harmon M., "Realism and Phenomenology," in *The Return to Reason*, ed. by John Wild, Chicago: Henry Regnery Co., 1953.

———, *Phenomenology and Sensations*, Bloomington, Indiana University Press, 1966.
Chappell, V. C. *The Philosophy of Mind*, Englewood Cliffs, N.J.: Prentice-Hall, Inc. (Spectrum Books), 1962.
Chisholm, Roderick, his article on intentionality and his correspondence with Sellars, *Minnesota Studies in the Philosophy of Science, Vol. II. Concepts, Theories and the Mind-Body Problem*, ed. by Feigl et al., Minneapolis: University of Minnesota Press, 1958.
Chomsky, Noam, "Review of B. F. Skinner's *Verbal Behavior*," *Language*, Vol. 35, January–March, 1959, p. 26ff.
Copleston, F., *A History of Philosophy*, Garden City, N.J.: Doubleday & Company, Inc. (Image Books), 1964.
Dewey, John, "The Vanishing Subject in the Psychology of William James," reprinted in *The Problems of Men*, New York: Philosophical Library, Inc., 1946.
Downes, C. B., "Husserl's Theory of Other Minds: A Study of the Cartesian Meditations," unpublished doctoral dissertation, New York University, 1963.
———, "On Husserl's Approach to Necessary Truth," *The Monist*, Vol. 49, No. 1, 1965.
Edie, James, Introduction to *What Is Phenomenology?* Chicago: Quadrangle Books, Inc., 1962.
Edwards, Paul, *The Logic of Moral Discourse*, Glencoe, Ill.: The Free Press, 1955.
Farber, Marvin, *The Foundation of Phenomenology*, Cambridge, Mass.: Harvard University Press, 1943.
Frege, Gottlob, "On Sense and Reference," *Translations from the Philosophical Writings of Gottlob Frege*, ed. by Geach and Black, Oxford: Blackwell, 1952.
Gurwitsch, Aron, *Théorie du champ de la conscience*, Belgium: Desclée de Brouwer, 1957.
Hebb, D. O., *Textbook of Psychology*, Philadelphia: W. B. Saunders Co., 1958.
Heidegger, Martin, *Kant and the Problem of Metaphysics*, trans. by James S. Churchill, Bloomington: Indiana University Press, 1962.
Husserl, Edmund, *Logische Untersuchungen*, 3d ed., 2 vols, Halle: M. Niemeyer, 1922.
———, *Die Krisis der europäischen Wissenschaften und die transzendantale Phänomenologie*, The Hague: M. Nijhoff, 1954.
———, *Cartesian Meditations: An Introduction to Phenomenology*, trans. by D. Cairns, The Hague: M. Nijhoff, 1960.
———, Ideas: *General Introduction to Pure Phenomenology*, trans. by W. R. Boyce-Gibson, New York: The Crowell-Collier Publishing Co. (Collier Books), 1962.
Hook, Sidney, *The Metaphysics of Pragmatism*, Chicago: Open Court Publishing Co., 1927.

James, William, "Remarks on Spencer's Theory of Mind as Correspondence" (1878), in *Collected Essays and Reviews*, ed. by R. B. Perry, New York: Longmans, Green & Company, 1920.
———, "The Sentiment of Rationality" (1879), in *The Will to Believe*, New York: Dover Publications, Inc., 1957.
———, *The Principles of Psychology*, Vols. I and II, New York: Henry Holt and Company, Inc., 1890.
———, *Psychology: Briefer Course*, New York, Henry Holt and Company, Inc., 1910.
———, *Some Problems of Philosophy*, New York: Longmans, Green & Company, 1948 (originally published in 1911).
———, *The Letters of William James*, ed. by H. James, Vols. I and II, Boston: The Atlantic Monthly Press, 1920.
———, "The Tigers in India" (see below, *Pragmatism*).
———, *Essays in Radical Empiricism and a Pluralistic Universe*, New York: Longmans, Green & Company, 1942.
———, *Pragmatism* (and four essays from *The Meaning of Truth*), New York: World Publishing Company (Meridian Books), 1955.
———, *The Writings of* . . . , ed. with an intro. by John J. McDermott, New York: The Modern Library, 1968.
Kenny, Anthony, *Action, Emotion and Will*, New York: Humanities Press, 1963.
Kneale, William, *Probability and Induction*, Oxford: Clarendon Press, 1949.
Knight, Margaret, *William James*, Penguin Books, 1950.
Lauer, Q., *The Triumph of Subjectivity*, New York: Fordham University Press, 1958.
Lewis, C. I., *Mind and the World Order*, New York: Charles Scribner's Sons, 1929.
Linschoten, Johan, *Auf dem Wege zu einer phänomenologischen Psychologie: die Psychologie von William James*, trans. from the Dutch by F. Monks, Berlin: Walter De Gruyter, 1961.
Lovejoy, A. O., *The Thirteen Pragmatisms*, Baltimore: The Johns Hopkins Press, 1962.
Mach, Ernst, *The Analysis of Sensations*, Chicago, 1897.
McGilvary, E. B., "The 'Fringe' of William James's Psychology, the Basis of Logic," *Philosophical Review*, Vol. XX, 1911.
Merleau-Ponty, Maurice, *The Structure of Behavior*, Boston: Beacon Press, 1963.
Metzger, Arnold, "William James and the Crisis of Philosophy," in *In Commemoration of William James*, New York: Columbia University Press, 1942.
Natanson, Maurice, *Essays in Phenomenology*, The Hague: M. Nijhoff, 1966.
Otto, Max, "The Distinctive Psychology of William James," in *William*

James: Man and Thinker, Madison: University of Wisconsin Press, 1942.
Perry, R. B., *Recent Philosophical Tendencies*, New York: Longmans, Green & Company, 1912.
———, *The Thought and Character of William James*, Vols. I and II, Boston: Little Brown & Company, 1935.
———, "James the Psychologist as a Philosopher Sees Him," *Psychological Review*, 1943.
———, *In the Spirit of William James*, Bloomington: Indiana University Press, 1958.
Pitkin, W. B., "A Problem of Evidence in Radical Empiricism," *Journal of Philosophy*, 1906.
Place, U. T., "Is Consciousness a Brain Process?" in *The Philosophy of Mind*, ed. by Chappel, Englewood Cliffs, N.J.: Prentice-Hall, Inc. (Spectrum Books), 1962.
Russell, Bertrand, "On the Nature of Acquaintance," *The Monist*, 1914.
———, *The Analysis of Mind*, London: George Allen & Unwin, 1921.
Ryle, Gilbert, *The Concept of Mind*, New York: Barnes and Noble, Inc., 1949.
———, "Formal and Informal Logic," in *Dilemmas*, New York: Cambridge University Press, 1954.
Santayana, G., in *William James: Philosopher and Man*, ed. by C. H. Compton, New York, Scarecrow Press, Inc., 1957.
Sartre, J.-P., *The Emotions*, New York: Philosophical Library, Inc., (Wisdom Library), 1948.
Schuetz, Alfred, "William James's Concept of the Stream of Thought Phenomenologically Interpreted," *Philosophy and Phenomenological Research*, June, 1941.
———, "Multiple Realities," *Philosophy and Phenomenological Research*, 1945.
Sherover, Charles, "The Kantian Basis of Heidegger's Conception of Time," to be published by Indiana University Press.
Skinner, B. F., *Verbal Behavior*, New York, Appleton-Century-Crofts, 1957.
Smith, John E., *The Spirit of American Philosophy*, New York: Oxford University Press, 1963.
Spiegelberg, H., *The Phenomenological Movement: A Historical Introduction*, Vols. I and II, The Hague: M. Nijhoff, 1960.
Strawson, P. F., *Individuals: An Essay in Descriptive Metaphysics*, New York: Doubleday and Co., Inc. (Anchor Books), 1963.
Thévenaz, Pierre, *What is Phenomenology?* Chicago: Quadrangle Books, Inc., 1962.
Wahl, Jean, *Les Philosophies pluralistes d'Angleterre et d'Amerique*, Paris: Librarie Félix Alcan, 1920.

Wild, John, "Exploration of the Life-World," *Proceedings and Addresses of the American Philosophical Association*, 1960–1.
———, "William James and Existential Authenticity," *Journal of Existentialism*, Vol. 5, No. 19, Spring, 1965.
Wilshire, Bruce, "Reality and Art," in *Art and Philosophy*, ed. by Sidney Hook, New York: New York University Press, 1966.
Wittgenstein, Ludwig, *Philosophical Investigations*, New York: The Macmillan Company, 1953.
Woodbridge, F., *The Realm of Mind*, New York: Columbia University Press, 1926.

NOTES

Introduction

1. See particularly, Johan Linschoten, *Auf dem Wege zu einer phänomenologischen Psychologie: die Psychologie von William James* (Walter De Gruyter, 1961). Also see Aron Gurwitsch, *Théorie du champ de la conscience* (Desclée de Brouwer, 1957).
2. See below, p. 107.
3. I. Kant, *Critique of Pure Reason*, 2d ed., sec. 40.
4. J. D. Watson, *Behaviorism* (Univ. of Chicago Press), 1.
5. E. G. Boring, *American Journal of Psychology*, 55:310–27, 1942.

1. James's Dualistic Program for a Natural Scientific Psychology and Its Failure

1. James, William, *Psychology: Briefer Course* (Holt, 1910; originally pub. 1892), 467. This will be referred to as the "Abridgment"; the main work, *The Principles of Psychology* (Holt, 1890), Vols. I and II, will be referred to as the *Principles*, while in the footnotes only volume and page will be cited, e.g., I, 55.
2. I, vi.
3. I, 218.
4. I, 183ff.
5. Abridgment, 467.

6. Op. cit. 468.
7. Op. cit., 464–5.
8. William James, *Essays in Radical Empiricism* (Longmans, 1942), 134, 197.
9. Abridgment, 465.

2. The Puzzling Opening of "The Principles of Psychology"

1. I, 1.
2. I, 5.
3. I, 6.
4. Ibid.
5. Ibid.
6. I, 9.
7. I, 8.
8. Perry, R. B., *The Thought and Character of William James*, 24.
9. I, 2.
10. Ibid.
11. See also, I, 184, where he speaks of "false knowledge."
12. I, 552–3.
13. I, 6.
14. See "Remarks on Spencer's Definition of Mind as Correspondence," in *Collected Essays and Reviews;* see also I, 145ff.

3. Initial Difficulties of Psychophysical Dualism: Inadequacy of Causal Theory for the Specification of Mental States

1. I, 177.
2. I, 134.
3. I, 102–3.
4. I, 86.
5. I, 24.
6. I, 26.
7. I, 24.
8. I, 24 fn.
9. I, 30.
10. I, 554ff.
11. I, 477.
12. I, 128.
13. I, 126.
14. I, 447.
15. II, 518ff.
16. I, 104.
17. I, 135.
18. I, 136.
19. I, 145.

20. I, 137.
21. I, 144.
22. I, 140.
23. I, 142.
24. I, 144.
25. I, 145.
26. I, 434.
27. I, 444.
28. I, 447.
29. I, 222.
30. II, 7.
31. Ibid.
32. This turns out to be a touchy example. Perhaps saying the cat is tired is part of what we mean by saying it is asleep, although we do not think so. The complete adjudication of this problem would require a separate analysis.
33. It does not necessarily follow that sensations are private, since they are caused by neural processes which can be made public. I only say that James might be tempted to infer this because of the usual closure and separateness of any one person's nervous system.
34. Hebb, D. O., *Textbook of Psychology*, index, under "sensation."
35. II, 33–4.
36. II, 34.
37. Ibid.
38. I, 232–3.
39. I, 231.
40. I, 232.
41. I, 232.
42. Ibid.
43. Ibid.
44. Ibid.
45. I, 232–3.
46. I, 183.
47. I, 140–1.
48. Ibid.
49. See *Collected Essays and Reviews*, 43 fn., in which the editor, R. B. Perry, characterizes this work as seminal and prophetic of James's later work. I agree.
50. Op. cit., 64–5.
51. Ibid.
52. I, 225.
53. I, 286; II, 243.
54. See *Minnesota Studies in the Philosophy of Science*, ed. by Feigl et al. (Univ. of Minnesota Press, 1958), II, 518.
55. I, 450–1.
56. I, 402ff.

57. I, 145.
58. I, 146 (italics mine, B.W.).
59. I, 151.
60. I, 158.
61. The view of physics James held at that time required him, evidently, to say that this must apply to physical states as well.
62. I, 161.
63. Just as did the rationalist critic of associationism, F. H. Bradley. See his *Principles of Logic* (Oxford, 1922), according to James's references to it, as indexed in the *Principles*.
64. I, 604. Notice how late this statement comes in the first volume.
65. I, 603.
66. I, 554.
67. I, 591.
68. I, 163, 174.
69. I, 163.
70. I, 186.
71. I, 278.
72. I, 474.
73. I, 163. It should be noted, however, that James held with Janet that some conscious states could be "split off" and become unreportable by the person having them (see I, 202ff). Furthermore, we will note his reference to transitory, fleeting, or marginal states of consciousness which do not or cannot occupy the focus of consciousness.
74. I, 480.
75. I, 219.
76. I, 459.
77. I, 182.

4. Further Difficulties of Dualism: The Stream of Thought

1. I, 183.
2. I, 183–4.
3. Ibid.
4. I, 216.
5. I, 184.
6. Ibid.
7. I, 185.
8. I, 190.
9. I, 197.
10. Ibid.
11. I, 331–2.
12. I, 628.
13. I, 186.
14. I, 187.
15. Ibid.

16. I, 191.
17. I, 194ff.
18. I, 194–5.
19. I, 195.
20. I, 241.
21. I, 276.
22. I, 196.
23. I, 225.
24. I, 196.
25. I, 236.
26. I, 496.
27. I, 231.
28. I, 214.
29. I, 241.
30. Ibid.
31. James is here anticipating the phenomenological notion of that which is present nonthematically in the field of consciousness. In James's terms, it is "on the margins of consciousness." Some current reinterpretations of the "unconscious mind" have proceeded along these lines.
32. I, 240, 241.
33. I, 274.
34. I, 275.
35. G. Frege, "On Sense and Reference." The *sense* of "morning star" is different from the *sense* of "evening star"; the *reference* of each is the same, i.e., the planet Venus.
36. See the next chapter.
37. I, 275–6.
38. I, 281.
39. Ibid.
40. A juicy example of psychologism: "Psychology is by far the most independent and stable of the sciences. And if all the sciences were ever to be absorbed in any one, psychology is best fitted to be that universal science. For what are the other sciences but orderly or half-disordered systems of conceptions? And are not all conceptions facts of human consciousness?" James Baldwin, *Handbook of Psychology* (Holt, 1890), 15.
41. I, 462.
42. I, 280.
43. I, 279.
44. I, 281.
45. I, 265.
46. I, 269.
47. R. B. Perry, *In the Spirit of William James* (Indiana Univ. Press, Midland Books, 1958), 90.
48. Ibid.

49. R. B. Perry, *The Thought and Character of William James*, II, 75ff. Quoted in Alfred Schuetz, "William James's Concept of the Stream of Thought Phenomenologically Interpreted," *Philosophy and Phenomenological Research*, June, 1941, 451. Schuetz evidently agrees with Perry on this point.
50. I, 471.
51. The first sense of "feeling." Object (No. 3) is felt.
52. I, 259.
53. See also "The Sentiment of Rationality" (1879–1880) in *The Will to Believe* (Dover, 1956), 80ff.
54. I, 463.
55. I, 472ff.
56. I, 259.
57. Ibid.
58. II, 509, *passim*.
59. See chap. 3, note no. 54.
60. I, 281–2.
61. I, 260.
62. I, 260, 269.
63. I, 243. "Transitional" would have been a better word than "transitive." James is not talking about a logician's "transitive relations."
64. Ibid.
65. I, 174.
66. Regarding the alleged movement of thought, see my remarks on Aristotle and intentionality in chap. 7.
67. I, 254 (also 246, 249).
68. I, 246.
69. I, 254.
70. Ibid.
71. This is as old as Plato, and James makes Plato relevant to his discussion by agreeing with him on the changelessness of meaning (Ideas). One cannot say that a meaning changes, because in saying that *it* changes he implies that it is the *same* it, so contradicting himself.
72. I, 247.
73. I, 627–8.
74. I, 250–1.
75. I, 252.
76. I, 251.
77. I, 253.
78. I, 259.
79. I, 245.
80. I, 459ff.
81. I, 183.
82. I, 258 fn.

83. I, 186.
84. I, 477.
85. I, 231.
86. Ibid.
87. II, 243.
88. Ibid.
89. I, 253ff.
90. I, 253.
91. E. B. McGilvary, "The Fringe in William James's Psychology: The Basis of Logic," *Phil. Review*, Vol. XX, 1911, 144ff; Milic Capek, "The Reappearance of the Self in the Last Philosophy of William James," *Phil. Review*, October, 1953, *passim*.
92. I, 266.
93. I, 269.
94. II, 1.
95. This distinction has been made famous by Bertrand Russell, but James introduced it first.
96. I, 221.
97. I, 620.

5. The Phenomenological Breakthrough in James's Psychology: Psychology as Field and Horizon as Well as Stream

1. *Die Krisis der europäischen Wissenschaften und die transzendentale Phänomenologie* (Nijhoff, 1954), 267. Writes Husserl: "W. James war, soviel ich weiss, der einzige, der unter dem Titel fringes auf das Horizontphänomen aufmerksam wurde, aber wie konnte er es ohne das phänomenologisch gewonnene Verständnis der intentionalen Gegenständlichkeit und der Implikationen befragen? Geschieht das aber, wird das Weltbewusst zein von seiner Anonymitat befreit, so vollzieht sich schon der Einbruch ins Transzendentale."
2. Downes, Chauncey B., "Husserl's Theory of Other Minds: A Study of the Cartesian Meditations," doctoral dissertation, New York Univ., 1963, 48.
3. In *Commemoration of William James* (Columbia Univ. Press, 1942), 209.
4. *Logische Untersuchungen*, 3d ed. (Niemeyer, 1922), II, 208. Translation is mine (B.W.).
5. *Théorie du champ de la conscience* (Desclée de Brouwer, 1957), translated as *The Field of Consciousness* (Duquesne, 1964), 185. As actually printed, this statement is a bit misleading. The "topic" for James is only the "kernel" of the Object of thought, and is precisely not correlatable to the full "noema" in Husserl. The latter corresponds substantially to James's Object. The Object is "the full noematic correlate," the "sense" in Husserl.

6. Op. cit., 185.
7. Ibid., 186.
8. Husserl, E., *Ideas: General Introduction to Pure Phenomenology*, (Collier Books, 1962), 83, para. 24.
9. I, 275.
10. Note the order of the relevant chapters in the *Principles*.
11. I, 579.

6. James's Conception of the Self: Phenomenology in Embryo

1. I, 226.
2. I, 225.
3. "It seems as if consciousness as an inner activity were rather a *postulate* than a sensibly given fact, the postulate, namely, of a *knower* as correlative to all this known; and as if '*scious*ness' might be a better word by which to describe it. But 'sciousness postulated as an hypothesis' is practically a very different thing from 'states of consciousness apprehended with infallible certainty by an inner sense.' For one thing it throws the question of *who the knower really is* wide open again . . ." Abridgment, 467. Sometimes James identifies the self with the procession of thoughts, e.g., "if that procession be itself the very 'original' of the notion of personality, to personify it cannot possibly be wrong." I, 227.
4. I, 291.
5. I, 294, 324, 373, 384.
6. I, 294. Evidently James subdivides the social self: there are as many different social selves as there are persons with images of oneself.
7. I, 296.
8. I, 297.
9. I, 298.
10. I, 299.
11. I, 320.
12. I, 299–301.
13. I, 304.
14. I, 305.
15. I, 341.
16. I, 319.
17. I, 340.
18. I, 241.
19. I, 241; cf. I, 320.
20. I, 341.
21. I, 330–4, 372.
22. I, 134.
23. I, 363.
24. *Essays in Radical Empiricism*, 170 fn. (italics mine, B.W.).

25. I, 300.
26. If a sense organ—in contrast to an agent—can be said to feel anything at all.
27. I, 300.
28. I, 301. This is a mere topic for discussion.
29. I, 173.
30. *Philosophical Investigations*, 124–5.
31. For an account of Wittgenstein's lengthy preoccupation with James, see John Passmore, *A Hundred Years of Philosophy* (London, G. Duckworth & Co., 1957), 428. After suggesting the *Principles* as helpful background reading for Wittgenstein's *Philosophical Investigations*, Passmore writes, "One of his former pupils, Mr. A. C. Jackson, tells me that Wittgenstein very frequently referred to James in his lectures, even making on one occasion—to everybody's astonishment—a precise reference to a page number! At one time, furthermore, James's *Principles* was the only philosophical work visible on his bookshelves . . ."
32. I, 319–20.
33. I, 320.
34. In my judgment this is what James means by "warmer."
35. I, 373, 385.
36. I, 325.
37. See Johan Linschoten, *Auf dem Wege* . . . , (Walter De Gruyter, 1961), 194.
38. See the first note to chap. 5.
39. A conversation reported to this writer by William Barrett. But Barrett corrects me: The word was "mind" rather than "self."
40. I do not know the original source of this story.
41. I, 233.
42. I, 478–9 fn.
43. To be perfectly consistent he should have said Object.
44. II, 286.
45. Again James is not perfectly consistent on this point: We will note below that in some passages his dualism seems to take hold and he attempts, however, sporadically, to construct Objects out of sensations.
46. I, 360.
47. Or overemphatically, as he seems to relish nothing more than a chance to attack Kant.
48. I, 363.
49. I, 363, 365.
50. I, 361. Note my criticism in chap. 7 of James's interpretation of Kant.
51. I, 331 fn.
52. I, 331.
53. I, 332.

7. Phenomenology: Intentionality and Worldiness of Thought

1. I, 459.
2. I, 460.
3. II, 655.
4. I, 480.
5. I, 461.
6. I, 473.
7. I, 462.
8. I, 478 fn.
9. I, 479 fn.
10. I, 480.
11. Linschoten, J., *Auf dem Wege* . . . , (Walter De Gruyter, 1961), 136.
12. Herbert Spiegelberg, *The History of the Phenomenological Movement* (Nijhoff, 1960), 115. He says that Husserl conceives intentionality as an active and creative achievement, rather than just a static or passive directedness.
13. Book III, chap. 8, 431b, 20.
14. I forego comment on his idea that individuals can also be intuited in their particularity; I also do not comment on the distinction between the object *simpliciter* and the object for reflection. See H. Chapman, "Realism and Phenomenology," in *The Return to Reason*, ed. J. Wild (Regnery), 20.
15. *De Anima*, 431b, 29. Also 425b, 22ff.
16. 415b, 15.
17. 416b, 23.
18. *Nicomachean Ethics*, 1174a, 13.
19. I have qualms about using "mental state" in any reports of Aristotle and St. Thomas. It is redolent of Descartes, modern philosophy and subjectivism, and is anachronistic.
20. Cf. James's notion of the mental state as "vehicle"—I, 461.
21. *Action, Emotion and Will* (Humanities Press, 1963), 189.
22. See Chapman, "Realism and Phenomenology," 10ff; Kenny, 16, 191; Raziel Abelson, *Philosophy and Phenomenological Research*, XXIV, no. 3, 442. The latter is a review of Kenny's *Action, Emotion and Will*.
23. Rhetoric, 1398a, 30ff. Cited in Kenny, 193.
24. This is translated by Kenny from *Summa Theologica* Ia, 18, 3 and 1. He admits that his translation of *perfectio* as "bringing about a state" may be questioned. I think this admission is judicious, for the whole modern notion of "mental state" is suspect, as we have seen so vividly in the case of James.
25. This is translated by Kenny on pp. 194–5, of *Action, Emotion and Will*. I have never seen an "s" used for the second "t" in "inten-

tion," and I think it is misleading. The spelling suggests the intension as opposed to the extension of a concept. While phenomenologists are assuredly interested in intensions or "senses" (*Sinne*), they mean more by "intention" than by "intension." Intention has two aspects: as psychical act in the stream of consciousness, and as intentional object, which latter is often prominently *Sinn* or intension. Thus Kenny's spelling suggests a slighting of the act-aspect, or in James's terms, psychical aspect. He may be right philosophically, but Brentano and Husserl, who are mainly responsible for the use of the term today, would not think so.

26. Marvin Farber, *The Foundation of Phenomenology* (Harvard Univ. Press, 1943), 341.
27. *Ideen*, para. 4.
28. *What is Phenomenology?* (Quadrangle Books, 1962), 43.
29. *Ideen*, para. 44. It might be said that the word "appear" is not quite the right word to be used for *Erlebnisse* and acts of consciousness, because they are given "absolutely." I do not pause on this point, however.
30. *Ideen*, para. 84. *Lebenswelt* becomes central in Husserl's last work.
31. *Ideen*, para. 36.
32. Op. cit., para. 84.
33. As Spiegelberg writes (Ibid., 115): "Intentionality is the character of mental acts which allows different acts to have identically the same object; intentionality is linked to the form or essence of a thing—what other things could in principle share."
34. *Ideen*, para. 36.
35. I do not discuss the allegation that Husserl becomes an idealist in his later writings.
36. Farber, 335ff.
37. Husserl, *Cartesian Meditations*, trans. by D. Cairns (Nijhoff, 1960), 24.
38. Husserl, "Persönliche Aufzeichnungen," hg. von Walter Biemel, *Philosophy and Phenomenological Research*, XVI, 1956, 267.
39. Farber, 277.
40. II, 1–2.
41. Although we notice that James does not mention the total Object of thought but instead speaks of object in the sense of topic or individual thing; he also simply says "fact" rather than saying "something perceived as a fact."
42. II, 8.
43. Op. cit., 68.
44. "Exploration of the Life-World," *Proceedings and Addresses of the American Philosophical Association*, 1960–1, 7–10.
45. Introduction to Thévenaz, *What is Phenomenology?*, 34–5.
46. II, 134ff.

47. Kenny, op. cit., 5.
48. I obviously do not accept Kenny's flat assertion that James held a causal theory of perception; op. cit., 40 fn.
49. II, 301.
50. II, 134–5.
51. II, 35.
52. I, 631.
53. I, 605.
54. *Essays*, 193.
55. Op. cit., 182.
56. Op. cit., 167–8.
57. Op. cit., 184.
58. Op. cit., 193.
59. II, 313.
60. *Problems of Men* (Philosophical Library, 1946), 390.
61. I, 630.
62. Perry, *Recent Philosophical Tendencies* (Longmans, 1912) 365; E. Mach, *The Analysis of Sensations* (Chicago, 1897), 14, 23.
63. Perry, *The Thought and Character of William James*, Vol. II the Letters to Strong.
64. A. O. Lovejoy, *The Thirteen Pragmatisms* (Johns Hopkin Press, 1962), 131.
65. *Philosophical Review*, October 1953, *passim*.
66. This is the formula that the *Principles* tends toward: Al thought is thought *of* something; all somethings are somethings think able *of*. The common ground of thought and reality begins to appear.
67. II, 287, 291. See also Gurwitsch's criticism of any attempt t equate James with the phenomenalism of, say, Mach: *Field of Con sciousness*, 19.
68. II, 286–7.
69. II, 293.
70. II, 287.
71. II, 297.
72. II, 290.
73. II, 297ff.
74. II, 283.
75. II, 286.
76. II, 287.
77. II, 290 fn.
78. Sydney Shumaker, *Self-Knowledge & Self-Identity* (Cornel Univ. Press).
79. Instead of "ourself" as the "subjective" pole of the relationship I think James would have been better advised to say any possibl practical subject.
80. II, 35.
81. II, 297.

82. Furthermore, James adds the note, "I use the notation of the Ego here, as commonsense uses it. Nothing is prejudged as to the results (or absence of results) of ulterior attempts to analyze the notion."

83. One of James's later, popular phrases. I indulge myself in precious few of these.

84. II, 293.

85. II, 293–4.

86. II, 299.

87. *Journal of Philosophy*, XXXVII, no. 221, 589.

88. *Journal of Existentialism*, XIX, Spring, 1965, 255.

89. II, 283.

90. II, 319–20.

91. II, 297.

92. *Philosophy and Phenomenological Research*, Dec., 1940.

93. Author's Preface to the English edition, in *Ideen*, 6. When page number is cited we refer to *Ideas* (Collier Books, 1962).

94. *Cartesian Meditations: An Introduction to Phenomenology*, trans. by D. Cairns (Nijoff, 1960), 151.

95. In his cardinal publication of 1913, *Ideas: General Introduction to Pure Phenomenology*, Husserl uses the word "pure" synonymously with the word "transcendental," 5.

96. Ibid., para. 16.

97. Yet Husserl maintains that in some sense intuition can be mistaken; this sense is not clear to me.

98. *The Triumph of Subjectivity* (Fordham Univ. Press, 1958), 106.

99. *Ideen*, chap. 3.

100. *Cartesian Meditations*, 21ff.

101. *What is Phenomenology?* 47–8.

102. *Ideen*, chap. 9.

103. In the later *Ideen II* and *Ideen III* Husserl more completely discusses the problem of the rational grounding of psychology.

104. "The meaning of thing is given in thing-perception," *Ideen*, para. 44.

105. Thévenaz, 90.

106. *Ideen*, chaps. 2 and 3. See also Farber, 271.

107. Author's preface to English edition, *Ideen*, 6.

108. See *Probability and Induction* (Clarendon Press, 1949), indexed under "Phenomenology."

109. Introd. to Thévenaz, 35.

110. Op. cit., 167.

111. II, 35.

112. II, 293.

113. I, 275.

114. *Critique of Pure Reason*, 2 ed., sec. 40, as cited in Copleston,

A History of Philosophy (Doubleday, Image Books, 1962), VI, 36.
    115. II, 661 fn.
    116. II, 662 fn.
    117. Lauer, 72.
    118. Concerning the point that phenomenology only uncovers what is already there, see Farber, 270.
    119. I, 606.
    120. I, 641.
    121. James, *Collected Essays and Reviews*, 437.
    122. Individuals: *An Essay in Descriptive Metaphysics* (Doubleday, Anchor Books, 1963), 30.
    123. Ibid., 29.
    124. I, 272.
    125. *A History of Philosophy*, VI, 46.
    126. *Ideen*, para. 62.
    127. II, 639.
    128. II, 659.
    129. II, 644–5.
    130. II, 650.
    131. II, 655.
    132. II, 646, 669.
    133. II, 646.
    134. II, 659.
    135. James even speaks of "universal objects" (I, 479 fn.); cf. Husserl, *Ideen*, para. 59, in which essences as "general objects" are discussed.
    136. II, 650.
    137. It is not my concern to elucidate the differences between phenomenology and linguistic philosophy; I think the similarities are much more important. Chauncey Downes has written that, "there is an extremely close parallel between Husserl and linguistic philosophy. In Husserl's phenomenology we use the method of fictive variation to obtain necessary connections between senses. In linguistic analysis we use the method of variation in the uses of words to obtain rules governing the connections between words." (*The Monist*, Jan., 1965, 104–105). And after all, J. L. Austin himself has written, "In view of the prevalence of the slogan 'ordinary language,' and of such names as 'linguistic' or 'analytic' philosophy or 'the analysis of language,' one thing needs specially emphasizing to counter misunderstandings. When we examine what we should say when, what words we should use in what situations, we are looking again not *merely* at words (or 'meanings,' whatever they may be) but also at the realities we use the words to talk about; we are using a sharpened awareness of words to sharpen our perception of, though not as a final arbiter of, the phenomena. For this reason I think it might be better to use, for this way of doing philosophy, some less misleading name than those given above—for

Notes

instance 'linguistic phenomenology,' only that is rather a mouthful." (Quoted by Downes, 105–6.)

138. From *Dilemmas*, quoted by Jager, *Essays in Logic from Aristotle to Russell* (Prentice-Hall, 1963), 172.
139. Ibid., 175.
140. Ibid., 179.
141. II, 632.
142. Ibid.
143. II, 335.
144. *Varieties of Religious Experience* (Mentor Edition), 45.
145. I, 482.
146. See how this idea is developed later by Sidney Hook in his *Metaphysics of Pragmatism*, *passim*.
147. II, 335–6.
148. Doctoral dissertation, 40ff.
149. *Phenomenology and Sensations* (Indiana Univ. Press), 1966; see the whole section on Husserl. Of course, Husserl does talk about "fictive variation" as a method of disclosing essence.
150. Heidegger, *Kant and the Problem of Metaphysics*; see also Sherover, Charles, "The Kantian Source of Heidegger's Conception of Time" to be published by Indiana University Press.
151. For example, to be able to take a devil-may-care attitude toward my own death, I *must* be, essentially, a being-toward-death.
152. *Essays in Radical Empiricism*, 25.
153. James attests to this cluttering in his own description of the *Principles*: ". . . the enormous *rat* which ten years' gestation has brought forth," and again, this ". . . loathsome, distended, tumefied, bloated, dropsical mass, testifying to nothing but two facts: first, that there is no such thing as a *science* of psychology, and second, that William James is an incapable." (Perry, *The Thought and Character of William James*, II, 47–8.)
154. I, 471.
155. In 1895 James wrote (in an address which was later published as *The Tigers in India*): "Suppose, to fix our ideas, that we take first a case of conceptual knowledge; and let it be our knowledge of the tigers in India, as we sit here. Exactly what do we *mean* by saying that we here know the tigers? What is the precise fact that the cognition so confidently claimed is *known-as*, to use Shadworth Hodgson's inelegant but valuable form of words?

"Most men would answer that what we mean by knowing the tigers is having them, however absent in body, become in some way present to our thought; or that our knowledge of them is known as presence of our thought to them. A great mystery is usually made of this peculiar presence in absence; and the scholastic philosophy, which is only common sense grown pedantic, would explain it as a peculiar kind of existence, called *intentional inexistence*, of the tigers in our mind. At the very least, people would say that what we mean by knowing the tigers is mentally *pointing* towards them as we sit here.

"But now what do we mean by *pointing*, in such a case as this? What is the pointing known-as, here?

"To this question I shall have to give a very prosaic answer—one that traverses the prepossessions not only of common sense and scholasticism, but also those of nearly all the epistemological writers whom I have ever read. The answer, made brief, is this: The pointing of our thought to the tigers is known simply and solely as a procession of mental associates and motor consequences that follow on the thought, and that would lead harmoniously, if followed out, into some ideal or real context, or even into the immediate presence, of the tigers. It is known as our rejection of a jaguar, if that beast were shown us as a tiger; as our assent to a genuine tiger if so shown. It is known as our ability to utter all sorts of propositions which don't contradict other propositions that are true of the real tigers. It is even known, if we take the tigers very seriously, as actions of ours which may terminate in directly intuited tigers, as they would if we took a voyage to India for the purpose of tiger-hunting and brought back a lot of skins of the striped rascals which we had laid low. In all this there is no self-transcendency in our mental *images taken by themselves*. They are one phenomenal fact; the tigers are another; and their pointing to the tigers is a perfectly common-place intra-experiential relation, *if you once grant a connecting world to be there*. In short, the ideas and the tigers are in themselves as loose and separate, to use Hume's language, as any two things can be; and pointing means here an operation as external and adventitious as any that nature yields.

"I hope you may agree with me now that in representative knowledge there is no special inner mystery, but only an outer chain of physical or mental intermediaries connecting thought and thing. *To know an object is here to lead to it through a context which the world supplies*. All this was most instructively set forth by our colleague D. S. Miller at our meeting in New York last Christmas, and for re-confirming my sometime wavering opinion, I owe him this acknowledgment." *Pragmatism* (World Pub. Co., Meridian Books, 1955), 225–7.

Of course, there is some vagueness even here. What does James mean by the subjunctive "would lead" and the conditional "if followed out" and the talk of the "ideal context of the tigers"? But he seems to be saying that it always *does* lead if followed out, and his contention that the "pointing" is "an operation as external and adventitious as any nature can show" is quite emphatic.

156. Certainly there are contingent elements in our experience, but that is because we live in a contingent world. The sun might not rise tomorrow, and we would experience this and the shock. But we would still know what it *meant* to think, "The sun rises tomorrow."

157. See "Is Radical Empiricism Solipsistic?" in the original version

Notes

of the *Essays* (1912), 234. Perry omits this key article from the most recent edition.

158. Ibid., 238.
159. Ibid., 239 fn.
160. This is a subject for another study.
161. I, 606.
162. I, 609.
163. *Ideen*, para. 77.
164. I, 606.
165. See above, 239 fn.
166. I, 627ff.
167. *Pragmatism* (World Pub. Co., Meridian Books, 1955), 224.
168. I, 481–2.
169. Ibid.
170. Note the tangled web which lingers on in James's last book, *Some Problems of Philosophy* (Longmans, 1948), particularly the chapter on "Percepts and Concepts."
171. All thoughts are intentional, but are sensations thoughts? I recognize the validity of the question. I also recognize that the "tradition of intentionality" has not always been comfortable in its treatment of sensations (e.g., Husserl's "hyletic data").
172. See his chapter on "The Perception of Things" in the second volume. See also I, 478, fn., next-to-last paragraph. This is in blatant contradiction to what we have already quoted from the last paragraph of this footnote.
173. See C. I. Lewis, *Mind and the World Order* (Scribner, 1929), Appendix D, 414. James anticipated Lewis on this point, but he was certainly not consistent.
174. Recall what we noted about sensations as a limiting conception.
175. I, 258 fn.
176. I, 253.
177. II, 449.
178. II, 455.
179. II, 453.
180. II, 454.
181. Ibid.
182. II, 313.
183. II, 450–1.
184. Kenny, 40ff.
185. In C. H. Compton, *William James, Philosopher and Man* (Scarecrow Press, 1957).
186. *The Letters of William James*, ed. by H. James; letter to D. S Miller, July 8, 1893.
187. II, 453.

188. *Essays*, 141.
189. Ibid., 143.

Conclusion

1. Margaret Knight, *William James* (Penguin Books, 1950), 50.
2. *Philosophical Investigations*, last paragraph of the book.
3. James intended to return to the mind-brain problem. He died before he could do this. *Some Problems of Philosophy*, 217 fn.
4. In this I merely extend James's notion of the psychologist's fallacy.
5. "Is Consciousness a Brain Process?" printed in *The Philosophy of Mind*, ed. by V. C. Chappell (Prentice-Hall, Spectrum Books, 1962), 101ff.
6. Ibid., 106.
7. Place argues that the usual rule, that the logical independence of two descriptive expressions involves the ontological independence of entities described, breaks down in the case of brain state and consciousness, because in this case it just happens to be true that the operations which have to be performed in order to verify the two sets of characteristics can seldom if ever be performed simultaneously. Ibid., 104.
8. Abridgment, last page.
9. By "map" is meant the correlation of mind with definite physiological states of the brain *via* the correlation of languages. I do not mean to suggest that brain neurology is so advanced that neurologists are on the verge of finding the physiological correlates of advanced mental or psychological behavior. But if this is ever to happen we must clear away philosophical or conceptual muddles first.
10. *Verbal Behavior* (Appleton-Century-Crofts Inc., 1957), 108. see Noam Chomsky's review in *Language*, XXXV, Jan.–March 1959, 26ff.
11. Perhaps Skinner's statements have some veiled significance for genetic psychology—the study of the sources of our language. But to think that a study of sources illuminates the significance of the final effect is to be guilty of the genetic fallacy. Language, as we actually use it, has a life of its own independent of the present and actual physical environment—*and* the actual environment of the past.

INDEX

Aristotle, 31, 42, 124, 156–158, 204, 240
Associationism, 59–61
Austin, J. L., 244

Baldwin, J., 235
Barrett, W., xi–xiii, 239
behaviorism, 7–8, 20, 27, 34, 50, 99, 124, 136
belief, 68, 171–175, 178
Bergson, H., 180
Berkeley, 170
Boring, E. G., 8
Bradley, F. H., 40
bracket, 5, 7, 182ff.
Brentano, F., 75, 155ff.

Capek, M., 171, 237
causal conditions/logical conditions, 41–42, 44–45, 49, 59
Cerf, W., 180
Chapman, H., 17, 201
chemical-therapy, 221
Chisholm, R., 54, 95
Chomsky, N., 248

Churchill, J. S., 203, 227, 245
consciousness, 22, 30, 53–54, 58, 67, 125; reinterpretation of, 134, 138, 143
Copleston, F., 194

Darwin, C., 50–51
Descartes, R., 159, 162
Dewey, J., 169, 177
Downes, C. B., 201, 244

Edie, J., 163, 186
emotions, 212ff.
essence, 3–8, 184, 199–201
existence, 174, 198–200
existential phenomenology, 199–203
external relations, 15ff.

Farber, M., 244
field of consciousness, 82, 108, 128, 134–135
Frege, G., 86–87, 144
fringe, 87ff., 94, 108, 178

Galileo, 193
Gurwitsch, Aron, 120–121, 237

Hebb, D. O., 43
Hegel, G., 186
Heidegger, M., 180, 198, 203
Helholtz, 46, 100–101, 207
Hume, D., 15, 79, 110, 175
Husserl, E., 3–8, 86, 120–121, 148, 154–162, 180–202

idealism, 14, 17, 170
identity theory of consciousness, 11, 219–221
informal logic, 186–197
intentionality, 8, 17, 19, 26–27, 52–53, 61–62, 117, 130–131, 152ff., 203, 214; as mental acts, 28, 148–149, 156ff., 161
internal relations, 6, 9, 15, 154, 161–162
intuition, 5, 181
introspection, 7–8, 21, 71–76, 83; paucity of its report, 128, 154

Janet, P., 234

Kant, I., 4–5, 74, 141, 145ff., 161, 175, 181, 191, 198, 203, 245
Kenny, A., 157, 240–241
Kierkegaard, S., 199
Kneale, W., 186
knowledge by acquaintance/by description, 115
knowledge (or cognition) in generic sense/in specific sense, 26

Lauer, Q., 182
Lebenswelt, 7, 19, 107, 117, 123, 166, 171, 179–180
Lewis, C. I., 247
Linschoten, J., 155, 163, 207
Locke, J., 79, 164
logical conditions/causal conditions, 41–42, 44–45, 49, 59
Lovejoy, A., 170

Mach, E., 170
mapping the cortex, 221, 248
margin, concept of, 108, 120
meaning intentions & meaning fulfilments, 206
Merleau-Ponty, M., 132, 141, 212
metaphysics, 10–11, 14, 57
mind, criterion of, 22
Moore, G. E., 142

McGilvary, E. B., 237

necessary truths, 5, 18, 160, 187–196
noesis-noema, 121, 154, 184–185

object of thought as topic and as Object, 86ff.
open-textured concepts, 204

Passmore, J., 239
perception, 114–115, 121, 181ff.
perceptual object of thought, 83, 121
Perry, R. B., 25, 90–93, 96, 170, 233
phenomenal body or body-subject, 79, 132ff., 165, 175–176; as supplying rules of being, 148
Place, U. T., 219–221
Plato, 88, 98, 152, 199, 222, 236
physiology, 21ff., 47, 50, 55; limitations of, 26, 126; and associationism, 60; and the view that it supplies a sufficient explanation of all thinking, 26
primary and secondary qualities, 164
psychologist's fallacy, 77ff., 80, 99, 103–104

radical empiricism (philosophy of pure experience), 8, 14, 167–171, 204, 215–216
reality, sense of, 171ff., 183
regressions to dualism, 55, 96–105, 196, 202–211

satisfaction of thoughts, 94
Sartre, J-P., 141, 212
Schuetz, A., 236
self-identity, 132ff., 140
self of selves, 127
sense of the same, 109, 150ff.
sensations, 42ff., 58–59, 116, 162–163, 165–166, 247; as to their being, 109ff.; as bodily sensations, 45ff.; as detected by painters, 110ff., 122
Sherover, C., 203, 245
Shumaker, S., 174
Skinner, B. F., 222ff.
social self, 127, 238
space, 154, 162–167
Spencer, H., 29, 51–52
spiritual self (inner self), 36, 128
Spiegelberg, H., 155, 240
St. Thomas, 157–159, 240

Index

Strawson, P. F., 193

teleology, 22–24, 49–54, 99, 122; and essence, 200–202
tendency, feelings of, 102ff.
Thévenaz, P., 160, 184, 193
time, 100–101, 167, 169, 192, 206
transcendental investigations, 4–5, 17, 184–194
transcendental phenomenology, 188–202

unconscious mind, 63

Ueberweg, 200

Varieties of Religious Experience, 140
vagueness in mental life, 98–99

Watson, J. D., 7–8
Wild, J., 163, 178
will, 36, 54, 178
Wittgenstein, L., xiii, 137–138, 217
world of practical realities, 18–19, 176